... BUT WITH RESPECT

also by the same author

Television: a Personal Report (1981)
The Case for Televising Parliament (1963)
Day by Day: A Dose of My Own Hemlock (1975)
Grand Inquisitor (1989)

Sir Robin Day was one of the original newscasters for ITN in 1955. In 1959 he joined the BBC's *Panorama* to which he has been a contributor for thirty years. From 1979–87 he presented *The World at One* on BBC Radio 4, and from 1979–89 he chaired *Question Time* on BBC1. Awards for his work in broadcasting have included the Guild of TV Producers' and Directors' Award, 'Personality of the Year' in 1957, the Richard Dimbleby Award in 1975, and the Royal Television Society's 'Judges' Award in 1985. Sir Robin was knighted in 1981. His memoirs *Grand Inquisitor* were a best-seller on publication in 1989. He has two sons and lives in London.

Day with Nasser

Day with Macmillan

Day with Wilson

SIR ROBIN DAY

... BUT WITH RESPECT

Memorable television
interviews
with statesmen and
parliamentarians

Weidenfeld and Nicolson · London

First published in Great Britain in 1993 by
George Weidenfeld & Nicolson Limited
The Orion Publishing Group
Orion House, 5 Upper St Martin's Lane,
London WC2H 9EA

A catalogue reference is available from
the British Library

ISBN 0 297 81302 1

Filmset by Selwood Systems, Midsomer Norton
Printed in Great Britain by
Butler & Tanner Ltd
Frome, Somerset

To my sons
Alexander Day
and
Daniel Day

Illustrations

The photographs are from Camera Press, except as follows: Lord Lambton (Hulton-Deutsch), Margaret Thatcher and John Major (Press Association), Robin Day with Bernard Levin (BBC). The trio that appear as a frontispiece: Nasser (ITN), Harold Macmillan (ITN), Harold Wilson (BBC).

CONTENTS

Introduction   I
Gamal Abdel Nasser 1957   II
Harold Macmillan 1958   21
Sir Alec Douglas-Home 1964   33
Roy Jenkins 1966   49
Edward Heath 1972   65
Lord Lambton 1973   81
Harold Wilson 1974   103
Lord Shawcross 1975   121
James Callaghan 1976   151
Lord Hailsham 1979   163
Enoch Powell 1979   177
Dennis Skinner 1979   191
Margaret Thatcher 1983   207
Margaret Thatcher 1987   229
John Major 1992   253
Neil Kinnock 1992   271
Robin Day interviewed by Bernard Levin 1980   287
Afterthought   301

Acknowledgements

My thanks are due to all those eminent persons who readily agreed to their interviews with me being included in this book.

I am deeply grateful to the British Broadcasting Corporation, and also to Independent Television News and to Thames Television for granting permission to publish these interviews.

Robin Day

INTRODUCTION

The selection of interviews in this book is from the hundreds done by me during the last thirty-eight years. The interviews are with statesmen or parliamentarians. Several were occupants of Number 10 Downing Street at the time – Macmillan, Douglas-Home, Wilson, Heath, Callaghan, Thatcher, and Major. There are interviews with other politicians of brilliance and eloquence who never reached the top of Disraeli's greasy pole – Roy Jenkins, Enoch Powell, Quintin Hailsham, Hartley Shawcross. And there is Neil Kinnock, poised for the victory which eluded him.

But politics is not only about Right Honourables, about those who have sat in Cabinet. Much of the charm and colour of politics flows not from position and influence, but from personality and individuality, from (say) the rugged proletarianism of Dennis Skinner, or the aristocratic sophistication of Lord Lambton.

The television interview has provoked more controversy, generated more headlines, and illuminated more personalities than anything else on the British television screen. The serious political interview dates from the second half of the fifties. Early examples were my ITN encounters with Nasser (1957) and Macmillan (1958). On BBC *Panorama*, Woodrow Wyatt and John Freeman were making their mark. Later, in 1959, Freeman followed with *Face to Face*. This brilliant series was, however, mainly non-political. His guests tended to be celebrities, exhibitionist 'characters' or entertainers of one kind or another. No British Cabinet Minister was seen to suffer Freeman's icy interrogation in *Face to Face*.

In the sixties, television interviewing established itself as a distinctive and dramatic branch of journalism, a force in politics, and a topical talking-point for viewers. British politicians, once suspicious and fearful of television, soon used their parliamentary skills to become masterful TV performers. Macmillan and Wilson became much more than accomplished House of Commons men. They were television stars, household faces.

The value of TV interviews has grown greatly since the questions became more challenging, penetrating and incisive. This stimulated the politician and entertained the viewer. The interviews became longer and deeper, producing portraits by cross-examination. Recently interviews of almost a whole hour by, say, Walden or a Dimbleby, have been frequent. Length, however, is no guarantee of quality or clarity.

The House of Commons itself has been televised since 1990. Margaret Thatcher or John Major could at last be judged by how they answered Neil Kinnock and others elected to question and challenge them. This was a most healthy development, for which I had campaigned for over thirty years. But televising the House has still left work for TV interviewers to do, particularly during an election campaign. Parliament then is dissolved, and there is no face-to-face debating between party leaders. So interviews with the Prime Minister and the shadow Prime Minister may still be significant events. This was so in the General Election of 1992.

In the sixties and seventies major television interviews, such as those on BBC *Panorama*, were newsworthy events of much value in the political process. They attracted big headlines, verbatim news reports, fierce editorials, strong political reaction, and lively viewer response. In the eighties political interviewing suffered a set-back. The significance, value and appeal of the big television interview declined. For different reasons, but with similar results, Margaret Thatcher and Neil Kinnock developed a technique which devalued the television interview as an instrument of democratic scrutiny. They were both determined to make the television interview a platform of their own. The interviewer's questions, or attempts at questions, were treated as tiresome interruptions to the statistical hammering of Thatcher, or the repetitious rhetoric of Kinnock. To prevent the monotony of a monologue, the interviewer was forced to butt in when he could, if he could.

Prime Ministers and party leaders are, of course, entitled to use whatever tactics they feel will be electorally advantageous to them. But democracy cannot flourish without fair and reasoned dialogue. If the nation's most potent means of communication cannot supply such dialogue, democracy will suffer. What we saw in the eighties were interviewers steam-rollered by preconceived answers, whatever the questions. This was not so in previous years, in the sixties and seventies. The interviews here with Macmillan, Douglas-Home, Wilson, Heath and Callaghan show how those Prime Ministers addressed themselves, in their different styles, to the interviewer's questions, though it is true that Heath and Wilson were sometimes apt to give lengthy answers.

All but three of these sixteen interviews were televised 'live', or were recorded as if 'live' and broadcast without editing. The interviews with President Nasser, Lord Lambton and Lord Shaw-cross were all filmed on location and had to be edited in the normal way. But there were no cuts of any importance.

In 'live' interviews, the interviewer has a responsibility heavier than may be imagined. He has to work in a combination of circumstances which few other journalists experience. He cannot write up his interview afterwards in his office or his hotel room. He has to perform in the presence of a world-famous statesman, a powerful Cabinet Minister or an accomplished parliamentarian. The moment may be one of political tension or high drama. The situation may be of the utmost gravity or fraught with intense emotion. Lives may be at stake.

The interviewer's words must be carefully chosen. He may have to speak without preparation by way of instant response, knowing that the interview is being watched by an audience of millions, daunting not only for its hugeness but for the fact that it includes many critical experts. The viewing audience, for instance, may include diplomats, dons, businessmen, economists, trade unionists, bankers, Cabinet Ministers, housewives, lawyers and doctors – all on the look-out for inaccuracy or distortion. The interviewer must express himself clearly and accurately.

He must keep his nerve. He must press his questions when a question has been evaded. He must discontinue a line of questioning which turns out to be irrelevant or ill-judged. He must avoid becoming involved in an altercation about a disputed fact or statement. An altercation merely muddies the waters.

All the while, the interviewer must also be conscious of the defamatory pitfalls into which a 'live' broadcaster can stumble. The television interviewer's responsibility for avoiding libel – and contempt of court – is personal and immediate. The unscripted dialogue of a 'live' television interview goes out to the audience at once, without any editorial or legal filter. Of course the newspaper journalist also produces his material under intense pressure, but he knows that lawyers, sub-editors, editorial executives and others can check it, alter it, cut it, and authorize it before publication to the world.

The television interviewer's responsibility is to make immediate and well-judged decisions in public which no one else can make for him at that precise moment. He has 'the autonomy of the instant voice'. In recent years, however, I have been shocked to find that the practice has grown up of interviewers being instructed what to ask by a producer through an earpiece. Producer's instructions may be necessary and unobjectionable in programmes where one item has to follow another, but they should not be used to control or guide the questions of an interview. Such prompting prevents the interviewer from being on top of his job. An interview cannot be conducted by two people simultaneously. Too many TV interviews are incompetent because the interviewer is treated by the unseen producer as a puppet and is told what to ask.

When political leaders are granted access to television's powerful platform, they should be subject to critical and informed questioning. Interviewers should therefore be knowledgeable political reporters, not disc-jockeys, chat-show hosts or showbiz 'personalities'. Questioning should be tenacious and persistent but civil. I shudder to watch interviewers who think it clever to be snide, supercilious, or downright offensive.

Recently the view has been heard in professional circles – from producers and broadcasting executives – that the straightforward political interview on TV has played itself out as a useful and informative form. Or as one wag put it, 'The set-piece television interview has had its Day.'

One such comment by a current affairs producer appeared in the professional journal *Broadcast* (June 1992): 'A presenter – relaxed, charismatic, incisive questioner – meets politician, confident and well trained in deflecting even minor questions. And so it goes, each understanding the other's strategy, but rarely being politically significant or revealing: more of a psychological gameshow than current affairs.'

But we have heard this sort of thing before. Establishment swordplay ... Political shadow-boxing ... Talking heads ... Meaningless middle-class fencing. And so it goes.

Of course, if the politicians get better at answering, the interviewers will have to get better at questioning. But there will always be a need to question those who rule us, or who aspire to rule us. Question-and-answer is not a passing fashion. It is a rudimentary historic method of conducting argument and imparting information. Socrates was right.

The value of the TV interview to our democracy should not be underestimated. Television interviews are one way by which political leaders can be genuinely open to questioning of a critical, informed and challenging nature. When a politician is interrogated on television it is one of the rare occasions outside Parliament where his or her performance cannot be completely manipulated or packaged or artificially hyped.

Some answers can be prepared or scripted or learnt by heart, but not all. The answers cannot be on a teleprompter as for a speech to camera. The spin-doctors, the image-makers, the PR wizards can advise on voice, on posture and on manner. Politicians can be professionally coached about what to say and how to say it, but once the interview has started the politician is alone. Questions can, of course, be predicted or guessed or anticipated by advisers, but the actual questions are chosen by the interviewer. At least one or two of his questions may come as a surprise.

Thus an interview on television is one public act which is not wholly in the hands of the ad-men, the propagandists or the marketing men. If a politician flannels or fudges in a TV interview, this can be seen and judged by the viewing electors. They can form some impression of the politician's credibility, candour and character.

The difference between TV interviewing and the work of other journalists who also ask questions is that a TV interrogation is conducted in front of the viewers. The interviewer's questioning is not part of research or exploration of a subject preparatory to the writing of a column, a feature, an editorial. Thus the TV interviewer's questions must not be (but too often are) rambling, or repetitive, or long-winded, or confusing. The TV interviewer's questions, whether they are carefully prepared or off-the-cuff, should be clearly expressed and factually accurate.

The TV interviewer has to perform his professional function in public, in close up, under the critical gaze of the vast TV audience. TV interviewing is one of the performing arts, like oratory, acting, singing, debating or advocacy. The writing journalist does his questioning behind the scenes – sometimes on the record, sometimes off, often a mixture of the two. Thus when he comes to write, he can add his own comment, description, analysis, interpretation, speculation, so as to offer something rounder and deeper than simple on-the-record questions and answers.

Does this not suggest that the TV interview has a limited value as journalism compared to a column, a feature or a news report? In my humble submission, if a TV interview is conducted with ability, knowledge and style, it can, through cross-examination of a public figure, illuminate problems or events as vividly and entertainingly as any piece of writing. A straightforward TV interview can often throw more light on an obscure subject than any number of graphics and diagrams. In a TV interview a personality is put directly under popular scrutiny without a writer's embroidery or embellishment.

The upshot is that these different forms of journalism have their advantages and their shortcomings. But each benefits from the other. The TV interviewer will draw deeply on the work of the writing journalist. Newspapermen, for their part, are not slow to make maximum use of the TV interview when they find it revealing or newsworthy.

In recent years the TV interview has become more argumentative than interrogative. The interviewers tend nowadays to put questions in the form of propositions and opinions to which the interviewee's

6

reaction is invited. The arch-priest of this technique is Brian Walden. Others have followed in his footsteps. The result is often sophisticated and sparkling, as the best intellectual conversation can be. But when the questions become too opinionated, too self-indulgent, the viewer's patience and comprehension may be sorely tried.

I make no apology for reprinting once again the code I first wrote for interviewers in 1961, after six years' work as an interviewer. I have tried to follow this code myself. My professional colleagues can judge whether their own interviews match up to the standards of this code. Viewers may wish to judge whether the interviews they see on television, by me or others, match up to the standards of this code.

1. The television interviewer must do his duty as a journalist, probing for facts and opinions.
2. He should set his own prejudices aside and put questions which reflect various opinions, disregarding probable accusations of bias.
3. He should not allow himself to be overawed in the presence of a powerful person.
4. He should not compromise the honesty of the interview by omitting awkward topics or by rigging questions in advance.
5. He should resist any inclination in those employing him to soften or rig an interview so as to secure a 'prestige' appearance, or to please Authority. If after making his protest the interviewer feels he cannot honestly accept the arrangements, he should withdraw.
6. He should not submit his questions in advance, but it is reasonable to state the main areas of questioning. If he submits specific questions beforehand he is powerless to put any supplementary questions which may be vitally needed to clarify or challenge an answer.
7. He should give fair opportunity to answer questions, subject to the time-limits imposed by television.
8. He should never take advantage of his professional experience to trap or embarrass someone unused to television appearances.
9. He should press his questions firmly and persistently, but not tediously, offensively, or merely in order to sound tough.
10. He should remember that a television interviewer is not employed as a debater, prosecutor, inquisitor, psychiatrist or third-degree expert, but as a journalist seeking information on behalf of the viewer.

My conviction is that if interviews are guided by this code the value of television as an instrument of democratic scrutiny will be enhanced.

Each of these interviews should be read in the context of its time. Each is different in style, with its own topical significance, and its own historical setting, which is explained by way of introduction to each interview.

The full transcripts have not been published before. The printed word, even with clarifying punctuation, cannot convey the manner and tone of speech, or facial expression. These texts, like *Hansard*, are the record of what was said, if not *how* it was said. There has been no amendment or editing, except to clarify or omit those confusions and repetitions which invariably arise in transcripts of extemporaneous broadcast speech, especially where voices clash, or grammar is imperfect.

As a postscript, there is an interview, not by me, but by Bernard Levin, in which the great columnist, my old friend, turns the tables on me.

My assorted selection* is published to offer some very different examples of interviews which are memorable to me, and which may now be revealing, or nostalgic, or astonishing, or entertaining for others to read. This book, with its historical texts, may be seen as a companion volume to my memoirs *Grand Inquisitor*.

---

* It may be asked why I have omitted my 1982 interview with the then Defence Secretary John Nott, who walked out of the studio. This notorious incident has already been fully and fairly recounted in my memoirs, with all relevant quotations. Moreover the Nott interview, which is memorable only for the walk-out, was a short (three-minute) item. Hence it has no place in a book of in-depth feature interviews.

'I'm sorry about the bad relations between Britain and Egypt and we hope that both countries will work for good relations to be friendly again.'

PRESIDENT NASSER

This was my first important interview. It was an ITN exclusive which made front-page news, not only in the British press but all over the world. It was the first interview which President Nasser had given to any British or American reporter since the Suez crisis. Only nine months earlier, in the autumn of 1956, Anglo-French forces had invaded Egypt. The background to this interview was difficult and sensitive. Britain and Egypt were not in diplomatic relations. Two British businessmen had been convicted on espionage charges. The situation was tense.

Five years earlier, as a young army officer, Nasser had been prominent among those who led the revolution to remove King Farouk. He had replaced Neguib as President of Egypt in 1956. Later that year he announced the nationalization of the Suez Canal, which had been internationally owned by Britain, France and others. In the ensuing Suez crisis the Anglo-French attack on Egypt, condemned by the UN and the United States, was halted. Nasser's prestige was enhanced and the reputation of the British Prime Minister, Sir Anthony Eden, destroyed.

It had been agreed in negotiations for my interview that I would be free to ask Nasser anything within the broad areas of questions which we had submitted, and in return his answers would be shown in full. I had with me the written authority of ITN's editor, Geoffrey Cox, that I was to withdraw if my right to question was restricted.

We had to wait a long seven days in the Semiramis Hotel in Cairo for the interview appointment to be confirmed. Officials warned against raising certain matters. I took note and steeled myself to raise these warnings with Nasser himself at the time of the interview. When I did so, he quickly said he did not mind what I asked him.

This was an interview which made television history. Its significance was appreciated by the veteran reporter James Cameron, who wrote a front-page story in the *News Chronicle* under the banner headline COLONEL NASSER DROPS IN:

> Sitting in the garden of his Cairo home, President Nasser leaned forward last night into British television screens. And he asked that we reunite in friendly relations. He thus did something that had never been done before in the history of international diplomacy.
>
> For the first time on record, a national leader submitting a major point of national policy, by-passed all protocol and sent his message into the homes of another state *at a time when the two were not in diplomatic relations.*

Time magazine reported the interview thus:

> Sitting before the cameras of Britain's Independent Television News – as Russia's Khrushchev did for CBS in the US – Nasser sent an amiable grimace into several million British living rooms ...
>
> Robin Day, the shrewd British interviewer who asked the questions for Britain's ITN, wanted to know how Nasser reconciled his stand against Communism at home with his overseas dealing with Russia ...
>
> Confronted with a direct question on Egyptian policy toward Israel – whether he really wanted to see its destruction as a state – Nasser tried desperately to fight his way between the Charybdis of a yes that would please Arabs and the Scylla of a no that would mollify the West.

Regrettably, this interview with President Nasser was transmitted at the off-peak hour of 11.05 p.m. So it had a minority audience, but it won professional acclaim.

ITN had given me a great opportunity. Interviews with world figures were not then commonplace as they are now. I had been in television for less than two years.

President Gamal Abdel Nasser

Interviewed for Independent Television News
Filmed at his home in Cairo, 29 June 1957
Transmitted 1 July 1957

ROBIN DAY President Nasser, the first thing I want to ask is this: What is your feeling towards Britain now?

PRESIDENT NASSER Well, I'm sorry about the period of the bad relations between Britain and Egypt and we hope that both countries will work for good relations in order to be friendly again.

RD Do you want to resume normal diplomatic relations?

NASSER I think that is the duty of each country. We have to return to normal relations.

RD Could I ask about your attitude to American policy now, in particular the Eisenhower doctrine for preventing the spread of Communism in the Middle East?

NASSER Well, we look to the American policy in connection with National-ism in the Middle East, because we feel that what is dominating in the Middle East now is Nationalism not Communism. There is no spread of Communists in the Middle East. But the Americans insist that Nationalism is Communism and try to stand against Nationalism, thinking that they are standing against Communism. They will turn the Nationalists to be Communists, because Nationalism is an open movement. Communism is an underground movement. They attack Nationalists and try to stand against Nationalism. The result will be turning Nationalism into an underground Communist movement.

RD You don't allow Communism to spread inside Egypt, do you?

NASSER Well, according to my information and my experience during the last five years, I think that Communism was neutralized in Egypt because of adopting Nationalist policy. Because the people are aiming at their national aspirations, they feel they are not able to adopt and fulfil their national aspirations and they come underground and form Communist elements. Now, because of the national policy of Egypt, I think that the Communist movement was neutralized.

RD Can you explain to people who watch this interview why it is that you fight Communism at home and yet appear to work very closely with it in your foreign policy?

NASSER Well, Communism at home, local Communism, is illegal.

RD In Egypt?

NASSER In Egypt, yes. But dealing with Russia is another thing. Our policy is a policy of non-alignment.

RD Non-alignment?

NASSER Non-alignment.

RD Similar to that of India, do you mean?

NASSER Similar, yes, to that of India. We want to have trade and commercial relations with all the world. We want to be friendly to all the world, we want to participate in the case of peace, we want to participate in the decrease of the cold war, we want to co-operate with the world to avoid war.

RD Do you feel that you are running any risks if Russia strengthens its foothold in the Middle East?

NASSER Well, of course we are against any domination in the Middle East.

RD Now you have often been criticized in the West for spending money on armaments which might have been devoted to improving the Egyptian standard of living. Do you have any comment on that?

NASSER Well, building an army which will be able to defend Egypt is not at all spending money on heavy armaments. We have to defend our country against aggression. We were saying that always. We declared that we are not aiming at aggression but we have to defend our territory against aggression. Now you know that aggression was against us. We were attacked by Israel, by Britain and France, of course at the same time.

RD Isn't it arguable that if there was a state of war with Israel, that her attack was merely a continuation of the state of war and not a separate act of aggression?

NASSER But there was an armistice at the same time. An armistice is a transition period between a state of war and the end of war.

RD You said that Egypt needs arms to defend herself but one question that has been prominent in the public mind in Britain and America in the last two or three days has been why Egypt should need three large Russian submarines?

NASSER Well, you know when we made our arms deal we asked for submarines. We want to build up our navy, as we build our army and air force. We asked for these submarines, well why not have submarines?

RD But Israel has interpreted this as a further threat to Israeli shipping. Is that a fair interpretation?

NASSER No, Israel is always interpreting everything to make noise and propaganda in order to deceive the Western world. They want to isolate the Arabs from the Western countries. So they have to raise their voice and make this noise. If you follow the Israeli propaganda they take each incident to make from it a big cause.

RD Is it still your policy to refuse Israeli shipping the right to go through the Suez Canal?

NASSER Really we cannot isolate the passing of Israeli shipping in the Suez Canal from the whole Palestine problem. We realize now in the Western countries that they are concentrating on the passing of the Israeli ships through the Suez Canal, neglecting the other problems. I mean the rights of the Arabs of Palestine who were expelled from their territory. The Arabs have the right to return to their home, to return to their territory as it was decided by the United Nations. Israel is asking to use the Suez Canal. According to the Constantinople Convention of 1888, Article 10, Egypt has the right to defend herself and defend her territory. According to this article, we stopped the Israeli ships from using the Suez Canal from 1948 until now.

RD Are you going to go on doing that?

NASSER Well, we feel that this is a part of the Palestine question.

RD You say that you cannot isolate this question, but as you remember the Security Council of the United Nations did isolate it in 1951, when they ruled that the stopping of Israeli shipping, and I quote, 'cannot be justified on the grounds that it is necessary for self-defence'.

NASSER In 1951 in the Security Council, they said that stopping the Israeli shipping from using the Suez Canal is not in the spirit of the armistice agreement. We take it as a legal question, we say that we have the right.

RD Then if you take it as a legal question are you prepared to accept a ruling on the matter by the International Court of Justice?

NASSER We said that in our declaration about the Suez Canal.

RD Now it has been frequently said of you, President Nasser, that you want to see the destruction of Israel as a state. Is that true?

NASSER Well, you can read my speeches. You can read all my statements. We said that we have to defend our territory against aggression and we insist about gaining the rights of the Arabs of Palestine, the one million refugees. There is a difference between the rights of the Arabs of Palestine and the destruction of Israel. I don't believe in war, and I don't believe that any small country can raise war because we cannot neglect the whole public opinion and the world moral and we cannot gamble a big war.

RD One quotation which has been used against you, President Nasser, is this: that in a telegram for instance to President Kuwaitly of Syria in December 1955 you said this, 'Egypt will be glad when her army and that of Syria meet on the ruins of this treacherous people.' Now is that implying the destruction of Israel?

NASSER Is it true? Are you sure of this telegram?

RD Those were the words I have.

NASSER All right, we can see it after this interview.

RD You think that might be an unfair translation?

NASSER Of course.

RD Then is it right that you now accept the permanent existence of Israel as an independent Sovereign State?

NASSER Well, we don't recognize Israel because there is a problem between us.

RD That is a diplomatic matter. But do you accept the permanent fact of its existence as an independent Sovereign State?

NASSER Well, you know – you know you are jumping to conclusions –

RD No, I'm asking a question. I appreciate, President Nasser, that you don't recognize Israel but surely that is a purely diplomatic technicality. Are you prepared to accept the existence of Israel as an independent Sovereign State apart from the question of frontiers?

NASSER Well, you know Israel for us is a problem because Israel to us now is a Palestine problem. We are aiming to solve the problem of the refugees. We are insisting and we are calling to give the Palestine refugees their rights – their territories, their land and their homes. We don't recognize Israel. We feel that the Israeli problem is the problem of Israel and the problem of the Palestinians. We said before that we are ready to accept the United Nations resolution of 1947 – that is to give the Arabs their rights and to give the Jews their rights.

RD Do you ever see a time when you and Mr Ben Gurion might get down by a table and talk about this problem?

NASSER Well, you know every time that Ben Gurion has said that he is ready to talk with us he was planning something. Seven days before the aggression, Ben Gurion said, 'Our policy is peace. We want negotiations with Egypt,' but he was trying to mislead us in order to raise his attack. One time before he said that he is ready to meet with Nasser to talk for a settlement. Next day there was aggression against Egyptian troops. It is a matter of trust and confidence.

RD To take your book. Is it a correct interpretation to say that you dream of the Arab countries becoming one great power from the Persian Gulf to the Atlantic ocean?

NASSER Well you know this book was published in 1956, after, one year after the revolution. I put this part about the Arab countries as a result of our studies, strategical studies. From the histories we can see that if the Arab countries are co-operating together they can defend themselves against aggression, if they are divided, if there is a dispute between the Arab countries, they will be under foreign domination. That's why I said in this book that the Arab countries must co-operate and must unite their policies.

RD You say a little more than that, don't you, President Nasser? According to this translation you say that 'the role of Egypt is to spark this tremendous power latent in the area around us'.

NASSER Yes.

RD That's a little more than co-operation.

NASSER Well, you know it is a power, maybe weakness or power. It was weakness. If we look through the history we can find that sometimes power was used as weakness elements against the Arabs. I said that we have to change these factors of weakness to be factors of power, that is, factors of strength to defend ourselves against aggression and against domination.

RD One of our British papers, the *Manchester Guardian*, which was very critical of Sir Anthony Eden's policy, says last week that your foreign policy towards the Arab States is now in ruins. What do you say about that?

NASSER Well, it was said many times in your newspapers, many things which are not the truth. Once it was said that I am making conspiracies all over the Arab world. I answered the question once that I don't think I am a genius to organize conspiracies and activities all over the Arab world. I would be the best organizer in the world.

RD Are your relations with Saudi Arabia and Jordan as satisfactory as you would like at the moment?

NASSER There are some difficulties, according to some suspicions in Jordan. It was said in Jordan that we are really participating in the plots. Of course it is nonsense. Of course your papers said that before. Hundreds of times the American papers said that before. It was said we were supporting some elements against the government. Well of course it is not true. I think in Jordan they will realize that, the Jordanian people will realize that we were not supporting a part of the Jordanian people against the others.

RD How about Saudi Arabia? Are you satisfied with King Saud's attitude at the moment?

NASSER My personal relations with King Saud are friendly relations, I look to King Saud as a friend. Sometimes there may be some suspicion but I think the facts will be known.

RD Do your policies have the support of the majority of the Egyptian people?

NASSER Well, I think so because they stood beside us during the aggression, according to your information – British information – they are waiting for the Egyptian people to make a revolution against the Egyptian government. We distributed 4,000 pieces of small arms to the people to stand beside the army during the aggression. We were able to collect these pieces of arms after the end of the aggression. The people were really ready to fight and to die for the liberty of their country. This was a proof for me that the people are supporting the policy of their government.

RD Can you answer the question which has been asked in the last few days in the West as to why it is necessary for you to strike out about half the candidates in the next month's elections?

NASSER Well, you know, if you return to history – if you return to American history during the days of Washington, or Oliver Cromwell in Britain, you may see that we are now facing this period of building up democracy. We have now a vacuum. We have no political parties because democracy was used for domination in this country. The minority was dominating the majority. The landlords and the Feudalists – we liquidated feudalism – we put an end to the domination of the landlords. We liquidated the parties – there was a vacuum. We want to build a new democracy for the interests of the people. We have to go on step by step.

RD Now most important of all, President Nasser, may I ask you about your plan for running the Suez Canal which you have deposited with the United Nations. Are you prepared to reconsider those proposals to bring them more into line with the famous six principles which the Security Council said were essential for any settlement of the Canal?

NASSER Well, we feel that our last declaration is fulfilling the six principles. The main point of conflict was the insulation of politics of any one country. We feel we want the insulation of the politics of the other countries, the other countries want the insulation of the politics of Egypt.

RD Could I put to you the point made by Mr Macmillan in the House of Commons last month. He said your proposals were a unilateral declaration. In other words not an agreed system but something Egypt could go back on at any time and therefore it was not right to say that the Canal was insulated from Egyptian politics.

NASSER No, but we said in this declaration that we want to register this declaration of the United Nations as an international obligation and it was registered in the United Nations as an international obligation. We were informed by Mr Hammarskjöld.

RD But the position at the moment is that Egypt should go back on the declaration if it so chose.

NASSER No, no, it is impossible – it is impossible after the declaration and after we said that it is an international obligation. Why we go back? For what reason? To make trouble?

RD Do you expect the great maritime countries of the world to be satisfied with that answer, without some international guarantee?

NASSER If they want to ease the tension and they are great powers, we are small country so they have the initiative. I don't think that small country like Egypt will try to create trouble with big powers.

RD But don't you think it is better and more profitable for a small country like Egypt to have a system which does not force great maritime countries to seek alternative routes of supply?

NASSER Well, we said we are ready to have a system of co-operation, but not a system of foreign domination because the Suez Canal is part of Egyptian territory. So we are ready about any sort of co-operation but not domination, whether it is international domination or single domination of any one of the big powers.

RD Mr President, thank you.

'*At home you are a politician, abroad you are a statesman.*'

HAROLD MACMILLAN

Macmillan's official biographer, Alistair Horne, records: 'His first breakthrough as a "television personality" had come with a full-length interview staged by a young, brash and virtually unknown journalist called Robin Day on 23 February 1958, immediately on his return from the Commonwealth tour.'

This ITN interview was a landmark in the premiership of Harold Macmillan, and in my own career. Next morning the *Yorkshire Post* observed, 'Certainly Macmillan is no longer just a House of Commons man.' It was the first time that a Prime Minister had been vigorously questioned on television. Apart from perfunctory interviews at airports, it was also the first time that a Prime Minister had been interviewed by a single questioner. No such interview would ever have been contemplated by Eden, Attlee or Churchill.

For me, this interview with Macmillan was the moment when I began to realize that my work as a TV journalist would turn me into a highly-exposed figure of controversy at the centre of political events. But not until much later did it really become clear that my television career had gone into orbit that Sunday evening in February 1958. I was thirty-four. I had been in television for less than two and a half years.

The reader of this Macmillan interview after thirty-five years may wonder why it was a front-page sensation at the time. My questions may not now seem particularly penetrating or forceful, or (with respect to Alistair Horne) brash. But remember that here, for the first time, a Prime Minister was being interrogated by a reporter in front of the mass TV audience. If my questions do not today seem vigorous, that was not the contemporary reaction. According to a sophisticated observer, Derek Marks of the *Daily*

Express: 'This was the most vigorous cross-examination a Prime Minister has been subjected to in public.'

Cassandra of the *Daily Mirror* took me severely to task in his celebrated column:

> Mr Day, who is a formidable interrogator, suddenly asked Mr Macmillan how he felt about criticism in Conservative newspapers 'particularly of Mr Selwyn Lloyd'.
>
> At once the Queen's First Minister was put on the spot. What *else* could he say about his colleague? How *could* Mr Macmillan be anything but complimentary to his colleague – and to his accomplice in the Suez escapade?
>
> So here you have the ridiculous situation of how the British Prime Minister can suddenly be put on a Morton's Fork which forces him into defending and maintaining a colleague who is obviously a disaster to British foreign policy.
>
> Mr Robin Day by his skill as an examiner has been responsible for prolonging in office a man who probably doesn't want the job and is demonstrably incapable of doing it.
>
> The Idiot's Lantern is getting too big for its ugly gleam.

The Editor of the *Daily Telegraph*, Donald MacLachlan, was doubtful about what he had seen: 'Should the Prime Minister have been asked what he thought of his own Foreign Secretary, before a camera that showed every flicker of the eyelid? Some say Yes; some say No. Who is to draw the line at which the effort to entertain stops?'

The *Manchester Guardian* seemed to be disturbed by the sheer novelty of the occasion:

> Everybody wants to know what a Prime Minister thinks about his colleagues, and Mr Day asked the right questions; but Mr Macmillan is the first holder of his office to have satisfied public curiosity so bluntly. This may be judged a good or a bad development, according to taste, but it is certainly new. Could one have imagined Sir Winston Churchill when Prime Minister gossiping about Sir Anthony Eden or Lord Salisbury?

Pendennis in the *Observer* wondered nervously: 'Will the television screen begin to by-pass the House of Commons, or even (dread thought) the Press? This is the kind of question that has been sending a shiver down what's left of Fleet Street's spine.'

Macmillan had been in office for only just over a year. Under his leadership, the Tory Party had survived the shambles of Suez. He had brushed aside the resignation of Chancellor Thorneycroft and two other Treasury ministers as a 'little local difficulty'. A few days before this interview, there was yet another blow to Tory morale. The party suffered a major by-election defeat at Rochdale. Labour won it from the Tories who were humiliated into third place. Moreover 80 per cent of the votes at Rochdale had gone to candidates who opposed Britain's H-bomb deterrent. That was one reason for my emphasis on the deterrent in this interview. Another reason was a Commons debate on defence, due that week. And the future of the Foreign Secretary, Selwyn Lloyd, who had flopped in a debate the week before, was the subject of much critical speculation. It was a question about Selwyn Lloyd, carefully phrased after close consultation with ITN's Editor, Geoffrey Cox, which elicited the big news for the next morning's front pages.

This was Macmillan growing in stature. Not yet the triumphant Macmillan who was to win a landslide victory in the 1959 General Election. But it was Macmillan the consummate politician, who was soon to be dubbed Supermac by the great cartoonist Vicky. It was Macmillan's debut as the TV star who in his old age was to stage such a stylish come-back as a performer. At the age of ninety he was to be the matinée idol of the televised House of Lords.

Perhaps the reader will share my enjoyment of the wise (or was it cynical?) Macmillanesque aphorism: 'At home you are a politician, abroad you are a statesman.'

The Rt Hon. Harold Macmillan MP, Prime Minister

Interviewed 'live' in the ITN series Tell the People
23 February 1958

ROBIN DAY Prime Minister, we've read in numerous newspapers that
you've come back with a new personality from your Commonwealth
tour, that instead of the dignified, reserved Mr Macmillan, there's a
new, back-slapping one. One word that I saw: a 'barn-storming' Mr
Macmillan. Are you conscious of any change of that nature?

RT HON. HAROLD MACMILLAN MP, PRIME MINISTER Well, I don't think
very much, but you know one has greater opportunities abroad. At
home you are a politician, abroad you are a statesman.

RD Lady Dorothy Macmillan was quoted this morning as saying that she
had promised 'to parcel up a few grandchildren and send them to
Australia and New Zealand'. Now, would you like to see more
emigration yourself?

MACMILLAN Well, yes I would. And, of course, the Australians are
frightfully keen to get their country filled up, as far as possible, with
British migrants.

RD Would you like to see it on a very large scale?

MACMILLAN It's been on a pretty big scale, you know. It can't go too
fast because it's very important that there shouldn't be misfits and
that the people should be happy and settle down well. But it will be
easier, really, now because now that Australia's building up her
industries, and England after all is a great industrial country, it will
be easier because more people will be able to go to towns and
industrial work, rather than to the distant countryside.

RD You've spoken of the tremendous sense of partnership and loyalty
that you found on this trip, but is it not a fact that by far the largest
country you visited, India, is utterly opposed to the basic principle
of British policy, namely the deterrent power of the H-bomb?

MACMILLAN No, I think that isn't really so. They are opposed to the
H-bomb, certainly, they are opposed to the groupings in NATO,
and so forth, but on the really basic thing they are on our side, that's
to say, they are bitterly opposed to the Communists in every way,

they are trying to defend the parliamentary system, individual freedom and everything which is part of our tradition.

RD Could I ask you this, Prime Minister, why does Britain need the H-bomb on its own, duplicating American effort?

MACMILLAN Well, two reasons for that. First we made the A-bomb. We were first to make it, under Attlee's government, then we made the H-bomb, under Churchill's government, and think it's a good thing that we should have an independent contribution to the deterrent, and I'm rather interested to see some of the people who don't want to have it are the most hostile to the United States and most anxious that our policy should not be what they call subservient to the United States.

RD But if Russia is afraid of anything, it is American power it is afraid of. What difference to the deterrent does our contribution make?

MACMILLAN Well, I think the independent contribution is a help. It gives us a better position in the world, it gives us a better position in the United States, and it puts us where we ought to be, in a position of a great power.

RD Now you say it gives us a better position, but can you imagine any situation in which we would use our H-bomb alone?

MACMILLAN I hope I can imagine no situation in which we would have to use it at all. But I say that the fact that we are a nuclear power helps us with the United States and makes them pay greater regard to our point of view, and that's of great importance in my view.

RD Could I put it to you in another way, and it's a view held I think not only by anti-American people, who say this – what is the use of brandishing this weapon – having this weapon, which could only mean suicide for this island if it were used?

MACMILLAN Well, because the object of the deterrent is to deter, that's to say it shouldn't be used. Of course, if it is used, well then the whole world falls into a terrible state of collapse. The point of it is that it shouldn't be used.

RD What do you say to those who want Britain to give a moral lead by abandoning the bomb?

MACMILLAN Well, I can understand those who want to give a moral lead by abandoning all armaments, that seems to be quite logical. I have great respect for that. But I can't see the object of abandoning one form of armament and keeping the others; there's no moral distinction.

RD And what about the suggestion that for Britain to abandon the bomb would induce other countries, like France for instance, to make an agreement not to have nuclear weapons?

MACMILLAN I don't think that is so at all. I think if we could get what we tried to get in the summer, and we may get again out of Summit talks, some general understanding with Russia, America and ourselves for controlled disarmament, that would have that effect, but for just Britain to drop out now, wouldn't have the result we want.

RD You think the only way to stop other countries from getting the bomb, apart from the three who have it at the moment, is a comprehensive scheme?

MACMILLAN Yes, which we nearly got in the summer and I am not at all without hope of getting.

RD Could I go on to the second stage in which the government say the bomb might be used, and in the White Paper there is a sentence, the government's White Paper on Defence, there's a sentence which has caused considerable alarm – it said that if Russia were to launch a major attack on the Western nations, even with conventional forces, they would have to hit back, the Western nations would have to hit back, with strategic nuclear weapons. Can you explain that, Prime Minister?

MACMILLAN Well, I'm glad you've asked that, because I think it has caused some misunderstanding. Surely it is this. If there is a sudden attack on us by nuclear, on the West, the West must retort by nuclear, the only thing they've got. But if there was a conventional attack it may take different forms, it may be just crossing the frontier, a few incidents, well of course you wouldn't answer that with a full nuclear reply. But if 200 divisions are mobilized and are marching across Europe, if London is being bombed by bombers, with ordinary bombs, if the whole great battle has begun we must retort, and what we must do now is to make it clear to Russia that we would retort in those circumstances, otherwise you are merely inviting an attack.

RD Don't you think that if the Russians know they are going to be attacked with H-bombs, even if they use conventional forces only, that is a direct encouragement to them to strike with nuclear weapons, first?

MACMILLAN No, because in the conventional field we wouldn't have a chance anyway. They have got 200 divisions. What have we got? Twenty, thirty, we might get forty? What we've surely got to distinguish is between some frontier incident and some things which give opportunity for negotiation. Remember that a conventional attack on a great scale can't be done in a moment. It takes two or three months' mobilization. All that becomes known, that's the opportunity for discussion, debate, hoping to stop it, that's the advantage. But if they were really determined to make an attack on that scale, they must know, and we must let them know, that the West would reply with all the power they have. Otherwise you are inviting attack.

RD These arguments are powerful ones, Prime Minister, but the fact remains that in the recent Rochdale by-election, leaving aside party labels, 80 per cent of the voters voted for candidates who did not want Britain to have the H-bomb at all. Are you concerned about that?

MACMILLAN Yes, I am concerned because it is very important that the people should understand. Of course I remember it all so well before the last war. I remember the peace ballot. I remember the curious combination of people, some of whom wanted to stand up to Hitler, and others who didn't want to have any arms at all. We have got to teach the people the truth, but I am equally certain that the way we are proceeding now − try and get the Summit talks, try and get controlled disarmament, in conventional as well as unconventional − is the right way of approach.

RD Don't you think there is a valid distinction, to go back to a point you made a moment or two ago, between the extreme nuclear weapon and ordinary weapons?

MACMILLAN There is, of course, a distinction, but of course, don't let anybody think that conventional war was very pleasant. We had 360,000 men killed in the Passchendaele battles.

RD They weren't defenceless civilians, were they?

MACMILLAN Well, they were the people of this country. I saw it twice in my life. I wouldn't like to send five divisions against 200 Russian ones.

RD Could I go on to the question of Summit talks, Prime Minister. You've said that you want them and you want them to be successful. Don't you think it would be a good idea to have a General Election first so that the Prime Minister who goes to the Summit is sure that he has a solid majority of the British people behind him?

MACMILLAN Well, I don't think that's at all a good idea. I think the first thing to do is to get the Summit talks, and the date of a General Election might not happen to coincide with the Summit talks. We might get the Summit talks a good deal earlier.

RD Do you expect Summit talks this year?

MACMILLAN I hope so.

RD How do you feel, Prime Minister, about criticism which has been made in the last few days, in Conservative newspapers particularly, of Mr Selwyn Lloyd, the Foreign Secretary?

MACMILLAN Well, I think Mr Selwyn Lloyd is a very good Foreign Secretary, and has done his work extremely well. If I didn't think so I would have made a change, but I do not intend to make a change simply as a result of pressure. I don't believe that that is wise and [it] is not in accordance with my idea of loyalty.

RD Is it correct, as reported in one paper, that he would like, in fact, to give up the job as Foreign Secretary?

MACMILLAN Not at all, except in the sense that everyone would like to give up these appalling burdens which we try and carry.

RD Would you like to give up yours?

MACMILLAN In a sense yes, because they are very heavy burdens, but, of course, nobody can pretend that they aren't. We've gone into this game, we try and do our best, and it's both in a sense our pleasure and, certainly, I hope, our duty.

RD Prime Minister, could I turn to another point on the subject of unemployment. You felt very strongly about unemployment in pre-war years, didn't you?

MACMILLAN Certainly.

RD And you remember probably saying in the 1930s, when you were round about my age, that Mr Baldwin's government was 'a line of disused slag heaps which might well be tidied up'. Can I ask you this? Are you happy about the Cohen report on wages and prices which says that more unemployment may be necessary, if our economy is to work properly?

MACMILLAN I didn't write the Cohen report, and I am not responsible for it, but I do want to draw a distinction between the sort of unemployment that I saw at Stockton; you had half the population out of a job, three million men at one time; and what we now have, which is I think 1.8, and what I think Mr Gaitskell said was the sort of tolerable figure as high as 3 per cent. I wouldn't like that either, but there is a distinction, there must be some changes of employment, there must be some changes of industrial work and so on, but anything like mass unemployment would be absolutely tragic and fatal.

RD But are you, as Prime Minister, willing to see unemployment a deliberate instrument of policy to make the economy work?

MACMILLAN No.

RD That is what the trade unions are worried about.

MACMILLAN Of course, and I don't think it should be a deliberate instrument. On the other hand, they know themselves, the trade unions as well as us, that inflation and what is called over-full employment, five jobs for every three men, is equally bad, it's bad for discipline, bad for the trade unions, and what we want is a balance, exactly what that balance should be and how. But there'll always be movement in and out, that must be so.

RD Finally, Prime Minister, what do you say to the growing number of people who see the two main political parties simply as Tweedledum and Tweedledee?

MACMILLAN Oh! I think you have been reading *Alice,** even after nearly a hundred years! Of course there's a feeling, because we have had a good many troubles since the war, we have seen two great parties, each struggling with them, and, therefore, it is fairly easy to come along as a third party and say all sorts of programmes. There's bound to be that feeling. I don't think the way to cure it from our point of view is to do anything but to try to accept this, try and do our job decently and honourably, and when the time comes, go to the people on our performance and based on our performance and our hopes that we can give for the next period. That's the straightforward thing.

RD Thank you very much indeed, Prime Minister.

* *Alice in Wonderland* was first published by Macmillan in 1865.

'*The economy has seldom been stronger.*'

SIR ALEC DOUGLAS-HOME

1964

Sir Alec Douglas-Home was Prime Minister for less than a year. As the 14th Earl of Home (pronounced Hume) he had succeeded Macmillan in October 1963. He was preferred by the Tory Party (according to the soundings taken) to Rab Butler (who was vastly more experienced) and Quintin Hailsham (who was originally favoured by Macmillan).

After renouncing his earldom, Home was quickly found a Commons seat. In the House he was no match for Harold Wilson, then at the height of his parliamentary brilliance. But Sir Alec Douglas-Home had qualities – integrity, lucidity and incisiveness – which impressed both sides of the House, especially when he spoke on foreign affairs. These qualities are evident in this interview.

His short premiership was not particularly memorable. Why then have I included an interview with him in this selection? This interview was done at a time when politicians had become uncomfortably aware that television was a new force in the political process. In particular, the television interviewer was under attack for seeking to usurp Parliament.

1964 was an election year. Under the Quinquennial Act, the Prime Minister had to call a General Election by October 1964, five years after Macmillan's landslide victory of 1959. In the spring of 1964, when this interview took place, programmes such as the BBC's *Panorama* were a regular platform for leading parliamentarians. These programmes, with their interviews, had acquired increasing authority and influence. The television studio had become a commanding forum for political debate.

In January of that year, in a characteristic article headed 'Ballot Box v Goggle Box', Peregrine Worsthorne had observed: 'It is now primarily through favourite weekly or daily public affairs programmes that the voters meet their leaders face to face, and form their whole conception of what political debate and argument, discussion and analysis are all about.'

Brigadier Sir John Smyth VC, MP protested that 'television has really by-passed the House of Commons in its political interviews of Ministers, not even excepting the Prime Minister and the Leader of the Opposition.' The Brigadier went on to speak for many of his parliamentary colleagues when he asked: 'Are we really willing to allow the television interview, viewed admittedly by several million people, to assume greater importance than the proceedings of the House of Commons?'

After this *Panorama* interview with Sir Alec, the *Sunday Express* asked indignantly: SHOULD WE ALLOW A PRIME MINISTER TO BE TREATED LIKE THIS?

A cooler appraisal came from David Wood, the respected Political Correspondent of *The Times*. His report next morning was head-lined:

PRIME MINISTER ON TOP IN TV DUEL

MR DAY'S THRUSTS EASILY PARRIED

It may be a topsy-turvy development of representative democracy but there is no blinking the fact that the supreme test for a party leader these days has become the ordeal by television. There is no blinking the fact either that last night Sir Alec Douglas-Home came through the ordeal of Mr Robin Day's particularly formidable inquisition in the BBC programme *Panorama* without a scratch.

In his appointed role of television Ombudsman in the service of the watching multitude, Mr Day set subtle traps and pitfalls along every yard of Sir Alec's path and never made him stumble once.

Opposition backbenchers would probably have given years of their life to have the Prime Minister full in their sights for twenty minutes, as Mr Day did, but it may be doubted whether their marksmanship would have been so rapid and penetrating.

Mr Day forgot nothing in his probing for an Achilles heel . . .

No parliamentary question-time or debate gives MPs anything like Mr Day's opportunities.

Sir Alec parried and returned every thrust with ease – not least when Mr Day raised the issue of amateurish and indecisive leadership, a description that with every passing minute seemed more absurdly inappropriate to his intended victim.

What had happened to our parliamentary democracy if a Prime Minister was to be judged by his ability in 'parrying the thrusts' of a TV interviewer? This was a question which worried me deeply, and reinforced my conviction that Parliament should be televised.

At Westminster, according to Walter Terry in the *Daily Mail*, this interview was a leading topic of conversation. As David Wood reported that week in *The Times*:

> ... a week in which Parliamentarians ruefully had to accept that big league politics had been played not at Westminster but in the television studio ... It has not been lost on Mr Harold Wilson and Mr Herbert Bowden [his Chief Whip], for instance, that single-handed a week ago Mr Robin Day had more scope and time to call the Prime Minister to account on a range of current fundamental political issues than the Leader of Her Majesty's Opposition, not to say all the rest of his front bench colleagues.

With the mounting political tension of an election year, coupled with the growing concern about the influence of TV, this was a time when an interviewer had to keep his nerve, while being careful to avoid disrespect, bias, or egotistical behaviour.

Not all the readers of the *Daily Telegraph* agreed with the judgment of its veteran TV critic, L. Marsland Gander: 'I regard Monday's joust with the Prime Minister as easily the best political interview ever seen on the TV screen.'

The attitude of many politicians was one of envy, fear, and resentment, summed up by one Sunday tabloid in the question 'Who the hell does Robin Day think he is anyway?'

But today this 1964 interview may well seem mild, polite and wholly unaggressive. Nearly thirty years later, the reader will scarcely believe that it could have been seriously described as a 'formidable inquisition', or as an 'ordeal' with 'subtle traps' and 'penetrating marksmanship'. Such was the climate of the time. Television interviewing, however restrained and respectful, was still regarded by parliamentarians and newspapermen as an intrusion into their own territory.

The Rt Hon. Sir Alec Douglas-Home KT, MP, Prime Minister

Interviewed for BBC Panorama
17 February 1964

ROBIN DAY I'd like to start, before I ask you about your Washington visit, by asking you about this grave Cyprus situation – what is the latest position on that this afternoon?

RT HON. SIR ALEC DOUGLAS-HOME MP, PRIME MINISTER Well actually on the ground things are not too bad today. You know there were 700 Turks trapped in a school. Well we've been able to release them and there is a truce in that part of Cyprus arranged. Of course the assumption on which we're in Cyprus at all is that both sides want us to be there to prevent civil war. And neither our force, nor any international force, can operate unless that assumption holds.

RD What is the point of our taking the matter to the Security Council?

DOUGLAS-HOME The point is to try and get the general approval and cover of the Security Council and the Secretary-General, without exposing ourselves to a Russian veto of any operation, or indeed for a Russian control of it. As you know the Turks are very afraid of that.

RD How can we do that? How can we get the one without the other?

DOUGLAS-HOME There are various processes, you know, in the United Nations. There is the consensus proposal which is sometimes made, where you get a consensus of opinion without a vote, and if the consensus was in our favour that we should try and contrive an international force, I think that would be the best way.

RD The Opposition have asked 'why you did not go to the United Nations in the first place, as they say they suggested seven weeks ago?' What is your answer to that?

DOUGLAS-HOME I really almost answered that, I think, in what I said just now. The Turks are very concerned lest there should be a veto on any operation, and secondly of course that we do not want to see Russia – in her present mood about Cyprus – operating in the Eastern Mediterranean and really preventing any solution.

RD Do you accept that Turkey has a legal right, under the Cyprus Treaty, to take military action?

DOUGLAS-HOME Oh certainly all three of the guaranteeing Powers have a right to do so if the constitution breaks down.

RD And what would happen if Turkey moves in, would we stand aside, or what?

DOUGLAS-HOME Well, I don't want to anticipate that, because I think that we must use every possible political means to try and see to it that there is a solution, within the framework of the present constitution, but with, no doubt, some amendments, if those are possible.

RD What is the next step now?

DOUGLAS-HOME The next step I think is going on just at this minute, as we're talking, and that is the Security Council meeting. If we get a resolution which enables us to form an international force, however it's formed, we're not dogmatic about that, that will be the first thing. And the second thing will be to renew political consultations on some level – I haven't made up my mind which is the most desirable level yet – in order really to get rules of living on the ground while a political mediator operates.

RD There's a report tonight that there may be some idea of partition in the British government's mind. What do you say about that?

DOUGLAS-HOME Well, we've always held a very clear view on this: that partition is the worst of all answers to this problem; in a small island where the line of partition could only run through, for instance, a place like Nicosia. It really is the last resort, and even at that wouldn't hold.

RD And you don't have such a plan in mind . . .?

DOUGLAS-HOME No, no such plan.

RD Turning to your visit to Washington, Prime Minister, what do you regard as the most important result of your talks with President Johnson?

DOUGLAS-HOME Well, I think the most immediate result with which I was pleased was the complete identity of view that we now have about the position in South-East Asia. There was a moment when I thought that the American preoccupation with preventing Indonesia going Communist, and our natural preoccupation and first concern – that is the integrity of Malaysia – might pull apart. Now there's no danger of that, whatever. And I was able to tell President Johnson that if, for instance, our troops had to leave the frontier of Borneo, Borneo would be subverted and overrun, and the next target would be Singapore.

RD Did you complain to President Johnson about American aid to Sukarno?

DOUGLAS-HOME No, I didn't complain about American aid. There was no need. The visit of Mr Robert Kennedy, you know, began to bring us very close together on this. There was no need at all to complain about American aid.

RD Did you and President Johnson agree on any new steps towards easing cold-war tension? I'm thinking of this so-called 'Peace Offensive' which we've heard about.

DOUGLAS-HOME Well, we reviewed every possibility and I think I would still hold the view, after seeing President Johnson, that I really held before, that the area of anti-surprise attack is the most profitable area now. President Johnson made a proposal himself about freezing nuclear weapons. We have made a proposal to put observers in the whole NATO and Warsaw Pact area, and I think it is a combination of those kind of moves which might gain support from the Russians. Always, as you know, they've broken down before on one thing and that is the Russian fear of inspection.

RD How are we going to get over that, do you think?

DOUGLAS-HOME Well, that remains to be seen, but I would have thought it was so clearly to Russia's advantage to have observers really in West Germany, and in Europe, that they might be willing to consider this limited amount of inspection that would be required to prevent a conventional attack.

RD In defending British trade with Cuba, Prime Minister, do you think that you gave enough weight to the American view that the Castro regime might be brought down by economic pressure? Which is what they'd like to do?

DOUGLAS-HOME I know, but we've held a very consistent view about this and I hold it very strongly, that nobody of the nature of Castro is brought down by economic sanctions and boycotts, and I think they're very dangerous things. At the beginning the impact is not on Castro, the leader, but on the people, and on the whole people are willing to tighten their belts and back their national leader if they're really made hungry.

RD I came across a feeling in Washington, among quite a number of Americans, that if Britain had followed a different defence policy, one which included conscription, then Britain might have had more troops available to deal with problems like Cyprus. What do you say about that?

DOUGLAS-HOME Well, I don't think for these kind of operations that you want more troops. What you want are regular troops, very highly trained, with a very high degree of mobility, and that we've got, and I think we've demonstrated this in Malaya, in Cyprus, and in the three East African territories later. Of course, if you depart from police operations, to operations that are akin to war, then you have to call up reserves and do things of that kind, but I think for the police operations required of us in the modern world we've got enough and they're very highly trained. I'd like some more recruits for the Army, let's say that at once, but I think we shall get them.

RD When you say that our movements were swift and so forth, there was some criticism of our transport planes, wasn't there? I believe twenty-seven of them had to refuel on the way to Cyprus, which was said to be unsatisfactory. Don't you think we need more things like that?

DOUGLAS-HOME We shall get them, too, because we are thinking in terms now, of course, of improving our transport fleet, and we can do that. But I think that by and large the operations could hardly have been carried out more quickly and decisively after the word of command was given. I remember this vividly, because it was on Boxing Day about twelve o'clock at night when we first started this and within a few hours everything was on the move.

RD On the general subject of your defence policy, do you want to make the independent British deterrent the main election issue?

DOUGLAS-HOME No. I don't want to make it the main election issue, but it's bound to be the main election – well one of the main election issues if the Opposition insist on saying that they're going to deprive us of all control over our own nuclear arm. All I say then is that our electors must know that this is so and they must decide between us on this question.

RD May I put a number of points to you on that? If we depend on America for the sale of the Polaris missiles how can our deterrent be called, fairly, either British or independent?

DOUGLAS-HOME Well, America is an ally, has made a definite agreement with us at Nassau that they will provide us with the material to construct these submarines, and once we've constructed the submarines of course we go on making them ourselves. So we have this deterrent completely under our own control.

RD Do you think in an election the question of whether Britain can destroy Moscow will appear relevant at a time when attention is focused more on the problems of sending troops to these trouble spots in the world?

DOUGLAS-HOME I don't think that this will possibly loom very large in an election, except in this sense that I do believe that if we deprive ourselves of all control over our nuclear arm then Britain becomes a second-class Power. Now the Opposition may be prepared to contemplate this, I'm not. I think it's a ridiculous conception and I won't have anything to do with it. And therefore, this could be, in that sense, a major issue.

RD You have said several times that the British bomb insures us a seat at the top table in world councils, but if we recall the most serious crisis of the nuclear age, the Cuban missile crisis, there were, I think, then, only two seats at the top table, and we had neither of them.

DOUGLAS-HOME We can hardly get to the table but the modern methods of communication allowed us to keep in the very closest touch with both sides, all the time. But what I do mean, and seriously say, is this, that on all these matters of nuclear peace, and war – and there will be some from time to time – the question of Berlin is not out of the way. There are very serious questions in South-East Asia which might bring East and West into a clash. But then we must be at the table and I'm sure that the French are going to get a nuclear weapon; they will therefore be there. But no other nation that has not got nuclear power is going to be asked to take part in these discussions.

RD What do you say to the argument, which the Opposition think is extremely important, that your policy is an encouragement, if not an incitement, to the nuclear ambitions of other Powers?

DOUGLAS-HOME Well, you see, the French are going to get this thing. It won't make the slightest difference to them whatever our decision is. So are the Chinese going to get a weapon.

RD What about Germany?

DOUGLAS-HOME Well, yes, I was just going to come to Germany, and Italy. I think that the idea of a whole lot of countries queuing up to try and manufacture nuclear weapons is quite out of the question. To begin with this takes years and years to do and they haven't even made a start. I think that both Germany and Italy would far prefer to see some new arrangement in NATO which gave them, not a control over the firing of the weapon, but a really effective say in the strategy and deployment of these weapons, than they would try and get these things for themselves.

RD May I turn to domestic affairs, Prime Minister. Is it correct that you

41

have been warned by the Treasury that there is a danger of a serious Balance of Payments crisis in the autumn?

DOUGLAS-HOME Well, I can answer that in one word – and that word is no.

RD On January 1st of this year you said the economic outlook was very good, do you still think so?

DOUGLAS-HOME Yes, I think it's seldom been stronger. Of course, there's always a danger of the pressure on the economy of these great programmes of capital investment, on education, housing, roads and the rest of it on which we're engaged. But the economy is very strong; exports are going up. Almost everything depends on whether we can really maintain the 4 per cent overall increase in the national production, year in and year out.

RD But the head of Neddy warned, I think on Friday, that the economy is coming to a difficult period. Are you saying that no precautionary measures are necessary – between now and October?

DOUGLAS-HOME If the Chancellor judges that the economy is running into what you call a difficult period (which might be quite different from a critical period) if he judged that, he would take the necessary action – election or no election. This is a matter of the national interest and the national economy, not, I hope, of party politics.

RD But of course you might be in a dilemma, in that if you do take measures to prevent such a crisis these might be unpopular and harmful to your election chances?

DOUGLAS-HOME Well, there might be. You know it isn't really necessarily a Prime Minister's job to be popular. A Prime Minister's job and a Chancellor of the Exchequer's job is to do what is right for the country. We may be unpopular if anything had to be done, but I'm not saying that anything will have to be done, because that must be for the Chancellor to judge in the circumstances of the time.

RD Prime Minister, you may have noticed a number of criticisms of your record as Prime Minister, that your leadership has been 'amateurish and indecisive'. I want to put a number of points to you on which this criticism has been made. First of all, why did it take you three months to decide whether to have two Ministers of Education or one?

DOUGLAS-HOME Because we had to consult the universities, technical colleges, the educational authorities. And in November I said in the House of Commons, that I would give the decision in February, and I did.

RD But your opponents have suggested that delay was due to a clash between the rival ministers concerned?

DOUGLAS-HOME Yes I know, but you see my opponents are not in the Cabinet and I have been all the time. I simply haven't seen this clash. And Lord – Mr Hogg (we must remember to get this right, I must, certainly) – Mr Hogg is now the minister responsible over the whole field of education, and backed up very loyally by Sir Edward Boyle.

RD But why have you demoted Sir Edward Boyle?

DOUGLAS-HOME Well, because for this reason – when you say 'demoted' – I haven't. Sir Edward Boyle, because of his overall contribution, and very experienced he is, is a member of the Cabinet still. But Sir Edward Boyle – and indeed I myself – and everybody else were very anxious when we'd made the decision that there should be one Minister for Education that that decision should not be blurred in anybody's mind. So Sir Edward became a Minister of State for Education. He offered to go out of the Cabinet, but I brought him back in because obviously his opinions on much wider things are so valuable.

RD Of course it has been suggested that Mr Hogg was made education overlord as a result of a bargain made with you when you were trying to get him to join your government.

DOUGLAS-HOME I don't make bargains of that kind, but can you imagine anyone better qualified to fill this position than Mr Hogg? With every possible intellectual and – qualification?

RD I wouldn't quarrel with his intellectual qualifications but you would hardly expect me to answer your question which I don't think the viewers will want me to answer.

DOUGLAS-HOME No, I don't think so, one way or another.

RD Fair enough. May I turn to this question of the legislation to do with Resale Price Maintenance – what do you say to the criticism that these proposals were rushed in without adequately prepared legislation?

DOUGLAS-HOME No, they weren't rushed in, in that sense. What we felt we had to do, particularly at this time of our life, although you may think it's politically rash, was to throw the whole weight of the government's authority decisively on the side of lower prices. Now I think that – what I hope everybody will do now is to wait for the Bill, and that the criteria by which any manufacturer's claim that his Resale Price Maintenance Scheme is in the national interest will be fair, and seen to be fair, and if he can prove his case, well that's all right. This will be part of the national structure.

RD When do you expect this will become law?

DOUGLAS-HOME Well quite soon, as soon as they can print the Bill.

RD But when do you expect it will become law?

DOUGLAS-HOME Oh, become law, before – well, I'm not going to – I was going to say before we have a General Election – before the end of the session.

RD But before the General Election.

DOUGLAS-HOME Well, that is my intention.

RD How long will a Bill like this take to get through.

DOUGLAS-HOME That I can't tell you because you might deduce from that what the date of the General Election would be.

RD That might be a good thing. One Conservative Member of Parliament, Prime Minister, says he has never known such a large protest mail as he has had on the Resale Price Maintenance issue. Now, are you not concerned that these proposals will embitter many of your loyal supporters?

DOUGLAS-HOME I would be concerned if I thought that when the Bill is published anyone would find this unjust, but they won't. The criteria for judgment really will be fair, and do let me repeat the essential thing in our economy now is for British prices to be competitive. The government must set an example, and I believe we have done so by our most definite action, and definite indication to the country that the government is throwing its whole weight on the side of keeping prices down. And, after all, shopkeepers are also consumers. Every family is a consumer and interested in this.

RD May I put to you a question about which I think there is some confusion, the government's attitude on the emigration of these scientists, particularly to America? Now, does the government think it is a good thing which should be encouraged or a bad thing which should be prevented?

DOUGLAS-HOME I think it's over-simplifying it a little, perhaps, to put it that way, but it is a natural thing in a way that's been going on a long time that a proportion of our scientists and able men should go overseas, it's a European movement not only from Britain. But isn't the plain fact this, that America has 180 million people and therefore is three times the size of us? They're eight times as wealthy, and therefore there are certain sections, at any rate, of scientific research that they probably – in which they excel. Now that being so, some people are going to be attracted to go there.

RD But is it not a very serious thing that so many brilliant scientists –

however much we like to export our talent – should be leaving this country just at a time when Britain is trying to build up a massive programme of scientific education and development?

DOUGLAS-HOME Yes, and I hope that people who are thinking of going to America will take this into account, though I cannot imagine that any party or government could have put forward a more comprehensive scheme for higher education than we've done in the last few months. But many, many scientists, you know, are attracted here.

RD But do you plan any new measures in view of this recent wave of people saying they're going, to try and ease their problems even more, and to see what will make them stay?

DOUGLAS-HOME Well, of course we will do what we can. You don't think this is a revolt of the scientists, against the Socialist conception of society which would make all men equal. What they want is their talents rewarded and this is what I hope they're going to get under our system and organization of society.

RD Turning to your policy on Europe, Prime Minister, has the government decided whether Britain is going to try and enter the Common Market again, or not?

DOUGLAS-HOME You know, I told the House of Commons the other day that I'd have to have a gramophone record made of my reply on this. Because what I've said is that this is clearly not a live issue at present – it certainly isn't while General de Gaulle is there. I'm not sure it would be, even if he was succeeded by another French government. And therefore we have to wait and see, and then the government would have to give a lead to Parliament, and Parliament would decide.

RD But Mr Wilson has been seeking to make this an issue because he challenged you to give a pledge which read as follows – that no government of which you are head would consider entering the Common Market on any terms which would reduce Britain's existing freedom to trade with the Commonwealth.

DOUGLAS-HOME Yes, you see, but I gave the same answer to Mr Wilson as I've given to you.

RD And he wasn't very satisfied.

DOUGLAS-HOME No, but that's not my job.

RD Do you want to reform the process for choosing a Conservative leader?

DOUGLAS-HOME This is a little awkward for me, isn't it, because I am the last one who was chosen, and the processes were certainly as thorough as they've ever been on the traditional lines. I think the Party is capable of making up its mind about this, and will no doubt consider this between now and the time for choosing another Conservative leader, whenever that may be.

RD And on the question of whenever that may be is there not a strong case, very seriously, Prime Minister, for an early election, so that the country can have a government, of whatever party, invigorated by a fresh mandate, to tackle all these problems facing the country?

DOUGLAS-HOME I'm all for a fresh mandate when the time comes. But of course, if you're by that implying that we're not vigorous, just remember what we've done in the last few months ...

RD No, but any government would be invigorated by a fresh mandate ...

DOUGLAS-HOME Oh yes, I've heard this argument and I've been through a number of General Elections. And I've heard this argument used every time, and, you know, if we'd gone to the election last autumn we'd have been told that we were afraid of a hard winter. And if we go now we shall be – then we shall be told we're scared of an economic crisis in the autumn. And if we go in the autumn we shall then be told that we haven't dared to go before – you can't get it right.

RD I can see you've been thinking about this quite a lot, Prime Minister.

DOUGLAS-HOME I know, but this is old stuff.

RD Have you decided, Prime Minister, finally whether to take part in some kind of television debate or confrontation with Mr Wilson during the election campaign?

DOUGLAS-HOME My first reaction to this is that the British election is something in which something over 600 constituencies have to decide the issues, and the issues are issues of policy. Therefore I'm not particularly attracted by, so to speak, confrontations of personality. If we aren't careful, you know, you will get a sort of (what's it called?) Top of the Pops contest – I daresay I should win it, I'm not sure. But at any rate, I'm not really very much attracted by this. You'd then get the best actor as leader of the country and the actor will be prompted by a script-writer. I'd rather have our old ways, really, and put our policies firmly in front of our people.

RD But if you decline Mr Wilson's challenge – and after all debate between personalities is in the great British political tradition – might it not look as if you were running away?

DOUGLAS-HOME Oh no, I don't think so. After all, I debate with Mr

Wilson in Parliament. But I shall decide if I want to confront Mr Wilson, not Mr Wilson if he wants to confront me.

RD Thank you, Prime Minister.

'I would have found it almost an intolerable burden to be Home Secretary
had one had to decide whether people were to be hanged.'

ROY JENKINS   1966

I have interviewed Roy Jenkins, now Lord Jenkins of Hillhead, at
most stages of his complicated career – as Home Secretary (both
times), as Chancellor of the Exchequer, as Labour's Deputy Leader,
and as President of the European Commission. In the 1983 election,
after his ill-fated bid for a political comeback as Leader of the
mould-breakers in the SDP, I had a *Panorama* campaign interview
with him as 'joint Prime Minister designate' of the Liberal-SDP
Alliance. That occasion was described as 'Woy and Wobin wambling
on about the gwoss national pwoduct'.

A less portentous interview, and certainly the one which I recall
with most pleasure and amusement, is the one printed here. Roy
Jenkins was then a fledgling Cabinet Minister aged forty-five,
already a stylish Westminster figure, but without too much of the
grand manner which in due course he effortlessly acquired.

A few days earlier he had been appointed to the Home Office
by Harold Wilson. This was the first interview with Roy Jenkins
as a Cabinet Minister. I explore his Welsh upbringing, his family
background, his transition from Abersychan Grammar School to
Balliol College, Oxford. And why he chose Asquith and Dilke as
subjects for biographies. He explains why he found being a writer
harder than being a minister. Connoisseurs of the urbane Jenkins
style may enjoy the relaxed dexterity of his answers to the questions
about how Socialists should live and behave.

Roy Jenkins was about to make his mark as a reforming libertarian
Home Secretary, and as architect of the permissive society, which
he always preferred to call the civilized society. The central purpose
of the Home Office, he declares, is not 'the moral health of society',
but 'to hold the balance between liberty and order'.

This interview was one of an early BBC 2 series called *People to Watch.* That title was not inappropriate for Roy Jenkins, rising star of the Labour government. He was an elegant TV performer and, to some shrewd observers, a future Labour Prime Minister. In the end, however, this biographer of Prime Ministers failed to achieve the highest office, though there were times when it may have been within his grasp. A dignified consolation prize was his election to follow Harold Macmillan as Chancellor of Oxford University. He defeated his Oxford contemporary, Ted Heath, whom he here remembers as 'a solid, rotund figure ... with great political ambition, standing with his back to the fire in the Balliol Junior Common Room'.

Leaving aside Sir Winston Churchill, no other parliamentarian in this century has been, as Roy Jenkins was to be, not only an outstanding Cabinet Minister and a statesman of international repute, but an accomplished man of letters.

The Rt Hon. Roy Jenkins MP, Home Secretary

Interviewed in BBC 2 series People to Watch
2 January 1966

ROBIN DAY A shrewd observer of the Westminster scene, the Political Correspondent of *The Times*, wrote the other day that 'any minister who stays long enough in the Home Department will be lucky to escape damage to his liberal reputation'. True or not?

RT HON. ROY JENKINS MP, HOME SECRETARY I don't know, I've only been there for about ten days – two days in the office at the present time. Clearly it's regarded by a lot of commentators as a difficult and a dangerous department. It's not unique in that respect. The Ministry of Aviation, where I've just come from, was in some ways regarded as a rather difficult department but I enjoyed it very much. I'm sure there'll be a vast number of problems at the Home Office, and things which are very liable to blow up unexpectedly in one's face. But I'm not looking for a political graveyard, and at the same time I was very glad to become Home Secretary, so I hope one may be able to avoid it being this.

RD You used the phrase 'political graveyard', which has often been used about the Home Office – as a political historian yourself, is it accurate to say that the Home Office is a political graveyard in modern times?

JENKINS No, I don't think so, no. I think one could pick out a lot of offices from which people have gone down rather than up. But so far as the Home Office is concerned, in its whole period since 1782, when it was first established, a lot of people who've gone on to great success have held this office. Perhaps slightly less so in recent decades, though even so far as recent decades are concerned ... Lord Morrison of Lambeth held it for five years during the war and went on to a very considerable period of political success afterwards ...

RD Chuter-Ede's reputation was very high?

JENKINS Chuter-Ede's reputation, I would say, went up and he held the office of Home Secretary for a longer time than anyone since Lord Sidmouth, over 150 years ago.

RD Before I ask you to say whatever you feel you can say at this early stage about some of your Home Office responsibilities, may we talk a little about yourself? What kind of home did you come from – a poor one, was it?

JENKINS Well, it was certainly a poor one when I was born, or a fairly poor one, because when I was born in 1920 my father was still working as a miner in South Wales. He ceased to work in the pits before I can remember anything, when I was about eighteen months old, and he became a Trade Union official, which he was throughout my early childhood, and then throughout my later childhood he was a Member of Parliament. And certainly by South Wales standards – perhaps by any standards in the thirties as I grew up, it wasn't a poor home. It wasn't a rich home, but it was a perfectly comfortable, and even reasonably prosperous home.

RD You're somewhat unusual among the Home Secretaries in that your father in fact once went to prison . . .

JENKINS Yes, he did.

RD . . . in connection with his Trade Union activities. What were the circumstances?

JENKINS Well, the circumstances, which were rather carefully kept from me at the time, because they thought this would have a traumatic effect on me, aged six – the circumstances were that there was some riot which developed during the 1926 strike, and my father – quite unjustly, as he always thought, and he was basically a most law-abiding man – was sentenced to a short period of imprisonment.

RD Three months . . .?

JENKINS I think the sentence was nine months actually and I suppose he was there for a little less than that. He took the view, very strongly, that he was there as a leader, he was trying to restrain the position – the police took a different view.

RD You went to an elementary school?

JENKINS Yes.

RD And then a grammar school?

JENKINS Yes I did.

RD And how did you get to Balliol?

JENKINS I wasn't a scholar. I failed to get a scholarship, I got an entry. Balliol was fairly competitive then, not as competitive as it is now, but basically I got to Balliol because my father paid the fees, which, though he wasn't tremendously well off, he thought was the most important thing he could do at that stage.

RD And what did you read at Balliol?

JENKINS I read Modern Greats – philosophy, politics and economics.

RD And your tutor was?

JENKINS Well I had a variety of tutors. G. D. H. Cole was a tutor of mine. Lindsay – A. D. Lindsay, Master of Balliol – taught me ... Thomas Balogh taught me economics ... I was almost his first pupil.

RD He's now teaching the government economics?

JENKINS He's now teaching the government economics. He was an extremely good teacher in those days.

RD Did your political outlook – was it shaped by your early upbringing in Wales, the son of a miner, or was it formed intellectually as an undergraduate?

JENKINS Well, I've often tried to ask myself this question. I mean, I think I would have been appallingly insensitive if living in the South Wales of the thirties had had no effect on me. And yet if I honestly say had I lived in Surrey would I have been tremendously different in my views I think the answer is no, and to that extent, although I think the background had some considerable influence, I think the process was perhaps more an intellectual than a geographic one.

RD Your contemporaries at Oxford included Mr Heath, did they not?

JENKINS They did indeed.

RD And what impression did you form of him at that time – if any?

JENKINS Well, I remember him in a way quite well. He was President of the Balliol College Junior Common Room, and he became President of the Union in the term after I went up. I've a perfectly clear early physical recollection of him, standing in the morning, rather a rotund figure then, wearing a scholar's gown, he was an organ scholar, reading *The Times* – an appropriately statesmanlike paper for him to read – standing with his back to the fire against a club fender in Balliol JCR. A solid, rotund figure whom one thought had great political ambition and would fulfil at any rate some part of it.

RD Have you come across resentment, or suspicion, in the Labour Movement, that your manner, and speech, have in fact lost all trace of your Welsh origins? That you're now an urbane easterner, if you like, rather than someone from the Welsh hills, or valleys?

JENKINS Well, of course, one can never tell what thoughts there are in other people's minds. I don't think so, no. I've never been very consciously aware of this process myself. I came from a non-Welsh-speaking part of Wales. My parents, honestly, my father didn't speak terribly differently from myself. I've never been aware of a great change setting in.

RD You've never been aware of moving from one class to another?

JENKINS I don't think so, no. No, certainly not.

RD You're reputed, Mr Jenkins, to enjoy sophisticated and elegant living – do you see any conflict, as some people do, between this and being a Socialist?

JENKINS Well, I think we'd have to do a great deal of definition as to what sophisticated and elegant living amounts to. They are both adjectives which are rather carefully chosen ... It's not quite clear whether one wants to contradict them violently, or to regard them as flattering. They're both very much on the balancing line between adjectives which are – might be regarded as flattering but are in fact derogatory ...

RD I meant them as factual but I accept your point ...

JENKINS They're difficult ones to define. I don't – I don't lead a particularly extravagant life. I think – I mean, I enjoy a lot of things. If by elegant one means does one like things to be attractive rather than unattractive, yes I do. If by sophisticated one means does one like to know a wide range of people, inside and outside politics, then yes I do. But I think this is a good thing for anyone who's in an active position in life today.

RD To what extent do you think a Socialist's political beliefs should be reflected by the practice and example of his own life?

JENKINS Well, I think that somebody who claimed to be a Socialist but at the same time devoted his major central purpose to making money – or indeed to spending money – would be in a rather hypocritical position. But I think to some extent it's a question of balance. I don't think one should, or that many people would, take the view that somebody who has a reasonably comfortable standard of living ought not to enjoy it and be a Socialist at the same time.

RD So it's all right to be a successful Socialist author but not a successful Socialist stockbroker?

JENKINS No, no ... It wouldn't in my view be all right to be a successful Socialist author, if I thought about nothing but the money my books make.

RD On that point about practising in private life, do you think a Socialist should send his son to a fee-paying public school, for instance?

JENKINS Well, I think ideally the question of sending children to fee-paying public schools ought not to arise for any of us. But one of my children has been to what is certainly a public school, though he's left now, and gone at his own wish for a couple of terms to a comprehensive school. The others have gone to day schools in London, so we've had a fairly wide experience of education. No, I don't think it's any worse for a Socialist to do this than it was for my father to pay my fees at Balliol before the war.

RD You wrote biographies of Asquith and of Sir Charles Dilke, why did you choose those two personalities?

JENKINS Well, of course a lot of things one does in life arise largely through accident. I chose Sir Charles Dilke because my present publisher suggested him to me as a splendid subject for a biography – a figure about whom there was a great mystery which nobody had ever tried to investigate and I went home and read *The Times* report of the law case in which he was involved, and thought this was a fascinating subject and from there started to write about Dilke. Having written Dilke I was then looking for another book to write and I wanted to write broadly on this period between 1850 and 1914, because it's a period which interests me very much. On the whole I wanted to write about Liberals rather than Conservatives, because I prefer Liberals to Conservatives, and I wanted, at this stage, to write about a big figure, rather than a small, though extremely interesting figure, as Dilke appeared to most people. Asquith rather shone out as the obvious choice to make in these circumstances.

RD You also, I believe, hope to write the life of Hugh Gaitskell, of whom you were a devoted friend and follower. Since it's likely that you're going to be a member of the Labour Cabinet, or the Shadow Cabinet, for many years, do you think you'll ever be able to do this without reopening old wounds?

JENKINS Well, it's not so much this aspect of the matter which worries me at the moment, though I am becoming a little worried about my position in relation to this biography and I have a dual role, because I'm not only intended to be the biographer, I'm also, with Tony Crosland, the literary executor, and therefore have to decide what happens. I think there's an extremely interesting life to be written of Hugh Gaitskell. I'm not sure it matters it should be written this year rather than next year, but at some stage if I'm so occupied that I can't see an early opportunity of writing it, I shall obviously have to cease to be a dog-in-the-manger and let somebody else have a go. But I hope – I haven't quite come to that stage yet.

RD You're quoted as saying that it's harder being a writer than being a minister. Now, why did you say that? If you were accurately quoted.

JENKINS I think I was accurately quoted. I will, if I may, tell you exactly what I mean by this. Obviously in some sense the nervous strain of being a minister is far greater. What is not greater, what is far harder work about being a writer is this: ministerial work has a momentum. Supposing you wake up, as we always do, feeling not very vigorous on a particular morning, you go into your office and you have to deal with things, there are people to see you, there are meetings you have to hold, there are quick decisions which you have to take. You do perhaps not a perfect, but a fairly average morning's work, every morning when you're in your office, and you can't avoid doing it. But, when you're a writer – you know as well as I do – you sit down in the morning, and you have a blank sheet of paper in front of you, and in fact you can sit there the whole morning and put practically nothing on it. And the sheer deadweight effort, without any momentum of events to carry you forward, of writing when you aren't feeling fluent, and when the words aren't trying to come, is the hardest sheer intellectual work, harder than anything in a minister's life, which I've ever done.

RD The Prime Minister whose biography you wrote, Asquith – he was also the youngest member of the Cabinet when he was appointed by Gladstone to be Home Secretary. You record him in your biography as being an outstanding success as Home Secretary – did you learn anything from your study of him which might be of value to you as Home Secretary now?

JENKINS I think I – I learned a certain amount from my study of his period as Home Secretary but I would say in a way it's something which is of value to me as a minister rather than particularly as Home Secretary. I don't think the problems he had to deal with bear very close relation to those I have to deal with at the Home Office, but I think what I learned from him – from his period at the Home Office – was that you should concentrate on relatively few issues on which you think you really can do something decisive. And try and get a push on there, and not dissipate your energies over too wide a field, and I think that's extremely useful advice for any minister ... but not particularly for the Home Secretary.

RD Isn't it particularly for the Home Secretary because in fact he has got such a wide range of responsibilities over which he could dissipate his energies?

JENKINS Well, it may be that the Home Office, which is a slight rag-bag of government responsibilities, is peculiar in that respect, but I'd be very surprised if there was any government department in which a determined man couldn't dissipate his energies.

RD The image has grown up, fairly or unfairly, Home Secretary, of the Home Office as being a place where formidable civil servants bend ministers to their will. Now, does this alarm you? Do you think there's any substance in this?

JENKINS I don't think so, no. I think it's a rather formidable office physically, with a very high ceiling and a slight atmosphere of Victorian punishment about it.

RD Are you taking that modern painting you have at the Ministry of Aviation . . .?

JENKINS I don't think that will fit in but I hope to make certain changes in my room at the Home Office which will make it look a little more in accordance with how I see my role at the Home Office.

RD I'd like to ask you about how you see your role at the Home Office, in general, if I may, because you wrote a book in 1959, before the election, in which one of the things you said was this, that 'the wholesale reform of the Home Office is needed'. Now, that was six years ago – how far do you think that still applies?

JENKINS Well, I think some changes have occurred since 1959. I think probably if one looks at that book you'll find the thing I put absolutely in the forefront was the abolition of the death penalty, and I'm bound to say that I would have found it an almost intolerable burden to be Home Secretary had one had to decide whether or not people were to be hanged. That seems to me an enormous change and an enormous difference. But a number of – and there are one or two other changes, too.

RD You did refer, if I may remind you, to certain 'gross restrictions on individual liberty in urgent need of removal'. Now, some of these still exist. For instance, you referred to the fantastic position of the Lord Chamberlain's censorship – the ridiculous Sunday Observance laws; the harsh and archaic abortion laws; the divorce laws involving unnecessary suffering. Now, what are your views on those various things now?

JENKINS Well that was all good strong pamphletarian language but I'm certainly not going to say that having taken office I've changed my views – that I've turned round, in a phrase of Churchill's, 'like a squirrel in a cage', because I think there's nothing more humiliating than someone who advocates views when they have complete freedom and no responsibility and becomes an utterly different person when they have responsibility. And certainly my basic position, which, as you rightly deduce from this book, is a libertarian position, a view that the onus of proof is always very much on those who want to restrict the liberty of the individual, remains. And I hope that I can give some effect to that position as Home Secretary.

Of course, I mean, I've been a minister already, briefly, for long enough, for fourteen months, but long enough to realize that there are some new facts which become available to one, and that also, in order to, as opposed to making speeches or writing books about issues, in order to carry new important policies into effect, one has to have a certain consensus of opinion in the country. But I would be very disappointed in my period as Home Secretary, however short or long that may last, if I couldn't make some progress and some steady progress from year to year in dealing with some of these issues which I've mentioned.

RD May I ask you about one other specific issue? You talked in your book about the Conservative government's refusal to act on the homosexual law reform, and you called that refusal 'hypocritical'; Now, why did you call it hypocritical, and may we assume from that attitude that you will support Mr Humphry Berkeley's Bill on the subject, which is coming up shortly, I think?

JENKINS Well, I called it hypocritical because I thought, as I wrote then – I'm talking now about what I wrote six years ago – although I'm not saying there's a great change in my basic attitude, because I think it's hypocritical to take one view about conduct in private and another view about it in public, and I thought a lot of people did that on this particular issue. So far as government policy on Mr Berkeley's Bill is concerned, this is a matter not only for me, but certainly I will study the Bill very closely and I don't think you'll find a strong opponent of it in me. I hope I may be a little better than that.

RD Do you think, going back to a phrase you used a moment ago, that there is a consensus in the country for this particular change in the law?

JENKINS Well, what does one mean by a consensus? I don't necessarily mean that there is a solid majority in the country because there has rarely been this for most movements of reform of this sort, and I think that legislators have to give a lead. But I think certainly opinion in the country has moved very considerably – there was a great movement even in the House of Commons between the position when we had a debate on this issue in, I think, 1961 or 1962 and the position last year – and I think that movement in favour of reform here will continue, and I hope fairly fast.

RD Can I ask you to comment on the front-page report in Thursday's *Daily Express* which claimed that murders in 1965 went up to the highest ever total, what they say was 235, which according to their figures is more than 40 per cent more than 1963?

JENKINS Well, I think this was a premature and slightly scaremongering comment. I think one has to look at the figures much more closely when we've got the full statistics and see how they work out. And of course in relation to the abolition of the death penalty what we have also to see is to what extent the increase in murders, if there was an increase in murders, took place in the field where people would previously have been hanged but would not now be hanged, because the great majority of people committing murders were not hanged under the law as it stood, until this year. But, broadly speaking, whatever comes out of this, the House of Commons, after very long debate, very long debate extending over a great number of years, and great public discussion, the House of Commons, and the House of Lords, both of them on a free vote, took the view that the death penalty should be abolished.

RD Suspended . . .

JENKINS Suspended. They also – I was about to go on – they also took the view that it should, well I think it was actually abolition but that it should be looked at again by 1970, and clearly this being the view of the House of Commons it will have to be looked at, but what would be quite wrong would be to take the view that the House of Commons hadn't taken into account a great deal of statistical evidence from this and from other countries, and that because in a particular year something happened that one should make a sudden change back. I think the policy, although it's a very controversial policy, was taken after great consideration and clearly the period of experiment must without question be allowed to run.

RD Do you have any anxiety, Home Secretary, that the Obscene Publications law, which you were a prime mover towards getting changed, may have had a bad effect on people's morals?

JENKINS I don't think so. I've always thought it has been very difficult to show that preventing people reading things improved their morals. There was some worry about a flood of literature of no value into the country from abroad, and there was a small amending Act, last year, one aspect of which I didn't like, but which I was not broadly opposed to, and I think the present position in relation to the law of Obscene Libel is fairly satisfactory. Most of my Private Member's Bill stands, with a small amendment from my last-but-one predecessor at the Home Office, and I think that is a fairly quiescent issue at the present time.

RD Do you accept that one of the Home Secretary's concerns is to protect, and I quote, 'the moral health of society'. I'm quoting from Sir Frank Newsam's book on the Home Office, do you accept that? And how would you interpret it?

JENKINS Well I don't exactly see this as being the central purpose of the Home Office. And I'll tell you why, if I may. I see the central purpose of the Home Office as being that of striking a very difficult balance between the need to preserve the Queen's peace and the need to preserve the liberty of the individual. Now, the moral health of society is clearly a matter of the greatest importance, but I do not myself believe that this is primarily a matter for any government department. I think it's primarily a matter for other bodies. I don't think this is a thing which can be legislated about, moral health. No, I see the central purpose of the Home Office as holding this balance between liberty and order.

RD You, of course, have been an ardent campaigner in the past against many of the laws which were designed to protect the moral health, haven't you? May I deduce that you don't in fact think they did so?

JENKINS I don't think they did so. It's not in the least because I'm indifferent about – what was the phrase?

RD 'Moral health of society.'

JENKINS ... the moral health of society. I think this is very important, but I think that people can have different views about what constitutes moral health, and it's very easy for some people to try and impose their views of moral health on other people ...

RD You talked about keeping the Queen's peace. Of course what that means is, basically, preventing crime. Is not the rising crime rate becoming so serious that it may develop into a major political issue?

JENKINS Yes ... Well, a political – in a sense a party political, I don't know, but it certainly seems to me, already, to be a major issue, and one which I propose to devote a great deal of attention to in the course of the next few months, and I certainly don't regard the fact that I consider myself broadly a libertarian means that I don't consider myself as having a great responsibility for trying to do something effective about organized crime.

RD Do you plan any modification to the government's immigration policy?

JENKINS No. This, of course, was a policy which – a policy not of my predecessor but of the government as a whole, and it's something which – legislation has been for the moment postponed, and I've not yet had a chance to look at the position. But I think it would be a mistake to think that this matter as a policy is a matter for the Home Secretary and not for the government as a whole.

RD One more question on the Home Office. A former Head of the Home Office, a former Permanent Head, said that even if the Home Secretary was in office for five years he may well remain unaware of the full extent of his own responsibilities. After about ten days, Mr Jenkins, do you know, for instance, that you have responsibility for the protection of wild birds?

JENKINS Remarkably enough I do. I can't think why. I suspect very mainly because I've read a book written by that former Head of the Home Office. I'm better informed than I would have been before he wrote the book.

RD Turning away from the Home Office, you were commonly rated a great success as Minister of Aviation. What exactly did you achieve? Because you appointed a committee and no sooner had it reported than you moved to another Department, before you could do anything about it?

JENKINS Well, I appointed the Plowden Committee, I received the Report of the Plowden Committee, but I think that – what I would say, if I managed to do anything at the Ministry of Aviation, it was to try and concentrate the mind of the aircraft industry in this country, on the realities of their position, in a medium-sized, not a great Power, at the present time, and to realise that contrary to the position ten or fifteen years ago, they couldn't do everything on their own, if they did the result would be financial disaster. That they must concentrate their resources and that they must think of working with other European countries and not trying to do projects, big expensive projects, independently.

RD As one who resigned from the Labour Opposition front bench in order to advocate your views on joining the Common Market more freely, do you find any difficulty in belonging to a government which, apparently, at any rate, is rather slow in moving towards Europe, if it is at all?

JENKINS Well, I think in the first place it's a slight exaggeration to say I resigned. I was doing a very small job and I asked not to be reappointed ... It wasn't a very dramatic gesture, because I wanted, for the forthcoming year, to concentrate on the European issue, and I ...

RD It was a gesture of principle ...

JENKINS Well, I thought this was the most important issue at the time and I certainly don't in any way regret having done it. The European issue has been much more quiescent since the government came into power. I remain basically a European, without any question, in the sense that I think that the future of Britain lies in very close association with Europe, and if anything I think that the broad world developments over the past three years have strengthened me in that view rather than weakened me in that view. But, over the immediate past there's been no clear move which Britain ought to have made, and therefore, no, I feel no difficulty about being a member of the government and I don't think the many other members of the government who hold the same European views as I do feel any difficulty either.

RD Do politicians such as yourself today, Mr Jenkins, do enough diary-keeping and letter-writing, to provide material for the biographers of forty years time?

JENKINS No, of course ... One's got to be rather egocentric to think in terms of a biographer, and one's also got to be extremely energetic to think in terms of a biographer. We don't naturally write letters these days, there's no question about it, and it undoubtedly made the task of earlier biographers very much easier than is the case at the present time. This was very much so with Asquith, who was a prolific letter-writer, on the whole to women rather than to men, but still a very prolific letter-writer to women and this undoubtedly made my task very much easier. I don't think there are many people who write letters on this scale to either sex at the present time.

RD Do you keep a diary yourself?

JENKINS No I don't. Well, I'll tell you what I do keep – I keep very careful engagement diaries in which I write in events after they've happened and I keep these at the end of the year and I've got a great stock of those for fifteen years, so I could reconstruct fairly carefully what I was doing on any particular day.

RD Notes of phone calls?

JENKINS Not notes of telephone calls – goodness me, no! But occasionally after the ...

RD This is where a lot goes on now, isn't it?

JENKINS I know, yes. Quite. I keep letters which strike me as of real interest and occasionally after some series of events of unusual interest, to me at any rate, have happened, I try and dictate some notes about that to a dictaphone.

RD So you're trying to be of some help at any rate to your biographer of forty years hence?

JENKINS Yes. I'm not sure I've got that primarily in mind ... Of course one always thinks about one's autobiography. One has to live on something when one's retired.

RD Well, both your biographer, and yourself, will at least be able to look at this television interview in forty years time, which you weren't able to do in the case of Asquith. Mr Jenkins, thank you very much indeed.

'It applies right across the board to all incomes, to prices, to rents and to dividends.'

EDWARD
HEATH

This was a *Panorama* interview televised 'live' from Number 10 at one of the most critical moments in the Prime Ministership of Edward Heath. He had just performed his biggest U-turn. He had announced in the House that afternoon an immediate and compulsory freeze of prices, incomes, rents and dividends to last for three months if necessary.

I had in my hand the Counter-Inflation (Temporary Provisions) Bill which had been published just before the interview. Ted Heath had then been Prime Minister for nearly two and a half years. He had won the General Election of June 1970 against all expectations. At first he had pursued what would later be called a Thatcherite programme. He was pledged 'to change the course of history of this nation, nothing less'. The economy was to be set free. There were to be no more rescues of 'lame duck' industries. Incomes policy was to be discarded. Consensus was scorned.

But no Prime Minister had ever revised the whole thrust of his policy as fast or as completely as did Heath in 1972. The massive industrial force of the miners prevailed over his government in the strike of February 1972. Other workers followed with militant wage demands. Unemployment was rising towards the million mark. Heath abandoned his 'Thatcherism'. Contrary to his declared intentions, he abandoned the market economy for industrial interventionism, and on 6 November he took legal power to control prices and incomes.

Ted Heath was determined that inflation should be controlled, by statutory compulsion if necessary, and that his Tory government would not tolerate mass unemployment. It was an embattled Prime Minister in Downing Street that evening. Harold Wilson, the former Prime Minister and now Leader of the Opposition, warned him in the House that afternoon that the wages and prices freeze was unworkable and unfair. Enoch Powell, more brutally, asked the Prime Minister if he had taken leave of his senses.

The Heath U-turns of 1972 came to be seen as an evil betrayal of declared principles and as a disastrous venture into corporatism. But Margaret Thatcher, then a member of Mr Heath's Cabinet, if she deplored the U-turn, did not resign.

Anyone who does not remember the Britain of 1972 may well be astounded by the elaborate and detailed complexity of a statutory freeze of pay and prices, as explained here by Ted Heath. This was what came later to be disowned as corporatism by the Thatcherites.

This interview is one which destroyed a myth – namely the myth of 'ordeal by television', in which Prime Ministers and other politicians were allegedly harassed and bullied by aggressive interrogators. On this occasion it was the interviewer who deserved sympathy. This interview had to be conducted only half an hour after the new Counter-Inflation Bill had been put into my hands. The Prime Minister had been immersed in this matter for weeks. There was nothing I could ask him to which he did not have a ready answer. All the advantages were on his side. I had to soldier on as best I could on behalf of the viewing public to seek explanations for this massive U-turn, and to find out what it would mean. It was tough going that evening in Number 10. Edward Heath was vehement, impatient and angry.

The Rt Hon. Edward Heath MBE, MP, Prime Minister

*Interviewed 'live' in 10 Downing Street
for BBC Panorama
6 November 1972*

ROBIN DAY Prime Minister, why have you decided to do today what you have for so long refused to do and argued against?

RT HON. EDWARD HEATH, MP, PRIME MINISTER Because for three and a half months we have been trying to get a voluntary agreement with the employers and the unions to keep prices steadier and to allow wages to rise at a reasonable rate so that people could get the benefit of them. Last Thursday evening the talks broke down. The employers had made a large number of contributions as to how they would hold prices steady; the government had agreed to do the same with the nationalized industries. I had made a number of proposals to help the lower paid workers and so on. But the TUC found themselves unable to accept these proposals and in this situation it is the job of the government to govern and to do what is necessary to deal with rising prices.

RD May I ask about what you've decided to do, what prices are going to be controlled?

HEATH All prices – if you are talking about goods in the shops, with the exception of the non-processed foods. That means the fruit and vegetables which come into the shops and fish and meat. You see, there are seasonal variations – local variations in vegetables and fruit and so on.

RD Not fish?

HEATH I am just describing it ... and the different joints and so on. These will not be affected by the control for the simple reason that it isn't possible to control variations of that kind. It'll cover the processed food, the manufactured food and all the other manu-facturers.

RD Services? Things like going to the hairdresser's and all that sort of thing?

HEATH Services are included and also professional charges.

RD Fares?

67

HEATH Fares are covered because the government of course is responsible for the nationalized industries. That covers a large part of the fares; but fares are included as well.

RD Will this protect the housewife and the citizen against rises in food prices due to our coming membership of the Common Market?

HEATH Well – the question of food prices in the Common Market doesn't arise until the spring anyhow. And this is as you have said for ninety days from – it is effective today and the ninety days lasts from the time the Bill passes Parliament and it is possible for us to have a further short extension. But the purpose of this period of standstill for ninety days is then to enable us to bring in the Second Stage of fighting against rising prices which is what we have been discussing with the unions and with the employers.

RD I'd like to ask you about the second stage a little later. Can I ask you this? Who is going to police this price control?

HEATH Well – I think you have already read the White Paper and you have read the Bill. You will know that – that if prices are raised, of course the housewife or whoever is shopping can complain about them. They can complain to the government department which is concerned. If it is food it is the Ministry of Agriculture. If it is ordinary manufactured goods then it is the Department of Trade and Industry; and they can do this either to the head office in London or they can do it to local branches.

RD But Mr Jack Jones says that unless the Weights and Measures Inspectors are entitled to ... enabled to prosecute retailers and others who break the freeze, it will make a mockery of it – he says.

HEATH Well, he is quite wrong on that. Of course I know his view because he described it to us at very great length during these talks which we've had. The Weights and Measures Inspector isn't concerned with this aspect of control, and it does its job extremely well on weights and measures. But as far as this is concerned, the housewife can complain and then a notice can be given to the seller, to the shop to put the price back to where it was before today.

RD But if you are going to miss out – and I understand the reasons why you have – fish and meat and vegetables and perhaps other food items, isn't this going to make it pretty meaningless to the house-wife ...

HEATH I don't think it is at all. And of course, there are some spheres in food in which the government can help because there are some items in which we can help to keep down the prices ourselves. But I think the housewife realizes perfectly well what the seasonal fluctuations are with different vegetables and so on.

RD What is the position tomorrow? Is it against the law tomorrow for someone to sell, say, a pair of shoes at a more expensive price than he did today?

HEATH The law doesn't come into effect until it has passed through Parliament. But when it is effective then it is possible for a minister to give notice to a wholesaler or a retailer or a manufacturer to put his price back to where it was today.

RD But he can't be fined for putting it up ...

HEATH If he refuses to do so ...

RD He can be fined?

HEATH ... but no prosecution can be brought without the consent of the Attorney-General.

RD Now, people may not quite understand that this freeze which you are imposing is not to implement the deal you were trying to get out of the trades unions. It is nothing to do with the 5 per cent limit on prices and the £2 limit on pay increases?

HEATH That was the voluntary agreement that we were proposing. If we had had a voluntary agreement, that could have been put into effect straight away. The employers, the industrialists, said that they would keep their prices down to 4 per cent over the cost of the year. The retailers gave their undertaking. We gave our undertaking on the nationalized industries. All this could have come into effect straight away. If the unions had accepted this, then they would have had a general council meeting and a meeting of the executives of their unions and they could have put it into effect straight away. But if one was going to put this into legislation – the arrangement we have made – then the legislation is much more complicated than what ... would be much more complicated than what we have produced now, and would have taken longer to get through Parliament. Meantime we would not have had any control or influence over prices at all. You see – the CBI – who have carried out their undertaking very fully on prices over the last fifteen months – that undertaking expired on 31 October, and so there would have been this gap between 31 October and the time the new legislation was brought in on the basis we talked about voluntarily. And so to bridge that gap and to enable us to frame the next legislation and carry it through Parliament we have got this standstill.

RD Of course – all the lower paid people who were going to get that flat rate of £2, which was going to benefit them more than anybody else – aren't going to get it now. Are they?

HEATH No. But they are going to benefit from the standstill. They are going to benefit from the standstill. No. Not during this standstill. But what we do want then in the second phase is to get an arrangement which will enable the lower paid workers to benefit. Now – I just want to – amplify this because we agreed in the discussions on the objectives of our economic policy with the management and the unions and the first was to get steady expansion of this economy. Now we are getting that. This is quite clear. We are getting 5 per cent. The second was to ensure that the lower paid workers got particular benefit from it and also the old age pensioners. Now, when I put proposals to the TUC and the employers on Thursday, I made a number of concrete suggestions which we as a government would carry out and pay for from the taxpayers' money to help. This afternoon I told the House of Commons that we will carry those out.

RD Which part of your package are you going to put into operation now, which will help the lower paid? I am thinking of the pension increase.

HEATH As far as the pension increase is concerned, we said that we would make a lump sum payment and I told the House of Commons this afternoon that we will do this even though we haven't got a voluntary agreement.

RD And that is £10 ...

HEATH That is £10 for each pensioner and that means £20 for the married couple who are both of pensionable age.

RD Could you tell us what you weren't able to – or didn't – tell the House of Commons: when they will get that?

HEATH Well, I told the House of Commons that we would do it as soon as practicable and I have given instructions that the departments – and a number of departments are involved in this – must ensure that we get it paid if possible before the end of January. I do want people to realise that this is a tremendous task to ask the social service officials to do. There are eight million pensioners and paying out a lump sum like this does involve complications on top of all their usual work.

RD Can they expect an increase in the spring in addition?

HEATH Well, they had an increase in October and we are the first government to have said that pensions will be reviewed every year and so we review in the spring and we pay again next autumn.

RD Mr Vic Feather says that there is going to be much stricter control under your freeze on pay than on prices because of all the loopholes, particularly on food.

HEATH I don't accept this. But nobody has yet shown how you can prevent seasonal fluctuations in the price of fruit and vegetables, nor have they shown how if you get a shortage of a particular kind of meat you keep the price where it is. The only way you can do it is if the government buys all the food coming in to the country and then subsidises all the food coming into the country and what you'd very soon find is shortages and black markets and all the rest of it.

RD Mr Jack Jones called it a freeze for the little man but a bonanza for the big boys.

HEATH You know this really is absolute nonsense. Couldn't we keep this on a reasonable level?

RD I think what he has in mind – and I am only quoting what he said because he is an important trades union leader – I think what he had in mind is that ...

HEATH There's no bonanza here for anybody, it applies right across the board – to all incomes – to prices, to rents and to dividends.

RD May I put what I think he may mean? That people who have a large increment built into their pay, such as, let's say, a chief executive – a senior executive – might have, an increment of £1,000, £3,000 a year built into his pay, he will still get that. Whereas the ordinary worker will not.

HEATH This is not true. What we have said in there is that all incremental payments continue. Now the great mass of payments of increments are in teachers, the local government officers, the police and the Civil Service. And this is a very large number indeed, numbering millions. And the reason why we have done it is that the increment depends on age or on length of experience. And this happens because of those particular attributes of the person working. It is not a wage increase. I mean they have to negotiate. The teachers as you well know have to negotiate. The civil servants have to negotiate for their wage increases. And this they will not be able to do during the standstill, they will not be able to do during the standstill, they will not be able to receive it during the standstill.

RD But a lot of industrial workers don't have that system.

71

HEATH Industrial workers have an entirely different system. Let us take those who are working on piece rates. Now, if as a result of the demand for production during these next ninety days they are working more on piece rates, of course their take home pay will be more. Because as we've said specifically in the White Paper, it's the result of extra effort.

RD Agreements made before today but not yet implemented? What will happen to them?

HEATH Well, this is all set out in detail in the White Paper, because there are a very large number of different types of agreements.

RD Take the police, for instance . . .

HEATH Yes, that is carried through.

RD They will get it?

HEATH Yes.

RD But I thought it was coming into operation before the end of the freeze therefore it would be postponed until the . . . end of the standstill.

HEATH Some of it's come into operation already.

RD I see. Now could you answer Mr Wilson's point, the reason he thinks this freeze is unworkable and unfair, that it doesn't cover all food prices, it doesn't cover all rents, or school meal increases, or school clothing cost increases.

HEATH Well, Mr Wilson made his remarks before he'd read the White Paper. And he made them before he'd read the Bill. So he wasn't really in a very strong position to judge. As far as the individual items you mentioned, as far as school meals are concerned, it's outside the period of the ninety days which we've asked for here. And the school clothes, on the question of VAT; and VAT doesn't become effective until the time of the next Budget. Let us keep these things in proportion, and as far as fruit and vegetables and meat are concerned, when his government was dealing with this matter they didn't have a freeze on that either.

RD What about rents?

HEATH Rents are included in this.

RD All rents?

HEATH Well there are certain – I mean rents are a very wide variety of kinds, that's why I suggest that you deal with the White Paper instead of going into this mass of detail. But as far as local authority rents are concerned again, the next increase doesn't come until the spring. And as far as the private rents are concerned a very large proportion are controlled rents. Where a fair rent has been fixed but not yet come into operation, then a change won't be made.

RD What is your answer to the point made in the House of Commons this afternoon by Mr Enoch Powell, that it is fatal for any government or person to seek to govern in direct opposition to the principle on which he was entrusted with power?

HEATH Everybody in this country knows that no government could have tried harder than we have done in these past three and a half months to get a voluntary agreement – I think everybody acknowledges that. They agree that the proposal we put forward for £2 across the board allowing an increase of earnings up to £2.60 was fair to everybody, and it would have allowed us to have got steadier prices. We couldn't get it, and so our job now is to govern in the interests of all the people of this country. And that is what we are doing. The responsibility of a government at all times is to govern.

RD Do you deny that this policy is a reversal of the policy which you declared then to be in the national interest?

HEATH I declare that I've always wanted a voluntary agreement, that's what I've worked for and that's what I still want.

RD In the election manifesto, 'A Better Tomorrow in 1970', Mr Heath, you said, 'We utterly reject the philosophy of compulsory wage control.' You've really gone back on that haven't you?

HEATH No, because my philosophy is still that we should get this by voluntary means. I believe that in a free democratic society we ought to be able to get this and I still hope that in time we will. But meantime we've got to take this essential action to look after the national interest.

RD What is going to happen after this first stage which you've explained tonight, because people are a little puzzled as to what you intend after the first stage? Are we going to have more elaborate legislation, or a voluntary policy?

HEATH Well, during these talks with the TUC and the CBI we have covered a great deal of ground as to the sort of issues which are important and the sort of way in which we might solve the problems of wages and prices. And we shall now build on that when we're preparing our legislation for the second phase.

RD Legislation for the second phase?

HEATH Yes.

RD What kind of legislation will that be?

HEATH Well, it'll be legislation for dealing with prices and incomes, in a way, as I've said, which will allow us to take account of the discussions we've had in this – in the talks with the TUC and the CBI.

RD Why will you need legislation if it's going to be a voluntary system?

HEATH Well, you – I didn't say it was, I said that we'd failed to get a voluntary system, because of the refusal of the TUC to accept our proposals, and you asked me why we hadn't put our original proposals into legislative form. I explained that it takes time and it's a more complicated procedure than the standstill which we're having now. And so we now work on the second stage.

RD Why did you not get – try to get a voluntary prices and incomes policy of the kind that you offered the TUC much sooner in your time as Prime Minister?

HEATH When I became Prime Minister I offered consultation to both the CBI and the TUC. The TUC found it impossible to consult with us about the Industrial Relations Bill, and we were committed to carrying that through, absolutely rightly, by our election programme. And what we have done is to take the best time after that. In July I offered the talks and I'm very glad that they were accepted. But of course you must also remember that during that period we were dealing with rising prices. Although there was a wage explosion, at the time of the election when we came to power, which followed through for a period with great strength, we did succeed in getting prices, the rate of increase in prices, down quite considerably. It was 10 per cent in 1971, it was down to just under 6 per cent earlier this year. But the danger now is that the prices will begin to rise again, I'm talking about manufactured prices as well as the world food prices. And so this is why we've got – we've had the talks.

RD But wouldn't it have been better, Prime Minister, to have got the trade unions together round a table much sooner instead of –

HEATH But you can't get people round a table if they don't want to come.

RD No, but why didn't they want to come? They didn't want to come because you were alienating them with your – with what they regarded as a hateful Industrial Relations Act.

HEATH No, we were not alienating them because every government is entitled to carry through the measures which the country wants. And there was absolutely no doubt at all that the country wanted the reform of industrial relations. Now I don't want to discuss this in detail. I'm prepared to do so, but I want to maintain the atmosphere which we've been able to keep since the breakdown of these talks, in which there has not been – the groups have not been attacking each other – there have not been recriminations. Because, as I have said repeatedly since, and again in the House of Commons today, I want the three parties – the employers and the unions and the government – to be able to sit round a table and to talk about industrial problems. Now, it may not be possible to move very much further on this front straight away, but at least there are many other problems which we ought to be discussing. So I don't want to go into the past, as to whether the opposition to the Industrial Relations Act wasn't in fact political, rather than (if you like to call it) an industrial affair.

RD None the less the people, when they come to the election, will judge you on the past, that is to say your record. I must ask you this. Do you not have any regrets as to the way you have approached the unions in dealing with prices and incomes policy, and the Industrial Relations Act over the last two and a half years?

HEATH I have no regrets at all. Because, as I've said, we offered them consultation. I believe that that framework of the industrial relations legislation was vitally necessary for this country and history will show that was so. I've made a perfectly fair offer to the unions. If they come forward with any proposals for amending the Act, in any places where they think it's damaging to unions, or if employers say it's damaging to employers, or if either of them can show where it's damaging to the national interest, then as a government we are perfectly prepared to consider it, discuss it with them, and if justifiable, then we can ask Parliament to make the amendment – what fairer offer could there be than that?

RD May I put to you the question which you always used to ask, when anybody used to advocate to you a compulsory wage freeze, you used to say what good would it do, it's always proved futile, that the dam will break and there will be a great flood of wage increases. Why won't that happen now?

HEATH Because there are two differences. First of all this is for a comparatively short and limited period – the standstill – ninety days after the Bill is passed, with a possible short extension. And secondly, that when it was done before, it was done at a time of deflation and stagnation, when the then Chancellor of the Exchequer was trying to push down the standard of living of the people of this country. What we are seeing now is a time of expansion, in which the standard of living is improving in the country and what we are trying to do is to enable it to rise steadily instead of having a great increase in wages which pushes up prices, and that means we go back to the stop-go once again. Two very important differences.

RD But none the less a great many people watching may feel that they can have no greater hope of this freeze working ... a lasting solution than did the freezes of Stafford Cripps, Selwyn Lloyd or George Brown.

HEATH Then they should use all their influence with those with whom they are concerned to get a voluntary agreement and to show people this was a perfectly fair offer and the quicker we can get on to a sound voluntary basis the better.

RD What part will the Cabinet changes you made yesterday, Prime Minister, play in your new strategy – particularly the appointments of Mr Walker [as Secretary of State for Trade and Industry] and Sir Geoffrey Howe [as Minister for Trade and Consumer Affairs]?

HEATH I made the general changes in the government because we have been the government for two and a half years now and I thought it was the right moment to do this. And it is also taking account of the new task which we shall have when we go into Europe on 1 January [1973]. As far as ... Mr Walker is concerned and Sir Geoffrey Howe – Sir Geoffrey is going to have particular responsibility for consumer affairs and, of course, carrying through a policy like this, either in the standstill or in the later stage, or if we had a voluntary policy ... it does mean a great concentration ...

RD Yes ... because people don't quite understand. Do they?

HEATH I think they understand it very well ... they are all consumers ...

RD Yes – but you've never had a Department of Consumer Affairs.

HEATH You have always had a department which was responsible for particular aspects of consumer affairs – the Board of Trade of old, now the Department of Trade and Industry. But what I have done is to put a member of the Cabinet there in order to focus concentration on this and to look after the interests of consumers. He will be able to do this in particular during this standstill ... what's involved in prices and so on of all goods; foodstuffs will be dealt with by the Minister of Agriculture. And he will also be able to deal with the new legislation which we announced at the opening of Parliament which is dealing with competition policy, and the purpose of that is to keep prices steady.

RD And one final point on the consumer interest – how much should the housewife expect her food bill to go up now – roughly on a percentage? Or will it remain stable during the next six months?

HEATH Well, we are dealing first of all with this standstill ...

RD Yes.

HEATH ... and what I have said absolutely frankly is that the seasonal variations in food prices will of course continue. There are some in which we can help, which means putting extra taxpayers' money in, and where we can help with that we will help. But of course the food prices are bound to be subject to seasonal fluctuations and also to world influences. I am sure every housewife understands that.

RD A final point, Prime Minister, this reversal of policy – albeit temporary – does it depend for its success on the consent of the people and their compliance with the law? Do you think your chances of success would be greater if you went to the country in a General Election and asked the people to support you? And if they didn't to get out and let somebody else take over?

HEATH In these circumstances, I think the country will support us and they will support us whole-heartedly. I think they supported us over our attempt to get a voluntary agreement because they thought it was fair and a reasonable offer. They will support us now because not having achieved that, they believe the job of the government is to get on and govern and make the necessary arrangements and they will see quite clearly what we are doing and I believe they will support us whole-heartedly in this. Now, there is one other thing which I'd like to say. We are carrying this through Parliament as a Bill. It'll go through the parliamentary processes and then become a law and I believe that the duty and the responsibility of every citizen is then to obey the law. And I believe that from the great majority of citizens, whether they are retailers or wholesalers or manufacturers, whatever they may be – I believe we shall get support from them for the law. I hope this will also extend to every trades unionist and every worker in industry. And for this reason, it is not only that we are a democracy; it is not only that on the whole we are law-abiding; but it is also in the interests of everybody that this should be a success.

RD The proof of the pudding as regards that success, Prime Minister, will be in the price of it. Won't it? In the shops – to see whether it goes up or down ...

HEATH The general test of success will be in that it is part of the process of dealing with what we call inflation, which is really keeping prices steady so that the wages will in fact buy more instead of being frittered away in ever-rising prices. That will be the real test of success.

RD Prime Minister, thank you.

'If the call-girl had said to me suddenly, "please darling, tell me about the laser ray or something," I would have known that something was up.'

LORD
LAMBTON

My interview with Lord Lambton was utterly unlike any other that I have done. He was involved in the first ministerial sex scandal since the Profumo affair ten years earlier.

Antony Claud Frederick Lambton, MP for Berwick-upon-Tweed, was the son of the 5th Earl of Durham. He had renounced succession to the earldom to remain in the Commons, where he was still known by his courtesy title of Viscount Lambton. He was Air Force Minister (Parliamentary Under-Secretary for Defence) in the Heath government.

He resigned on 22 May 1973 after being interviewed by the police in connection with allegations relating to drugs and contacts with prostitutes. The *News of the World* had obtained compromising photographs of Lord Lambton. Two days later Lord Jellicoe, Lord Privy Seal and Leader of the House of Lords, also resigned because it had become known that he too had had affairs with call-girls.

The Prime Minister, Mr Heath, made a statement about these resignations to the House on 24 May, the day before my interview with Lord Lambton. He revealed that reports on these matters had reached him in April. He had immediately ordered the Security Service to watch the security aspect of Lord Lambton's connections. The PM also asked Lord Diplock, Chairman of the independent Security Commission, to verify that there had been no breach of security. Seven weeks later, the Commission confirmed that Lord Lambton had been involved with a Mrs Norma Levy and others in a way which could expose him to blackmail. But they found that Lord Jellicoe's affairs were of a casual nature and unrelated to Norma Levy's activities. The Security Commission concluded that neither Lord Lambton nor Lord Jellicoe had betrayed any state secrets, but that Lord Lambton had been a security risk owing to the possible danger of blackmail.

The whole affair, with two members of the government resigning (one a senior Cabinet Minister), seemed for a moment to be a tremendous scandal. But it proved not to be so. The storm blew over very quickly. Lord Lambton left politics but has continued writing articles and books. The unlucky Lord Jellicoe did not hold ministerial office again, but has been appointed to various public and political responsibilities.

Lambton's interview with me was extensively reported, indeed splashed, not only in the popular papers. *The Listener,* then owned by the BBC, carried a near-verbatim text. No other lengthy interview of mine (this lasted forty minutes) has been so fully reported.

Reaction was mixed. I was accused of 'impertinent and unwarranted intrusion'. But much of the press criticism of me was for being 'excessively sympathetic', 'even more anguished than Lord Lambton', and 'anguished to the point of tears'. I was, in fact, nowhere near to tears, but I must have given that impression. One minister was reported as saying, 'I thought Robin Day was going to break under the strain. Lambton never seemed to turn a hair.'

Having to ask a man in his own home about his sexual activities with prostitutes was a new experience for me. What was more, his eleven-year-old son was sitting in the room throughout, a few feet away from me. My producer, Chris Capron, had quietly suggested that it might be best if the boy left before the interview started. But Lord Lambton said if his son kept quiet it was fine for him to stay. We bourgeois men of television had not reckoned with the historical sense of an aristocratic family. That schoolboy, one day to be the 7th Earl of Durham, was thus able to witness an extraordinary, if painful, moment in the family history.

I have never in my interviews, before or since, asked people about details of their private life such as sex. But in the case of Lambton, sex had become a public matter because of his resignation from his ministerial position and the security enquiry ordered by the Prime Minister. Even so, to question Lambton about the whores he had been with was distressing, and gave me no pleasure. I had met Tony Lambton several times on journalistic assignments. Before joining the government he had written on politics for the *Evening Standard*. With his good looks and dark glasses, he always seemed more sophisticated than some of one's fellow reporters. We had dined together once, I remembered, while on some assignment in Cape Town.

I did not know him well, but we were on Christian-name terms. He was excellent company. This did not make my job of interrogating him any easier. On the contrary, his relaxed and friendly manner made it all the harder for me to put the painful questions which had to be put.

When, on the telephone, he had agreed to be interviewed, he made only one condition – that he should not be asked any 'prurient' questions. Since I had no intention of asking such questions, I agreed. But I thought it fair to give him a warning. I said, 'Tony, I will have to ask you the kind of painful questions you would have to ask if you were a reporter in my position.' He understood and immediately agreed, but I knew that some of the questions would be very painful for me to put.

Whereas I apparently looked strained, Lord Lambton won much admiration for appearing to be 'completely relaxed', and for his 'courage and candour'.

The *Daily Telegraph* recorded in its front-page account: 'Occasionally sipping a drink from a tall glass, he showed no embarrassment when questioned about his visits to the Maida Vale flat where he was secretly photographed in compromising circumstances with prostitutes.'

Lord Lambton won high marks for nerve. Several of his answers qualified for 'sayings of the week', notably his much-quoted dictum about drug-taking: 'Taking opium in China is totally different from taking it in Berwick-on-Tweed.'

On the drive through the night back to London, we listened with stunned incredulity to the soundtrack. Neither Chris Capron nor I had fully realized just how stylish and cool Lambton would sound to some people, or how outrageous he would sound to others. We expected good press coverage, but not the huge front-page treatment which the interview got next morning, with headlines such as: LAMBTON'S AMAZING CONFESSION; LAMBTON'S TV SENSATION; WHY LAMBTON PAID FOR SEX.

Underlying the whole interview is that still much-discussed question: how much does the private sex life of public figures matter? The unsatisfactory answer seems to be that it depends whether national security is put at risk, and on the circumstances of each case.

Despite the headlines and the excitement, this sensation, this scandal, was forgotten within a month. But the interview was a scoop at that moment. No one else had interviewed Lord Lambton about the affair. It is included in this selection not for any political significance (it had none) but for the same kind of fascination and period charm as the court-room cross-examinations in some *cause célèbre* of a bygone age.

I am glad to record that, a few days after the interview, Lord Lambton declared: 'Robin Day treated me perfectly correctly.'

Lord Lambton MP

Interviewed for BBC series Talk-in Today
Filmed at Biddick Hall, Co. Durham
24 May 1973
Transmitted 25 May 1973 on BBC 1

ROBIN DAY Lord Lambton, I ask you to accept that I will want to ask you questions which you, as a journalist, would want to ask, were you in my position.

LORD LAMBTON MP Now I quite accept that. I mean the interview would be really useless otherwise.

RD What first of all is your reaction to what the Prime Minister said in the House of Commons about this matter?

LAMBTON Well, I haven't really had proper time to read his statement, but this seemed to me a factual account of events.

RD Do you think it is fair and reasonable that ... that the Prime Minister should have known that your name was involved in these allegations as early as 13 April but felt he could not inform you about it until several weeks later because, as the Prime Minister said, there was a possibility of involvement in dangerous drugs leading to criminal charges?

LAMBTON Well, I should say that the Watergate Enquiry on everyone has made everyone in the Prime Minister's position excessively conscious of the vital importance of keeping himself out of any interference of any kind with justice and I should think if I had been in his place I would have done the same thing.

RD But nonetheless you would have liked to have been informed earlier ...

LAMBTON Well, of course, it would have been better for me and it might have prevented things but on the other hand the Prime Minister's position and status is this vital thing to preserve.

RD What is your feeling about this matter in relation to the Prime Minister whom you ... who appointed you to your position?

LAMBTON Well, great regret to have undoubtedly let him down. I have a very great admiration for the Prime Minister and I've known him now for, oh, over twenty years. I think he is a very remarkable man. I think he's to a certain degree cold, but I think the most interesting

85

thing about him is his sense of purpose. That's what I never ... why I really fell out with his predecessor, Mr Macmillan. It never seemed to me that he knew quite where he was going but what I like about the Prime Minister is that I think he has got an intense sense of purpose and of destiny and he works towards it.

RD In this case, as far as you yourself are concerned, you feel he has treated you entirely fairly, do you?

LAMBTON Yes, I would say absolutely.

RD You did not see him in connection with this matter?

LAMBTON No. He was in Paris.

RD Yes ... Were you surprised that Lord Jellicoe has resigned over a similar matter?

LAMBTON Well, I had not any inkling of any kind that he was connected in any way with the same sort of thing.

RD And you've never met him in any of these circles or any of these things ...?

LAMBTON Never and ... I haven't seen him for several months.

RD Were you surprised at the general atmosphere of restraint and sympathy – that was certainly my impression having been there in the House of Commons when the Prime Minister made his statement – restraint and sympathy not merely to the Prime Minister in this difficult situation but to you and Lord Jellicoe?

LAMBTON Well, the House of Commons is ... and I've been there so long that it's a very generous place to people in distress. I think it realizes that there but for the grace of God go I in many circumstances, and though of course a lot of people I know wouldn't have done what I've done ... I think that basically people do have perhaps too much sympathy. I think you could say there's probably too much sympathy has been shown towards us in this case.

RD This is, I think, a feeling among some MPs that on the whole the atmosphere ... surrounding the Prime Minister's statement looked just a little bit too much like the Establishment coming to the aid of its own.

LAMBTON Well, I think that it always will, it always has done in all the times I've been in the House. The House is always ready to give great sympathy. It usually regrets it, or the Opposition side usually regrets its sympathy to the government after, and probably tomorrow one will see the Labour Party saying that they have been too nice to the Prime Minister but basically there is this freemasonry.

RD But looking back on that Profumo episode which you and I both remember so well as journalists and you as a Member of Parliament at the time, my recollection is that there was slightly less sympathy towards Mr Profumo in the House of Commons than there was in the atmosphere today when a member of the Cabinet had to go.

LAMBTON Well, I think that the thing that annoyed the House about the Profumo case, which was terribly sad, of course, was the fact that he ... Profumo lied to the House and this was ... I think the House thought breaking these ... its own rules and therefore it had no pity for him because it had let them down not only in a human way but it had then let them down in the traditions of the House.

RD And this was then, your first reaction when this matter came to your notice was to ... was to tell the truth and at least avoid that particular misdeed of John Profumo.

LAMBTON Well, my absolute determination was to say as far as I could then exactly what had happened, how there was no excuse for what I had done and I didn't wish to make any, that I had great regrets about what had occurred and the consequences ... have on my life, constituency and the government and the Conservative Party.

RD Ten years ago, Lord Lambton, exactly ten years ago this summer, in 1963 during the Profumo scandal, you as a journalist were writing in the *Evening Standard* this: 'One cannot doubt that the harm which this will do to the Conservative Party will be enormous.' Do you think the same applies to the resignation of yourself and Lord Jellicoe?

LAMBTON I think that the fact that we have both come out at once with an admission and regret of what had happened will have some way palliated the harm, but there still will be harm and that of course one can't pretend, I mean one has got to look at this matter unbiasedly now. I mean I have to look at it unbiasedly and it obviously will harm the Conservative Party and of that I am very regretful.

RD You also wrote in one of your articles at the time of Profumo that you had warned the Conservative Party before the matter became public that Profumo ought to be asked to resign because of what he was up to. Now if then you could foresee what was wrong in his case why couldn't you foresee that what you have been doing in this matter would endanger your position?

LAMBTON I think unfortunately one of the frailties you might say of human nature is that one can very often see things in other people which one cannot see in oneself.

RD Far be it from me to object to a human frailty, Lord Lambton, but there may be some people watching who find it inconceivable that

87

someone who holds a ministerial position in the Ministry of Defence should not foresee the obvious risks involved in consorting with call girls.

LAMBTON But the risk is really what?

RD The risk is, I would assume, as you yourself pointed out in the case of the Profumo matter, the risk of a man being exposed to blackmail, not a question of a leak but a risk that security might be endangered by a man putting himself in a vulnerable position.

LAMBTON Well, I think there is this to say about this side of it, that perhaps one of my failings over this matter has been my absolute knowledge that in no circumstances whatever would I have ever consented to blackmail. And that had these films or things been shown to me, instead of shown to the *News of the World*, and a demand for money followed I would inevitably have gone to the police instead of the police coming to me. Therefore in my own mind, though I admit that this was quite wrong, I knew that I would never give in to blackmail and therefore there was no, in that sense, security risk.

RD You say that you knew that you would never give way to blackmail and that you would report it immediately to the police, but does that mean that you had considered the possibility of blackmail?

LAMBTON No. I never did. I mean subconsciously I regarded what I was doing as a private affair and I suppose subconsciously I neglected the risks because as far as ... as far as I myself was concerned there wasn't a security risk in that I would not ever put ... though I put myself in a position to blackmail I would have never ... could have never been blackmailed.

RD Are you saying that it had never crossed your mind that doing this kind of thing with this kind of people might put you in a vulnerable or embarrassing position?

LAMBTON No ... I can honestly say I regard it as a private affair.

RD Then you don't ... you take the view that the private life of a public man with particular responsibilities need not be more strict than that which is expected of ordinary people.

LAMBTON I don't think there's any doubt that it has to be today but I think that this does bring one to a really rather interesting point in that I wonder how long this can go on being so much the case in the relaxed society in which we all live, because I don't think that people can be expected to be one type of person for the first thirty-five or forty-five years of their life and suddenly become a totally different type of plaster saint. I don't think you can expect people to change their personalities and ... and their way of life, and in the society really in which we are living I think there is a danger that the rulers could become totally divorced and separated from the rulees.

RD From the people?

LAMBTON Yes.

RD In the sense that all people indulge in what for public men are disastrous things?

LAMBTON Well, I should think a great number of the people, a great number of the men watching this programme would know that they have done themselves at some time or other what I have done without endangering their jobs or anything. I think the question which will have to be met fairly soon is whether this sort of thing should be a blackmail ... should be considered, as it were, a blackmailable offence. Now, I'm not for one moment arguing at the moment that it isn't. It is. The rules as they are at the moment have to be interpreted as they are and I accept them absolutely as they are but I do think that some time in the future there will probably have to be a reconsideration of this outlook.

RD Many people might sympathize with that view but they might also think that if you go into public life you accept public responsibility of your own volition. Nobody asks you to become a Member of Parliament, nobody forces you to hold public responsibility. In making that choice you accept a code by which you have to set an example and be not as other men. A judge of the High Court, for instance, might well have been a rake in his twenties and thirties but he doesn't go around with whores when he's on the Bench.

LAMBTON No. I mean, I think that really rather proves my point, the point that I was going to make. Those are the rules now. I wouldn't deny that and I'm not making a personal present point but what I'm saying is that I think there is a considerable danger that if the rules are out of tune with the rules of the country then there will be a danger of a separation from the democracy of the country, as it were, that the same sort of people won't be ruling the country as are in the country themselves.

RD Did you have any knowledge or inkling as to whether these girls were part of a ring, whether international or not, of prostitutes?

LAMBTON None whatsoever.

RD Would it have been what you would have described in your journalistic capacity – this place you went to – as a brothel?

LAMBTON I didn't take it as such.

RD What do you mean by that?

LAMBTON Well, I regarded it as a private flat.

RD And were the girls people whom you had met ...

LAMBTON ... I met there ...

RD ... entirely socially?

LAMBTON I'd never met them before outside.

RD When you said in your original statement, Lord Lambton, that you had had a casual acquaintance with a call-girl and one or two of her friends, what exactly does that mean?

LAMBTON Well, I just met these people there and the acquaintance was totally casual and it was confined to the purpose of going to the room.

RD You were not then ... the word casual implies that you were not a regular client or visitor.

LAMBTON ... casual implied that it meant really nothing in my life.

RD But were you a regular client?

LAMBTON Not very.

RD But you say it wasn't a brothel but ... money was paid?

LAMBTON Yes, I wouldn't deny that and, as I said, they were call-girls ...

RD Yes.

LAMBTON ... and call-girls, as you know, are girls whom you call, I suppose, and pay money.

RD Yes. Do you know who took the photographs?

LAMBTON I've been told by the police that the husband of the girl did.

RD Do we know what his name is?

LAMBTON I understand he is called Levy.

RD Was he the man who tried to sell them?

LAMBTON I understand so, but this is pure hearsay.

RD Yes. Do you know if he succeeded in selling them?

LAMBTON I don't know.

RD If a newspaper were to have bought them, what would be your view of that?

LAMBTON Well, I would like to buy them from the newspaper.

RD What would you think of their action in buying them?

LAMBTON Well, I think again that this opens an interesting field because if national newspapers do make it plain that they are prepared to buy pictures of this sort, of public men in moments of indiscretion, then they are basically aiding the blackmailer.

RD Do you feel that the newspapers who originally told about this, or newspaper, should have told you about it?

LAMBTON It would have helped if they had done, but I've no complaint that they didn't.

RD Have you seen the photograph or photographs?

LAMBTON The police showed me the photograph.

RD You mentioned earlier 'film', did you mean film or was that just a slip of the tongue? Was this a still picture or were there moving pictures?

LAMBTON I don't know. I don't know what ...

RD But what you were shown was a still picture.

LAMBTON Still picture.

RD Do you wish to comment on reports in the London press that the photograph showed you in bed with two girls, one white, one coloured...?

LAMBTON No, I wish to comment on no part of it or ...

RD You still say that when you were doing this you didn't ... it never struck you at all that this could, as a minister in a sensitive department dealing with secret and important matters, that this could have put you in a position of risk or vulnerability?

LAMBTON Well, as I said, I regarded this as a private matter. Now a lot has been made of the fact that call-girls are a security risk in the sense that they might get knowledge. Now I think that this is extremely doubtful. People don't go to call-girls to talk about business affairs or secret affairs and anyone, for instance, who was with a call-girl. If the call-girl had said to me, suddenly, 'please darling, tell me about the laser ray or something or what do you think of the new Rolls Royce engine for the MRCA?' I would have known that something was up, that this was a deliberate plant. I should have thought that the last sort of person who is ever able to extract information from a minister or an official or anyone of any position is the sort of girl whom a man purely goes to see for one reason, and it would be immediately suspicious if the girl started talking about other reasons.

RD I understand what you say about how silly it would be if a call-girl asked you about some secret matter, but are there not, in the history of espionage cases, a good many examples of prostitutes being used in espionage in order to get close to people and to put them into positions and perhaps have conversations bugged and all that kind of thing? Isn't it standard Communist procedure?

LAMBTON ... If the conversation is bugged and it's ordinary conversation it's rather a waste of time ... I mean, if you talk about something else for a quarter of an hour, well, what does it matter if it is bugged? I mean, for instance, if our conversation here was bugged tonight it wouldn't be much secret to anyone.

RD I think it probably is being ... being bugged for the benefit of a substantial audience, Lord Lambton. Did you ever consider, or have you ever considered since this matter arose, since last Monday, that these girls might have been a party to this photography business, that they were part of it, that they were in league with the man who was taking the picture?

LAMBTON I can't tell. I mean, I think there's a great temptation after something like this to try and think back and think what you thought then, but I was unconscious of anything odd at all at the time.

RD Did these girls know who you were? That you were a minister?

LAMBTON I think, no. I don't think they knew I was a minister.

RD But they knew you were an important man? A politician?

LAMBTON I don't ... I don't know if they did. They may have done ... I never regarded myself as a very important man ...

RD But obviously in these circumstances you have become one.

LAMBTON Ah yes.

RD You said in your statement that ... you used the word pimp of the man who had taken the photographs and tried to sell them, doesn't that imply that these girls were managed and part of an organization and not merely freelance ladies who made their favours available?

LAMBTON The actual word that I used was sneak-pimp ...

RD Yes.

LAMBTON ... which I thought was rather more offensive, because it seems to me that a man who does this sort of thing is really fitting of any epithet. I gather, but again this is purely from hearsay, that this girl whose flat it was was completely under his power and it seems to me that the idea was profit. I suppose on adding it up he looked at the situation and thought, now I have got embarrassing evidence about this man, what shall I do with it to make most money for me? Shall I blackmail him or shall I tout it round? And I suppose he decided that he was likely to get more money touting it round because that I might have declined blackmail.

RD And when you were vising these girls, you never saw any other individual, a man who ... aroused your suspicions?

LAMBTON No, I was never conscious that anyone else was there.

RD Do you have any idea, even though it may be speculation, as to how these photographs were taken?

LAMBTON Well, I imagine they were taken either through the wall or through a cupboard or something.

RD Through a mirror or through an aperture?

LAMBTON I would imagine that might have been it.

RD May I come to another point which again may be in the minds of many people watching you now, Lord Lambton? One of your parliamentary colleagues, Maurice Edelman – Labour Member of Parliament – says this, 'why Lambton, a highly personable and attractive figure should have bought his sexual entertainment is more mysterious'. Can you say anything to explain the point?

LAMBTON Maurice wrote this?

RD Yes, in the *Daily Mail*.

LAMBTON Well, I must take attention to that because he is a great expert on these things ...

RD You mean he writes about them in novels?

LAMBTON Yes.

RD Why should a man of your social position and charm and personality have to go to whores for sex?

LAMBTON I think that people sometimes like variety. I think it's as simple as that and I think that impulse is probably understood by almost everybody. Don't you?

RD I think a great many people may understand it, Lord Lambton, I think that is so. But can I ... whether they would agree with it is, of course, another matter. Can I ask you this, when you went to your job at the Ministry of Defence as Under-Secretary for the Royal Air Force, you were vetted for security?

LAMBTON Yes ... I think you are vetted, yes, you are certainly vetted.

RD What do you mean you think you are?

LAMBTON Well I know I was vetted, yes.

RD But what they call positively vetted?

LAMBTON Yes.

RD I don't know whether I'm asking you to break the Official Secrets Act, which would not be a good thing to do on top of everything, but what exactly did it consist of?

LAMBTON I can't remember now.

RD It can't have been very thorough.

LAMBTON Oh, I think it ...

RD I mean so far as you knew. And you weren't asked a lot of questions.

LAMBTON I had to sign a lot of things as far as I remember but it's three years ago and I probably wrongly, but automatically I think one takes something like that as a formality though it's probably wrong to do so.

RD Were you, as far as you remember, given any special warning that although men of the world are men of the world, when you have a job of this nature you have to beware of being a man of the world as you may have been?

LAMBTON I think what makes my case worse is that the Prime Minister did send a memorandum round on this subject some time.

RD About what? Call-girls or behaving discreetly?

LAMBTON No, no, about I think a general code of conduct.

RD Supposing somebody had wanted to blackmail you – and I understand your point that you are confident that you would never have allowed yourself to be blackmailed – did you in fact have a great deal of secret defence information of value to an enemy which would have been blackmail-worthy?

LAMBTON I don't really know. One doesn't know what ... have no idea what the Russians know. Certainly I would rather doubt it but there are obviously, I think, things that the Russians would obviously have liked to have had confirmed. I think the whole of intelligence really is almost sort of like a switchboard. You press and press and press and you get the right answers from numerous touches and I think there would obviously, certainly have been things that they'd have liked to have known. But I can only repeat that never at any time did I mention anything vaguely in connection with defence.

RD Was drug-taking a part of the scene, the social scene in which these girls and yourself were involved?

LAMBTON Well I think that this is a case I can't talk about because it is *sub* ...

RD ... I'm not asking about your ... the charge which has been brought against you ...

LAMBTON ... *sub judice* but what, I think that I would like to say something about drug-taking because if anyone asks me, have you ever taken a drug I would have to say, upon occasions yes. Because I have travelled, like you, as you said to begin with, we've met in many parts of the world. I've been quite long periods in Singapore.

And once you go to a place like Singapore, try and understand the people there and the way of life, automatically you fall in with the customs of that country. So I have smoked opium in Singapore. Correspondingly I've been in a lot of Arab countries where hashish is a way of life. In certain of the North African countries, one doesn't want to insult anyone. You are offered cigarettes by the Arabs and I have taken those cigarettes partly for the experience and thing of the feeling. So I cannot say that I have not taken drugs. But, for instance, taking opium in China is totally different from taking it in Berwick-on-Tweed. One is, I think, an experience, 'be in Rome as the Romans do', and the other is a violation of the laws of the country.

RD And, without again commenting on the criminal charges against you which are *sub judice,* with regard to drugs, does this general attitude which you've mentioned as a result of your travels abroad, does that lead you to want a change in the British laws about drug-taking?

LAMBTON I don't really know about that but I would think that there's not the slightest doubt that there is a tremendous differential between types of drugs and I've had great friends, a great, great friend of mine died of heroin. And I've seen people rotted and destroyed by taking heroin. And there's no question that only the very severest laws for hard drugs should be enforced.

RD Going back to the main question, these girls and this form of employment they were in and the possible ring they were involved in, do you think it is possible, with hindsight now, that these were, as the papers have been suggesting, part of a ring penetrated by or even organized by, agents of a foreign power, basically possibly a Communist power?

LAMBTON I don't know but I suppose it is conceivable that this man might ask for some reward from them. For he's done his job for them quite well.

RD But the theme of much of the press reportage about this matter has been, particularly in the German press, has been a link of these establishments in various capital cities where important people go, in London, Brussels, Paris and elsewhere, and international agents keep an eye on them. Does that strike you as too fanciful?

LAMBTON I don't know but I imagine the vice world is rather like the Boy Scout movement in some ways.

RD I don't quite understand how.

LAMBTON I mean there are organizations in every country and naturally I should think that a madam in London will have relations with a madam in Paris and interchange each other's plans. My comparison to the Boy Scouts was purely organizational ...

RD You merely meant, hands across the sea is really what you meant?

LAMBTON Yes, any connection between the two activities could not, of course, possibly be contemplated.

RD When did you first realize that your activities had been discovered by the authorities?

LAMBTON When I saw the police.

RD This was on Monday of this week.

LAMBTON Monday of this week.

RD And you had up to that point no inkling of any kind?

LAMBTON None of any kind whatsoever.

RD It suddenly burst upon you on Monday.

LAMBTON Yes.

RD And did they come and see you at home or at your office?

LAMBTON No, the Permanent Under-Secretary of the Ministry of Defence, Sir James Dunnett, came to see me, obviously very embarrassed. He said the police wanted to see me and would I make the time. So I couldn't conceive why they wanted to see me, so I made the quickest conceivable time. It would be possible to have lunch and see them, which was 2.15, and, as you know, minute quantities of stuff were found in my house, for which I have an explanation. It never entered my head that the time I had, which was plenty to (I think they gave me any time that day) to destroy these things, because I had no sense of guilt whatever about them.

RD But this was when they brought the photograph and asked about the connection with the call-girls ...

LAMBTON This is when the whole story was told to me. Before I had no inkling of anything.

RD And what do you have to say about the way the police dealt with you?

LAMBTON I don't think that I could have possibly met two really finer men, or three finer men, in a service than the three really I met. I don't know what he is, something or other Commissioner Bond, struck me as a very exceptional type of policeman and so did his chief officer who served the summons on me today. Both seemed to me a very high type of officer. Their conduct to me was absolutely scrupulous. I mean when they came and searched the house ... I was a journalist like you ... found this situation so nightmarish, as you can imagine, that I really had to try and detach myself from it in order to look at it in an unbiased way. So I tried to look at them as if I was a stranger looking at people doing things which were nothing whatever to do with me. Their conduct I thought was impeccable, and I don't believe that anyone could possibly have complained about it, though I gather that certain things I said were taken to mean that. It certainly wasn't meant like that.

RD Lord Lambton, if you had been a minister in an entirely different kind of department, say the Ministry of Education or the Department of the Environment dealing with something like pollution, would you have had to resign in exactly the same way, do you think?

LAMBTON I think if I'd been an ... Under-Secretary in the Department of Environment I'd have left, resigned long ago without any reason like this.

RD But assuming you were in a Department and this had occurred and it was not a Defence Department, not a Department dealing with national security, do you think that your going with these call-girls, and the photograph ... would have been a matter calling for your resignation just as much?

LAMBTON No, I would have resigned.

RD Yes, but what I'm getting at is, do you think that your resignation would have been just as necessary?

LAMBTON I think it would because I think that you follow certain rules. Now, if you break those rules you break them at your own peril and you pay the price.

RD What price are you paying, Lord Lambton?

LAMBTON The price of the extinguishment of my career.

RD How do you envisage spending the next twenty-five years of your life? You are fifty, aren't you?

LAMBTON Yes. Well, I think that one of the lessons one learns, don't you, is that one never wants to make any decision in a hurry. I've always had a great many interests and I really haven't been very well in the last year or so. I think the life has been exceptionally busy for me and I certainly won't be bored because I have a great many interests, but I mean the ruling passion of my life will have gone.

RD Politics.

LAMBTON Yes.

RD And you're going to cut yourself off from that altogether.

LAMBTON Well, there's no doubt one should. I mean one can write, obviously, anything like that. But, as I say, one accepts the price of something.

RD But you accept the price of resigning from office.

LAMBTON Yes.

RD But does that necessarily mean leaving politics in this day and age, looking back on the number of politicians who in our public life have led lives by which your own might appear to be as pure as the driven snow?

LAMBTON I think that is largely irrelevant. There's all the world of difference, hypocritical as it is, in doing something and not being found out and being something and found out, because then you make a fool of your supporters. I mean, look: if you had said to an ordinary man in my division: 'Your Member went to bed with two call-girls,' he'd say, 'Good for him.' But if he was ... if he was put in the position that he is put in now of having his Member of Parliament publicly degraded for doing that, the position is totally different and the relationship could never be the same and he couldn't have the respect for his Member that must be the basis of a relationship between a Member and his constituency.

RD You think the ordinary person, lack of respect comes when the peccadillo is found out and not in the committing of the peccadillo?

LAMBTON Well, I say I think that my ... analogy is exact. I think if an ordinary man was told another man had been to bed with two pretty girls, he'd say 'Lucky dog', but if it was blazoned all over the newspapers that a minister had done that and brought his division in repute, he would say the man can't get away with it ... it's life, it's logic, that's what happens.

RD You've mentioned the ordinary people of your constituency, how do you think they do feel now about this matter and how do you feel about them?

LAMBTON They've been very nice but I have no doubt that underneath they are disappointed, that they feel I've let them down, and of course I have and this is very sad. I mean, I have a great, great many personal friends among constituents. If I go to a place like Rothbury, I mean, I'd meet forty people I would be pleased to see. Real friends and in a way I've known their parents and now their children and so it's immensely sad to break all these links.

RD Of course your constituency is not merely a constituency, as with many Members of Parliament. It is the area in which your family have been an important centre of the community for many, many generations.

LAMBTON Yes, yes.

RD Do you feel not only that you've let your constituents down. That you've brought disgrace on the name and the title which you were so anxious to keep?

LAMBTON Well, that is one of the sad parts of it.

RD You said you're going to resign from the House of Commons as well as from the government, why haven't you done that immediately ... ask for the Chiltern Hundreds?

LAMBTON Well I think one wants to wait a day or two. I mean, there is no immediate rush. The re-election won't be for a few weeks.

RD Is there any question that you would stay if your constituents were, at a less emotional moment, to ask you to stay?

LAMBTON There is no question.

RD You also mentioned in your statement that you issued to the press, Lord Lambton – I hesitate to ask you about it, but you mentioned it – your family? How do they react to this situation?

LAMBTON They have all been wonderful. Wonderful. A great, great support at a time like this and I couldn't have asked any more. Not a word of criticism for any of them and so one is very grateful for that.

RD Your wife had shown you the understanding which many wives might not?

LAMBTON Yes, I think, curiously enough, that most men would expect their wives over an incident basically unimportant like this to understand it.

RD One of the newspapers, I think the *Daily Express,* said that you were suffering a fate worse than you really deserve. Do you agree with that?

LAMBTON No. I think that would be wrong. I think that I had to accept a course of action and I have accepted it. It will make life obviously less pleasurable for me. I mean it will be a great loss for me – the House of Commons. I have many friends there. Conservative friends. Labour friends. I don't think I've ever managed to have a Liberal friend but I have many friends on the Labour benches. My pair, Ted Garrett, Bob Mellish – many people. I'll be very sad not seeing them any more.

RD You may not have ever happened to make a Liberal friend but I think if you had heard what Mr Thorpe said in the House of Commons after the Prime Minister's statement, you would have felt it was very warm and generous and sympathetic towards you.

LAMBTON Oh yes, he's a nice fellow Jeremy and always has been, a very nice fellow.

RD Are you relieved that there is not going to be a judicial tribunal of the 1921 Act character or a Denning-type inquiry as there was in the Profumo? To rake through everything in public? As a tribunal would have done.

LAMBTON What is there to rake through?

RD I don't know.

LAMBTON There are two cases of what I suppose you might call infidelity. It's not really a national issue. The Prime Minister has to deal with this country's recovery in the world, its trade position, its internal position, the trade unions. My petty problem compared to that is a personal one, and to overdo it or overstate it is to exaggerate very greatly my importance.

RD Will you co-operate with the Security Commission under Lord Diplock which is to inquire into the security aspect?

LAMBTON Of course. Of course, in every way.

RD Lord Lambton, you've obviously been through a tremendous ordeal in the last few days. I don't really know quite how to ask this question, but how has been your mood?

LAMBTON It's only three days ago and it seems certainly like years to me and the days have been almost unending. I don't think it's an exaggeration to say pain, but I think one has to face these things and survive them for the sake of those who are dependent on one.

RD I can't think of any other politician in the main stream of political life in this country who would talk about this matter as you have done with such frankness; and many people might say with courage too. Why did you want to ... why did you accept this invitation to do a television interview in which you could talk about these matters?

LAMBTON My first reaction when I got the producer's telegram was not to do it and of course my first reaction to the whole thing was that I will not really show myself again. I think that is the natural reaction of someone in these circumstances. But it really occurred to me when I re-read that letter that one has to face things again and this was perhaps the most direct and honest way of doing it in which one could show something of oneself.

RD You've made several statements and you've given this interview. Is there anything else which you would like to say to your constituents, to your friends, to the country, which you feel you've left unsaid in this interview?

LAMBTON No, I'd just like to thank all those who helped me and were so kind to me over the years in and out of Parliament and really you all for coming here to-day.

RD Lord Lambton, thank you very much.

'A Cabinet that has Michael Foot – one of our great successes in government – and Roy Jenkins all working together is the only hope for Britain.'

HAROLD WILSON   1974

In the television studio Harold Wilson always enjoyed the sword-play of a vigorous interview, just as he relished the much more savage cut-and-thrust at the dispatch box in the Commons. He was the Prime Minister I interviewed more often than any other. This interview in 1974 was during his second period as Prime Minister. He had been returned to Number 10 five months earlier, after the General Election of February 1974. That was the emergency election in which Heath had gone to the country on the issue: 'Who governs Britain'. The miners had challenged the Tory government's pay policy. No party won an overall majority in Parliament. Heath hung on for four days, but when he failed to get Liberal support, he had to make way for Wilson.

So in August 1974 Harold Wilson was presiding over a minority Labour government, having scraped back into power in February 1974. Wilson was now subordinating everything to win a working majority for Labour in the second 1974 election. This was to be in October, a couple of months after this interview. The miners' dispute, which had led Heath to impose a three-day week, was settled on the miners' terms. Labour repealed Heath's pay policy, and his ill-fated Industrial Relations Act. This was done as part of the so-called 'social compact' or 'contract', the deal struck by Wilson with the trade union leaders under which Labour brought in measures wanted by the TUC in return for moderated wage demands. Wilson's claim here that this 'social compact' would be an effective instrument for controlling the mounting inflation (15 per cent or so that summer) was, to say the least, over-optimistic. One year later inflation had rocketed to almost 27 per cent.

In that summer of 1974, after the inconclusive February election and with another like it in prospect, there was much talk of reforming the electoral system and of coalition government. The extensive press reports of this Wilson interview centred on his outright rejection of peacetime coalition and on his declaration that he would rather see a Conservative government than a coalition which fudged the big issues. 'Better Tory rule than a coalition' ran the *Guardian* headline. Another passage which intrigued political reporters was Wilson's reference to his 'brilliant Cabinet of head-strong horses', meaning Michael Foot, Roy Jenkins and Tony Benn.

There are flashes of the fabled political footwork that was the hallmark of Wilson's leadership, particularly on the Common Market issue. With a Cabinet and party deeply divided about being in the European Community, Wilson began his so-called renegotiation of the entry terms which Heath had negotiated in 1972. He is here ready to hold a referendum (previously condemned by him as 'a foreign device'). But Wilson is careful not to say whether his Cabinet will recommend a 'Yes' or a 'No' or make any recommendation at all. And he reveals that members of his Cabinet might be free to campaign on opposite sides. My spontaneous reaction ('This is an extraordinary way to conduct Cabinet government, isn't it?') was more than a mere question. But Wilson took it as fair comment and delivered a characteristic riposte.

In 1964 Wilson had been the first Prime Minister to reach Number 10 equipped with professional mastery of the techniques of television. This 1974 interview is Wilson at the height of his mature television style – relaxed, agile, humorous, masterful. But it is also Wilson as a great manipulator, brilliant at short-term party manoeuvring, rather than as a great leader. Behind these Wilsonian answers can be seen not the politics of principle but the politics of opportunism. Yet he did have one grand guiding purpose, to make Labour the natural party of government, which he seemed to be achieving in the sixties. But in the seventies the desperate efforts by him, and then by Callaghan, to keep the party united came to nothing. Not until the nineties, under the much stronger leadership of Neil Kinnock, did Labour again begin to look like a party of government.

Lord Jenkins suggests in his memoirs that Wilson's handling of the European question in the seventies did more than anything else to cause the Labour Party's disasters of the eighties. Others may dispute that sweeping claim, but this 1974 interview illustrates the pragmatic, unprincipled Wilson approach to the European issue.

The interview also recalls a sub-plot of the February 1974 election. Enoch Powell refused to stand as a Conservative and advised the electors to vote Labour to get Britain out of the Common Market. Whether Powell's advice helped Labour or not (Wilson denies that it did), the result of Labour's referendum was to keep Britain in the EEC.

It may be noticed that Harold Wilson calls me 'Robin'. He was the first Prime Minister to do so on television. This was alleged to be artificial mateyness, and part of his 'deliberately folksy TV manner'. Not so. It was quite natural for him to call me Robin, just as he had done ever since I became a TV interviewer in 1955. It would have been artificial for him to have suddenly started calling me *Mr* Day. But his 'Robin' caused comment, and gave the impression to some that interviews with the Prime Minister had become too cosy. I was careful, however, always to address him on television as 'Prime Minister', in the proper manner.

The Rt Hon. Harold Wilson OBE, MP, Prime Minister

Interviewed 'live' at 10 Downing Street
for BBC Nationwide
1 August 1974

ROBIN DAY Prime Minister, there will be a devil of a row – and I am quoting Mr Anthony Crosland on the radio this week – there will be a devil of a row (he says) if there is any question of there not being a General Election this autumn. Can you tell us what the position is?

RT HON. HAROLD WILSON MP, PRIME MINISTER Well – I obviously can't say anything about an election; but there certainly won't be a row.

RD Can you say you can't say whether there will be an election in the autumn – in view of all the –

WILSON Because these are matters that have got to be decided at the proper time and because in due course I will announce it in the normal way.

RD Are you simply preserving the constitutional proprieties? Or are you genuinely keeping your political options open?

WILSON I am preserving the constitutional proprieties. But whereas everybody else has decided the date – about seven different ones – I haven't.

RD But in considering when to hold the election – Prime Minister – can you see any arguments for holding on to office for a few more months in the situation you've been in –

WILSON I think we have in the past five months carried through more of our election pledges than any government since the war – even the Attlee government (of which I was a member). Nevertheless, when on major issues you cannot be sure – or you can have little expectation – of carrying essential legislation through, this is not a position in which, facing a grave economic crisis, a government can fairly be asked to carry on indefinitely. Particularly when we now understand that the Conservative leadership are entering in to discussions with the Ulster extremists whom they wouldn't be seen dead with when they were in government. It does lead to all kinds of rather disreputable Opposition coalitions.

RD Of course you owe your minority government perhaps – to someone you would regard as an extremist, namely Mr Enoch Powell. Don't you?

WILSON Not at all. No. He was not my problem. He was Mr Heath's problem ...

RD He won support for you ...

WILSON I doubt that. I think the support was on very different issues. It was on the three-day week and where confrontation and pitched battles between the then government and industry had led the country.

RD Don't the circumstances which you've just mentioned, Prime Minister, the economic crisis and the problems of dealing with a minority government – don't they represent overwhelming arguments for having an election as soon as possible after the holiday?

WILSON I think they are overwhelming arguments for having a government which can take decisions with the confidence that they won't be frustrated by manoeuvring. I said – I think in an earlier BBC programme on all this coalition talk – that I would rather have in this situation a strong Labour government or a strong Conservative government – however much we would deplore the things they would do and think them wrong – than have a coalition where all the big issues were fudged and where the necessary decisions cannot be taken.

RD Can we at least assume that polling day will not be before October?

WILSON You can assume just as much as you like; but I am not going to make any unconstitutional pronouncements on television.

RD Is there any truth – Prime Minister – following on what you have just said about the desirability of a strong government – is there any truth that you have decided that if there is another situation like we have now – that you will not continue as a minority Prime Minister – but you will hand over to the Tories?

WILSON I have not decided anything of the kind. We saw that undignified manoeuvring after the last General Election for three or four days, which proved to be very costly for the country; and I certainly do not intend to go through any process of manoeuvring, nor any of my colleagues either. But we are going for a majority government and I think that is what the country wants.

RD Talking of the Liberals, Mr Wilson, do you think that a system which gives the Liberals only fourteen parliamentary seats for 6,000,000 votes is fair?

WILSON I think they have got a case here; though no one has found, so far, a better solution. But of course – what and who are the Liberals? You see? If you can get someone like Mr Mayhew – (I don't want to spend much time on him) it proves you can be anything and a Liberal. The group of Liberals represent about fourteen different opinions and do not agree very much on anything.

RD But that – if I may say so, Prime Minister – is slightly off the point about the fairness, or otherwise, of the electoral system.

WILSON No, it isn't, of course. It isn't. Because if they represent a kind of loose conglomeration of every point of view in the country, then it is not unfair, since they have no identifiable separate existence and policy. It is not unfair that they – well – they divided up in the House last week – you see? I mean – they haven't got –

RD Of course, they would say – as indeed Mr Mayhew says and indeed Mr Thorpe often says – that they do represent a wide cross-section of people and classes, unlike either the Labour Party or the Tory Party.

WILSON ... We represent an extremely wide section of the country of every kind of class and interests and social backgrounds. They tend to get the Poujadist vote, of course. They tend to get the large number of Conservatives who regard Mr Heath as too progressive. Some of the Powellites you mentioned vote Liberal, of course.

RD Do you have any proposals as a majority government, if you were to be returned, to reform the electoral system?

WILSON We made it clear we are prepared to discuss it with all the other parties.

RD In what you call yourself, Prime Minister, the gravest economic situation Britain has faced since the war, what do you say to the argument that no single party – even with a working majority – can command the broad-based support which is necessary to unite the nation?

WILSON It is not only I who said it. The Conservative government said it before the last election and I think it is true. The last election (and the next) was fought (and will be fought) on the gravest crisis – partly through, as we would say, some of the Conservative policies. They would say some of the Labour policies, partly through this enormous oil surcharge with the quadrupling of oil – but I take the view – and it is true, I think, of the whole of our history that every coalition in peacetime (war is a different matter) has fudged issues, or has been – as in the case of the 1931 coalition right through to the beginning of the war – a positive menace both in social and economic terms and in international terms. In wartime, at least when they concentrate on winning the war, as in the last war, a coalition can work. Your decisions are narrowly confined to how to win the war and then organize the whole country. But in the last year of the last war – and I saw something of this – they couldn't take decisions on a single matter affecting the social and economic future of Britain because of their different political views.

RD So under no circumstances whatsoever, are you saying – you would not take part in or lead any kind of coalition government.

WILSON That is right. I have said that before. I say it again. If unhappily Britain was plunged into war, it would be the duty of every one of us to – if it was a question of saving the country in the war – to go into a coalition at any level and in any capacity that was required.

RD Some people do say, Prime Minister, that though we are not at war, the inflation is so serious that if it is not checked we shall be threatened with the collapse of the democratic system which is worse than anything that happened in war.

WILSON I have just drawn the distinction between the decisions you mean to take in peacetime and the decisions that are possible in war on a much narrower front. I think there are those at work today who would like to see the collapse of social democracy. I do not believe that any of the parliamentary parties take this view; but there is a devastating undermining – some of these smear campaigns against figures in public life – one has just been totally disproved this week – are designed to destroy public faith in politics and politicians and should be utterly repudiated by all parties.

RD Do you approve of the speech in which Mr Roy Jenkins warned that the Labour Party must win over, and not ignore, moderate middle of the road opinion?

WILSON I have been doing it all my life. I replied to all the speeches that I have read about and heard and listened to in a very lengthy speech myself to the parliamentary party – Labour MPs – which was almost universally acclaimed by all of them – earlier this week. And –

RD But only one line of it referred to Mr Roy Jenkins' speech, so you were not going to comment on it ...

WILSON Well, I think that some of those things that I said were regarded universally as commenting on his speeches, Mr Benn's speeches and other speeches; and what I said on that occasion is that the Cabinet must decide. I deprecate public debate about what the Cabinet should be doing, by members of the Cabinet; the Cabinet this week has taken many important decisions which will be published shortly in White Papers or in our policy. But of course I agree with Roy Jenkins that no government in this country can be successful or viable – or even get elected without a very much wider range of voters than those who are the acknowledged supporters of the party. That is what I have always tried to get. That is why I said the other night – and have done in all my years as leader of the party – try to keep together people of very wide differences of opinion, all of them socialists, in order to release the energies of people who have so much to contribute. I do not believe, as some party leaders of other parties – and predecessors perhaps of mine – believed, that you can run it with a very narrow team of like-minded people. I believe a Cabinet that has Michael Foot (one of our great successes in government) and Roy Jenkins – all working together as a Cabinet – I believe that is the only hope for Britain. That is in the best sense of the word a coalition.

RD Do you also agree with Mr Reg Prentice that British people do not want doctrinaire socialism based on out of date class war attitudes?

WILSON Yes. Of course I do. I have always pronounced that as well. But as I say, I believe that by distilling – which is my job – by keeping this very brilliant – this is the most experienced Cabinet we have had in this country since the war and the most talented – by keeping them together – a team of pretty headstrong horses – Attlee did the same with Aneurin Bevan then – I am enabling both the Cabinet and the country to have the benefit of the government that has all these points of view and then to see we speak as one Cabinet on our decisions.

RD ... It is all very well having a brilliant Cabinet of headstrong horses, and so on – but unless they are all racing in the same direction – let me ask you this then –

WILSON Let me just say that I've spent most of the last fortnight pushing on and driving the Cabinet – really driving them – to get decisions on all these important questions – public ownership of land, the industry White Paper on which there's been so much public debate, both by ministers and by the press; on superannuation, on disablement, on many other questions; on Kilbrandon. And we shall have united programmes on all these things. I am concerned to lead a Cabinet which is united on all our decisions. And this I have got.

RD A lot of people, I think, particularly in industry, would like to hear from you directly, Prime Minister, who is the authentic voice of Labour policy towards private industry, is it Mr Harold Lever who wants it to be vigorous, alert and profitable, or is it Mr Wedgwood Benn who continually threatens it with nationalization or state control?

WILSON With all due modesty the authentic voice is me – or I – whatever is the right grammar. I have taken charge of the whole of this operation, when I thought the thing was getting out of hand in too much public debate, and we have reached agreement now on the whole policy – every one of us, we are in agreement. I think at tomorrow's Cabinet we shall finalize the text of the White Paper. It will be published in the near future and then the country will be able to judge whether they like or don't like what we've got – it is a united policy in accordance with the manifesto which we've put before the country at the election.

RD Now in your recent Chequers speech, Prime Minister, you said that private industry must have the necessary confidence to maintain and increase investment and you went on – well, I won't go on, I think that makes the point ... let me ask you how can there be that confidence when there is a threat of widespread nationalization?

WILSON I also said in the same speech that they must have certainty ... that there will be a boundary between the public and the private sector ...

RD That's right.

WILSON ... which not everybody will agree with but we are agreed on it – and at the same time a frontier between certainty and uncertainty. Our paper – the White Paper will provide for a mixed economy, for an extension of public ownership – I can't of course disclose where the frontier will be today – and for a private sector which we want to see much more enterprising, much more responsible and accountable to the country and profitable. I believe that these things are essential. I'm particularly concerned – and there will be a reference to this in the White Paper – that we do something much more than any government has done for small industry, small firms, they've been badly hit, they're badly hit by the liquidity squeeze, they've been badly hit, for example, in Stage 3 in Mr Heath's policies by poaching of labour by richer firms, over the odds and Mr Heath's policy, and we're trying to work out something because I think there is an enormous contribution to come from private enterprise, small firms as long as they're enterprising.

RD But can you deny, Prime Minister, that the threat and talk of more nationalization – especially from Mr Wedgwood Benn – has damaged business confidence as a matter of fact?

WILSON I'm not dealing with individuals and public speeches. I made clear in my speech this week that I think the time – indeed I said this some time ago – the time for talk and debate, carrying on the argument of the last election on these matters is over and the time for action is here – those are the words I used. So I took charge of this operation: I have chaired all the meetings on it; I've taken a close hand in the drafting of it and now we're going to have action, we're going to have the thing utterly clarified and that I think is what the country wants.

RD When people read of the enormous debts of existing nationalized industries can you ask them to regard nationalization – whatever may have been the case for it in the past – as the way to achieve efficiency, solvency and good industrial relations?

WILSON Some of our nationalized industries, particularly electricity and coal, have got the highest record in productivity of any industry in Britain. As far as the debts are concerned, these are in large part due to the previous government – and indeed our own government – in holding their prices down below what private ownership would have done, in order to steady the cost of living. You see many of these industries have a very big labour content, so if wages go up there, as they should, equal with other industries, comparable industries, then prices are much more severely hit. So that is one reason. But the second thing is that the kind of thing that public ownership, public enterprise does – if you look at it in parts of the world where it's private – electricity, railways – the American railways are totally bankrupt – you are running services here which by their nature are very difficult to make viable. Therefore I do not accept the view that British public enterprise has been unenterprising, or in any way less effectively run than many private industries. And when you consider that so many private firms today are dominated not by the excellent management many of them possess – middle-management is very frustrated, they're looking over their shoulder whether they're going to be taken over by some Stock Exchange gambler related more to asset-stripping than to efficient production.

RD In view of all the large wage claims which are in prospect, Prime Minister, can you maintain that what you call the social contract ...

WILSON Yes.

RD ... is an effective instrument for controlling the very serious inflation?

WILSON Yes, I believe so. There are some claims which are themselves the result of the previous period of sort of tight ossification, of bureaucratic rigidities which already cost the country a three-day week and thousands of millions of pounds of lost output. But, of course, there are other cases – you've got the nurses, for example, who since 1970 haven't had a fair crack of the whip and now everyone knows their wage claim and their wage settlement will be greater than the average envisaged in the social contract. What we've learned, you know I introduced a big – a wage freeze – it worked by the way, there wasn't a single strike during that period and the cost of living rose by $1\frac{1}{2}$ per cent in the following year. But no democratic country, in my view, can do it twice. It's much harder each time. We've seen that with America ...

RD If you win the election, Prime Minister. Are you certain that you will be able to avoid having to impose a wage freeze?

WILSON Yes. I believe that this will not work. It led not only to confrontation, as we saw, it led to rigidities, to shortage of labour in some industries, to a degree of freezing of the economy, which is not what we need for solving our problems. There will be difficulties, no scheme is perfect. There will be, in the words, I think – was it a programme with you, Vic Feather and I when we announced the social contract eighteen months ago, we said there'd be some balls will get past the wicket-keeper but if they all get past, that wicket-keeper would have to be sacked, wouldn't he?

RD Yes, but Mr Healey, the Chancellor, said only last month that what happens to wages is the key to controlling inflation in the coming year. How are you going to do this if you're abandoning any reserve power in the event of the social contract not working?

WILSON Remember the reserve power and all that scheme won't work at all. That is a far worse proposal, even than for an only limited successful voluntary scheme. When he said that – I myself have said the same – that over the past year or two the cost of living has gone up partly because of world prices, partly because the then government wouldn't deal with food prices, partly because they forced up rents and all the rest of it, I have said, and Mr Healey has rightly said, that if we have wages going up – as under the threshold system which is proving very costly ...

RD ... which you were in favour of ...

WILSON Of course I was, yes, and I have said that – every time I've referred to this I said that I was not criticizing Mr Heath – I pressed for it – that it hadn't worked out as either of us thought ... But with the threshold scheme this of course increases wage costs and therefore will affect prices. That is why we have set out to tackle inflation at the price end – by the rents freeze, by holding mortgages down, by food subsidies, by a much tighter control over food prices in the shops. This means there will – and there's the Mini-Budget of Mr Healey – there will be fewer threshold triggers now than there would have been, because of that, and we have got to go further in that direction.

RD But despite all those measures like food subsidies etc. and the freezing of rents, Prime Minister, the fact is that inflation is now at a much higher rate than it was when you took office ... perhaps not due to you ...

WILSON Not at a higher rate than we knew it would be ...

RD ... a higher rate now than it was in March ...

WILSON But then the previous Conservative government when they fought the election knew that ...

RD But you added to it with your first Budget.

WILSON Well ... our first Budget net did not add to it ... Net – as Mr Healey proved very clearly in the House of Commons debate last week – when you take into account subsidies ... Then you had the other subsidies since, and the profits control and the price control ... But the previous government knew what rate of inflation we were facing: even pro-Conservative newspapers and the *Economist,* and you can't get higher than that in being pro-Conservative, forecast 18 per cent to 20 per cent increase in prices in January and said that is why the government, the Tory government, should have an election then, and of course they did, hoping to get out from under by one means or another. But I still believe – coming back to what you've said – that the right way to tackle inflation – even though we know wages aren't a problem for next year – is to hold back the wage situation by dealing with prices. That's what he's done in a small way in the Mini-Budget. He's made clear he hopes to be able to do much more in the autumn budget.

RD But by relying on that policy and on the social contract are you not leaving the government and the country without any defence against trade unions who may seek to use their industrial power against the national interest?

WILSON Yes ... There will be one or two ... Some with a long overdue grievance – as we now have referred to the Health Service; some where there's been a structural change due two years ago, as in the railways ... Yes, there will be problems. But you talk as though there is a cast-iron defence. For example under the Stage 3 thing ... there is no alternative in a democracy. It might work in a Communist country, it might work in a Fascist country – it will not work for very long and it has not worked in this country, it broke down in a democracy.

RD On the Common Market, Prime Minister, is it your position and that of the government that you want the renegotiations to succeed so that Britain can stay in, despite anything that Mr Shore may appear to say to the contrary?

WILSON The Foreign Secretary, with the full authority of the Cabinet, is negotiating with intent to succeed, in the hope of getting terms to replace the extraordinary terms that the Conservatives were satisfied with, so that these can then be put to the country, but the country will have the last word ...

RD In a Referendum or in a General Election?

WILSON In one of the two – we haven't finally decided. I've always kept this option open and I don't apologize for that. Of course, whether the country would want, shall we say, three General Elections in a row in a short period of time is a question to be answered ... A Referendum may be the answer, we shall be ready to have this.

RD But can you promise the people a choice in this way, Prime Minister, because you might not get a Referendum Bill through the House of Commons, even if you have a majority Labour government?

WILSON Oh, I don't think anybody in the House of Commons, when they are faced up with it, will say the British people should not have the last word, that the British people should not have the right to take a decision which would be final and binding on a major issue of constitutional importance – the most important for 300 years – on which Mr Heath broke his pledge to take the – not to take the country into the Market without the full-hearted consent ...

RD What would be the question in this Referendum, which of course you used to oppose strongly as a foreign device?

WILSON Well, I did oppose it in 1970 but then I would not – because I thought this could be left to Parliament – I would not have put to Parliament anything so manifestly unacceptable to the British people. The question – we'll have to draft it – will be something on these lines – I'm not drafting now, you understand – got to give consideration ... It would in effect say, following the negotiations, having got these terms, these new terms, or having failed to get any improvement, or whatever it is – the British people are now asked to decide whether you want to remain in the Common Market ... The question there will decide and there will be no fudging, it will be in or out. Their decision will be final and binding.

RD And the Cabinet will make a collective recommendation as to what ...

WILSON This is still to be decided. We shall wait until we had seen the result of the negotiations ... We shall then decide our attitude ... We haven't got there yet.

RD But you will make a recommendation one way or the other?

WILSON We shall decide what we're going to do. We may decide that this could be left to a free vote of the British people as a whole.

RD And have members of the Cabinet going on different sides?

WILSON This is possible. We haven't decided ...

RD That's an extraordinary way to conduct Cabinet government, isn't it?

WILSON It isn't. This is a matter of such transcendent importance that the people must be free to decide ... We haven't decided either to do it one way or the other ... We have been too busy carrying out election pledges – which is a thing that people haven't got used to over these last three years – and also we have been working very hard on the negotiations themselves.

RD In view of Labour's steady decline in the opinion polls since April, Prime Minister, what grounds have you got for confidence that the people will give you the majority vote and the majority in Parliament which they did not give you in February?

WILSON You know my view on opinion polls ...

RD Well, it's a broad trend ...

WILSON Well, it isn't a broad trend at all ... It hasn't in fact been proved very accurate a way of forecasting in the 1974 or the 1970 election and I personally – with some little experience of statistical matters – do not attach a great deal of importance to a poll of 1000 people, taken when about half of our people – much more than the Conservative supporters – are on holiday. I think if you went to my constituency with a public opinion poll this week and so many away, you would derive from that the fact that I am going to lose the next election there, and possibly my deposit ... In fact I got a majority of 15,000 last time and I shan't do too badly next time.

RD Well, forgetting the polls, can you give one ...

WILSON You raised them. I didn't.

RD Well, they do figure in discussion ... Indeed I'm sure with you in private ... too. But what ground, give us one ground for strong confidence – which you obviously appear to have – that you will get the majority. Something that will remain in people's minds ...

WILSON Political honesty ...

RD Political honesty?

WILSON Political honesty. Yes, we have carried out our pledges – as no government has done before and the whole country knows it. Secondly, we have policies relevant to the people as a whole. There'll be big arguments, you rightly said, about public ownership and the rest – some will say people should profiteer in particular in speculation, commodity and all the rest of it. Thirdly, because we have a recognizable government team. Mr Heath's team wasn't very good at the last election. They've most of them now either left him or have been sacked and don't even look like a potential government. There are three reasons. I could give you more if we had more time.

RD Just one point arising out of political honesty – which I think will be of interest to quite a lot of people. Does it arouse respect for politicians when a minister in your government [Sports Minister Dennis Howell] having condemned the Rugby Tour of South Africa then suddenly goes off to drink champagne with them simply because they've had a successful tour?

WILSON No. He went with my authority. I said he should go. I'm totally opposed to the tour going to South Africa. Unlike the Conservatives I've always been opposed to hobnobbing with South Africa, and Rhodesia ... and Fascist Portugal ... There was a great argument about those massacres last year. I authorized him to go simply to congratulate them on the way they played. They played very, very well indeed.

RD But they wouldn't have been able to play at all if you'd had your way?

WILSON Well, they'd have played just as well somewhere else – in Australia or New Zealand, I would have preferred that. But he said at the same time that we still deplored the fact that they went at all. I saw no reason why he shouldn't go and there's no – I hope on your part – imputation of dishonesty to him for going.

RD Not dishonesty but people will think it doesn't look really very straight and very – anything but rather hypocritical.

WILSON People like you will think that, Robin.

RD Well, I've heard a lot of other people say it ... I don't have a view on it one way or the other ... Prime Minister.

WILSON Yes, but you don't meet the country like some of us ...

RD Well, it depends who you mean by the country. A lot of people talk to me, Prime Minister ... sometimes about you ... But thank you very much ...

WILSON I'm talking about the grass roots ... I've spent every weekend going there ... I know I've got a different impression from you, Robin, but I'm sure we'll talk about it on another occasion ...

RD We'll meet again perhaps in September or October ... I forget which it was you said ...

WILSON I don't know when the BBC have arranged for my next interview.

RD Thank you, Prime Minister.

'I've said a lot of bloody stupid things in my life, and I think that was the most stupid thing I've ever said.'

LORD SHAWCROSS

Ever since I was an undergraduate at Oxford reading law, Lord Shawcross QC has been one of my heroes. I followed then with fascination his dazzling performance as Attorney-General in the post-war Labour government. No other law officer in my time has been such a star. His appearances in celebrated treason and murder trials made him a household name. In one of the now forgotten sensations of the post-war years, he was counsel to the Lynskey tribunal which investigated allegations of corruption. More importantly, Sir Hartley Shawcross was Chief Prosecutor at the Nuremberg War Crimes Tribunal.

In 1953, when I was a pupil barrister, Shawcross was the most fashionable silk of the time. I sat behind him at the Old Bailey and in other courts and observed his technique at close quarters. As an advocate, he was elegant and eloquent. As a cross-examiner, he was formidable. As a Labour politician, his utterances were not always well judged. As he readily admits, he had a capacity for dropping political bricks. His notorious boast, 'We are the masters at the moment', was, he confesses here, 'the most stupid thing I've ever said'.

This reminiscent interview, done in the summer of 1975, is about his life and times, about his forensic triumphs and his political gaffes. He talks about the Attlee government, and about his gradual disenchantment with socialism and the Labour Party. His parliamentary nickname, 'Sir Shortly Floorcross', was unfair because, though he moved to the right, he never joined the Tory Party. In the Lords he has always sat on the cross benches.

For the past forty years his contributions to public life have been indefatigable – in the City, on the Press Council, in Lords debates, and in pungent letters to *The Times*. His ninetieth birthday was celebrated in grand style in February 1992. Hartley Shawcross looked as debonair and sounded as silver-tongued as ever.

Our interview was filmed at his beautiful country home, Friston Place in Sussex. The completed programme was interlaced with historic film of events and personalities referred to in the interview. Production was by Christopher Capron.

The Rt Hon. Lord Shawcross GBE, QC

Filmed at Friston Place, Sussex
Transmitted in two parts, 7 and 14 August 1975, on BBC 1

ROBIN DAY Lord Shawcross, looking back on your long public career, which, of course, is still continuing, what was the most satisfying period of it? Was it the period when you were in the law, in politics, or in the world of finance? Or what?

RT HON. LORD SHAWCROSS QC I think probably the two periods that I found most satisfaction in were the period when I was actually in government. You know, one thought – I suppose this sounds terribly conceited and pompous – that one was doing a job reasonably well and that was a satisfying thing to do and that it was a job that was worth doing. Then, in the City, I think the work that my colleagues and I have done on the City Panel has been satisfying in the sense that I feel we've achieved something there.

RD Now, going back to your period in government and your activities then, do you regret that you didn't reach, in the course of that career, the highest positions in your profession, that of the law? I refer particularly to Lord Chief Justice, Lord Chancellor, or even Lord of Appeal, which are the professional pinnacles which lawyers traditionally aspire towards.

SHAWCROSS No, I think I can honestly say I don't regret that at all. I was twice offered appointment direct from the Bar to the House of Lords as a Lord of Appeal.

RD And why did you turn that down?

SHAWCROSS I didn't feel that I would like that position. I didn't want to retire into the backwater of the law and I don't think that I should have been a particularly good judge.

RD What about Lord Chancellor and Lord –

SHAWCROSS Lord Chancellor. I didn't want to be Lord Chancellor and Mr Gaitskell said that if he ever became Prime Minister, he would offer me that position. I found that a discouraging offer because I did not want to be Lord Chancellor. I would have liked other appointments under Mr Gaitskell, but not that one.

RD Would you have accepted the Lord Chief Justiceship had it been offered to you when you were at the height of your career?

SHAWCROSS Yes, I should certainly have accepted that. I think that is the greatest appointment in the law and I think that I might have enjoyed that but it wasn't offered to me at that stage and I don't regret that I am not Lord Chief Justice.

RD Why didn't you in fact get offered that post when Lord Goddard was coming to the end of his term in 1957 and 1958, because you were very much a strong contender by virtue of experience, weren't you? One has heard it said that Lord Goddard was anxious for you to succeed him.

SHAWCROSS I think Lord Goddard would have liked me to succeed him, yes. I believe that is true.

RD In relation to your political career, let me ask you the same question again. Do you regret not having held the higher positions in politics which you might have held had you not quit active politics and quit the Labour Party after the 1945 government.

SHAWCROSS No, I think I can say I don't regret that at all.

RD But you thought, at one stage, of contesting the leadership, did you not?

SHAWCROSS Yes. At the time that Mr Attlee retired or in the months leading up to his retirement, there was some question of my standing for the leadership of the party. But I didn't do so because Mr Morrison decided that he would stand and I had a great respect and affection for him and I wouldn't have thought of standing in opposition to him.

RD But you would have stood against Gaitskell as the choice of successor to Attlee in 1955, if Morrison hadn't come forward.

SHAWCROSS It's very difficult to know what would have happened if Morrison had not been in the ring. Gaitskell and I were friendly, we often talked about these matters, and it may be that there wouldn't have been a contest of that kind. I'm not sure.

RD What sort of support did you have for the idea that you should let yourself go forward in that leadership election?

SHAWCROSS I think probably my main support came from the trade union section of the party which in those days was, I must admit, rather on the right, called the solid section of the party.

RD Were there any political figures that one might know who were seriously supporting you or urging you to go forward?

SHAWCROSS Well, yes, there were a number. I suppose the one that occurs to mind most now is – is George Brown.

RD And what argument did he advance for your taking this plunge in this way?

SHAWCROSS Well, it's very difficult to say. He thought that I was perhaps qualified to do this thing. He certainly was very anxious that I should and very cross with me for not . . .

RD I'm trying to visualize the conversation more precisely.

SHAWCROSS Well, you know, George is a very robust person, he says what he thinks. And sometimes he – thinks wrongly, and he thought, in this particular regard, that I – I remember the phrase he used very well – that I was a natural for it.

RD For the leadership of the Labour Party?

SHAWCROSS Yes. I didn't think so. And I had no – I think I can say this with a fair degree of sincerity – I had no great ambition to be leader of the Labour Party, and I don't regret that I did not become leader of the Labour Party. I think it's a very good thing for me and no doubt for the country!

RD Going back five years earlier, to 1950, you very nearly became Foreign Secretary in that year, didn't you?

SHAWCROSS Yes. That I would have liked to be. It's really the one post in politics that interested me but as things turned out it didn't come my way.

RD But why not? Because one reads that in fact you were told at one moment that you were going to get the post and then something happened that Attlee gave it to Herbert Morrison.

SHAWCROSS Yes. It wasn't quite as strong as that. It was clear, I think, from what I was told, that the choice lay between me and Herbert Morrison. Attlee said that he would give it to me if Herbert didn't want it. Herbert didn't really want it. But he felt that if he didn't take it, people would regard this as a kind of confession of failure on his part and that it would tend to disqualify him from the leadership of the party later on and that of course he did want. And so he took it, in a way rather against his better judgment.

RD Why, in your very early youth, at the age of fifteen and from then on, were you a Socialist? This was – what? – at the end of World War I roughly. What made you –

SHAWCROSS Oh, it was in the middle of World War I really and at the end. Well, I'd been brought up in a pretty radical tradition. I suppose, basically, it was for humanitarian reasons. I was very much impressed by the great contrast that there was in those days, much greater then than now, between the rich and the poor. I thought the Conservative Party then was very remote from the realities in which the mass of the people lived; that one wanted to adopt a much more pragmatic approach. I was never a doctrinaire socialist, I'm afraid I was not a theoretical socialist in any serious sense.

RD Were you active in any way in Labour politics between the wars? Because you've always said that you joined the Labour Party at an early age and your critics say, yes, but what did he do before the Labour Party gave him a job in government.

SHAWCROSS No. It's perfectly true, I wasn't active in politics between the wars. I got adopted for a Birmingham constituency in the second half of the 1920s, but in those days, unless you had the support of a trade union, you had to put up the money for your election expenses. I had no money at all, and although I was adopted, when the time came, I had to withdraw.

RD And in the mid-twenties, you had not begun your career at the Bar, not begun to earn any money. You were married, weren't you?

SHAWCROSS Yes, I was married. That created some complications. Unfortunately my wife was seriously ill through the whole of our marriage. I had to make some money and I had no money of my own and, indeed, it was four years at the Bar before I made over £100 a year.

RD Do you remember the circumstances of your first brief?

SHAWCROSS I remember my first brief very vividly. Yes. It was a very simple case. About the delivery and non-payment of some wine, and I won the case but I haven't been paid the fee for that case even to this day.

RD But you made up for it later. Might I ask you whether the various statements are true that when you were at the peak of your career, in the 1950s, at the Bar, that you were earning over £50,000 a year?

SHAWCROSS Well, you mustn't get me into trouble with my tax inspector. But I think there was a period when probably I was earning that. Of course, at that time, most of it went away in tax.

RD Why did you start off your career at the Bar in Liverpool?

SHAWCROSS I didn't. I got called, of course, in London, and I stayed in London for about nearly two years, I think, but I made no progress there, and I couldn't go on living on the very small allowance that I had from my parents and my wife's parents and I got a job at Liverpool University which I was able to combine with practice at the Bar.

RD But you hadn't been to a university for a degree, had you?

SHAWCROSS No. I went to Geneva University for a short time, just to fill in time, as a matter of fact, because then I intended to become a doctor.

RD Then what made you change your mind and go to the Bar?

SHAWCROSS Well, while I was at Geneva they had the first meeting after the First World War of what was called the Second Socialist International, and I offered my services as an interpreter. I did this for free and I think the people there, like Herbert Morrison, whom I met there for the first time, Ramsay MacDonald, J. H. Thomas, all those people, were rather amused at this idea of a young, comparatively young boy doing translation work. So they took me on a trip on Lake Geneva at the end of the conference, and asked me about myself, and I told them I was going to be a doctor and Herbert Morrison, knowing from what I'd told him, that I'd been active in the local Labour Party in London, said well, if you want to go on in Labour politics, don't be a doctor. The thing is to go to the Bar, that's the easiest profession to combine with politics, and the best you can do for the Labour Party is to be a success in your own profession. And there's some truth I think in that.

RD And you –

SHAWCROSS So I wrote home to my parents and said I'm sorry, dear Pa and Ma, I've decided not to be a doctor, I'm going to get called to the Bar.

RD But you did not in fact stand for Parliament or become adopted as a Labour candidate, what, until 1943 or 1944.

SHAWCROSS Yes, I think it must have been in 1944. Of course, at that time I might have taken a different view, if I'd known what was going to happen. At that time, I didn't think there was the slightest chance of the Labour Party being returned to power at the next election. I thought Churchill would be likely to walk away with that.

RD So you didn't, when you got adopted in 1944 as a Labour candidate, you didn't say this is my way to become Attorney-General.

SHAWCROSS No, certainly not. I never had any great ambition to have one of the legal political posts, as a matter of fact.

RD What is your verdict now on Attlee as Prime Minister and that post-war Labour government in which you were such, if I may say so, a star figure in the public eye?

SHAWCROSS Well, I had a very great respect for Attlee. We called him the Headmaster. Perhaps he didn't inspire a great deal of affection from his colleagues. He was a rather withdrawn, monosyllabic person, but he was a man of tremendous integrity and I think history will say that he led a capable administration during a very difficult period of transition from war conditions to peace conditions. I am proud to have been a member of his government.

RD Of course, your reputation at that time was a very controversial one because although you were known as the brilliant Attorney-General, you were apt to drop political bricks with great regularity, weren't you? What was the explanation for the skilful lawyer being such a clumsy and indiscreet politician from time to time?

SHAWCROSS Perhaps I'm an indiscreet person. I suppose it's naïvety, I – I quite admit that I did drop bricks.

RD Well, let me remind you of one phrase which, apart from Aneurin Bevan's reference to Tories being lower than vermin, which came later, was probably one of the most legendary utterances of the post-war years, which has for ever been attributed to you, namely 'We are the masters now'. And in fact you didn't actually say that, did you?

SHAWCROSS Well, I've said a lot of bloody stupid things in my life and I think that was the most stupid thing that I've ever said. It was something very like that. In the context in which I used the phrase, it was perhaps understandable. As I recall it, I was speaking on the third reading or second reading of the Trades Disputes Bill, and I was quoting something that Churchill had said in the course of the General Election about trade unions, and I said, this being an equivocal phrase, 'What did he mean?' And then I quoted *Alice in Wonderland*: 'What do words mean? Words mean what the master says they mean,' said Alice. And so I said, 'We are the masters at present, I think.' Somebody picked it out a little later on and I then realized how stupid a phrase it was and very much open to misconstruction. What I really should have said and I think meant to say was that Parliament were the masters, they had to decide what these words meant. If I'd said that, it would have been all right, nobody could have disputed it.

RD Why did you leave the Labour Party in 1958, Lord Shawcross?

SHAWCROSS Well, I think there were a complex of reasons. I found being in opposition was very tedious. I was expected to do the Board of Trade things or the legal things and always to speak in opposition to the man who was doing that work for the government of the day. Now in point of fact, the then President of the Board of Trade or the then Attorney-General was often doing exactly what I would have done myself in the same position and I found it extremely tedious to have to attack him for doing it. I never believed in the theory that the duty of the Opposition is to oppose and I think that's one of the troubles in Parliament now. That was one reason.

RD And what was the other thinking in your mind? Was it the trend of the Labour Party –

SHAWCROSS Well, I certainly thought that the Labour Party, in spite of the fact that Gaitskell was then the leader, was clearly moving to the left. This appeared to me to be so particularly in relation to foreign policy, about which I'd always been very interested and about which I was concerned. Then I thought it might be some time before the Labour Party got back into power and I had any office. It was really being in office that I enjoyed, doing a job usefully. I knew that the only office I was likely to get was that of Lord Chancellor, as Gaitskell had in fact told me. I didn't want to be Lord Chancellor, and so I decided just quietly to fade out of politics, which is what I did.

RD Having left the Labour Party, why have you not joined another party, for instance the Conservative Party, which many people might think you were more suited to?

SHAWCROSS Well, I think there are two reasons. Perhaps my – my experience in the Labour Party showed that I was not a very good politician, I didn't like being in opposition, I only liked doing a job and, as I said with some conceit, doing it well. The other was I didn't like the idea of attacking my old colleagues and sort of stabbing them in the back. I think these were the two considerations.

RD I'd like to ask you, Lord Shawcross, about the office of Attorney-General in which you made your reputation in the years 1945 to 1950 and to ask you to explain what essentially distinguishes that office from other ministerial posts.

SHAWCROSS Oh well, essentially it is not a party post. You are appointed, of course, by the Prime Minister of the day but once appointed, the Attorney-General is the Queen's Attorney-General and it's his duty to be utterly independent of party considerations and to represent the public, the public interest. To represent in a sense the rights of every individual citizen, and he's got to do this with utter disregard of party considerations, with complete integrity. That's what he's got to try and do.

RD Do you think that the present Attorney-General in his attitude to the Clay Cross matter and his support of the recent Bill dealing with that, is consistent with the way you see the responsibilities of the Attorney-General that you've just described?

SHAWCROSS Everybody must answer to his own conscience, in matters of this kind. I wouldn't like to comment on the conduct of my successor.

RD Let me put it in another way, Lord Shawcross. If you had been Attorney-General, would you have consented to support or bring in or help draft a Bill to deal with the Clay Cross matter as the present government have done?

SHAWCROSS I think not. I think that it's rather an infringement of the rule of law in favour of a political view.

RD Let me illustrate, if I may, the point about the Attorney-General's responsibility by asking you about that famous matter in 1948, just after the war, which came to be known as the Lynskey Tribunal, because of the judge who presided over it. Now what responsibilities as Attorney-General did you have in that, and would you recall the extraordinary circumstances of that tribunal?

SHAWCROSS Yes. I can recall it very well. I was attending one of the assemblies of the United Nations at that time in Paris and the Director of Public Prosecutions, who works under the supervision of the Attorney-General, came over to me – sent me a message to say that he'd got something very grave to consult me about. He told me that there were these rumours going round Westminster that there had been grave corruption on the part of ministers and officials, including a very grave case, so it was alleged at that time, against a very close and very senior colleague of mine. He said you must come back at once and deal with this position. So I left Paris immediately and came back to London. Then the question arose what we should do. I discussed it with the Prime Minister, and we decided to set up a tribunal of inquiry under an Act which had been passed after the First World War, as a matter of fact, which would have inquisitorial powers, and which would have the authority, which Royal Commissions don't have, of summoning witnesses, for the production of documents and exposing people in however high a position to the most rigorous cross examination.

RD Now why were you so insistent, as Attorney-General, on leading the questioning before that tribunal, because many people at the time and since have said that in view of the fact that you'd got to deal with your own colleagues and your own political party and your own government you should leave that to somebody else?

SHAWCROSS Yes. I think that that would have involved discrediting the office which I then held. As I said a minute or two ago, I've always regarded it as the proper function of the Attorney-General fearlessly to represent the public interest and I wanted to demonstrate that that was the duty of the Attorney-General and that I was capable of discharging it.

RD You had to cross examine ministerial colleagues at that tribunal didn't you –

SHAWCROSS Yes, I did.

RD Such as Hugh Dalton and –

SHAWCROSS Yes. Dalton was right on the fringe of the case. His evidence was not really relevant to any serious issue but he insisted on giving evidence, and I cross examined him, certainly.

RD And, of course, the Junior Minister, John Belcher, who was one of the figures under suspicion.

SHAWCROSS Yes. Poor Belcher was much more involved although it turned out on investigation what he was involved in was, compared with what we've heard about more recently, very trivial stuff. Of course, when the thing started, and before the police investigations, which were very thorough, had got under way, there were rumours going round Westminster and the City that corruption of senior ministers on a much higher scale had taken place. But even so, I think that the tribunal was justified in the work it did, which went over a good many weeks, in exposing even these minor cases of corruption, because any corruption, even if it seems nowadays to be quite trivial in comparison to figures that we've heard of recently, any corruption in public life really goes to the root of the whole of our system of government and has got to be ruthlessly stamped out. That's what we sought to do. I think perhaps we treated these people pretty harshly, but the public interest in the purity of government demanded that.

RD Do you have clear recollections of the man who was the central figure in many ways of that tribunal, a character called Sidney Stanley, whom you cross examined, if I recall, for many many hours? Part of the national sport at that time was to find out at the end of the day whether Hartley Shawcross had been beaten by Sidney Stanley or the other way round in the witness box.

SHAWCROSS I think there's no doubt about that, he completely beat me. I did cross examine him for hours and hours, indeed I think days and days. But I had no success. I always remember one answer that he gave me in the course of cross examination. I asked him a question and he answered, smiling, as he always did, in a most good-natured way. 'Sir Hartley,' he said. 'Sir Hartley, you're trying to trick me with the truth.'

RD He was a kind of – how would you describe him? – a sort of black marketeer working in the underworld –

SHAWCROSS He was a spiv. A rather amusing spiv, working in the black market. As I said, those were the days when you had to get a licence for everything, a permit for this, a sanction for that, and of course it was calculated to produce corruption.

RD Coming back to your early days as Attorney-General, when you were a radical Labour politician you made some rather important changes in the Attorney-General's earnings. What exactly did you do?

SHAWCROSS It struck me, and my colleague Frank Soskice, at the time that we would be receiving far more money than even the Prime Minister and I thought that was extremely hard to justify.

RD Why was that?

SHAWCROSS Well, in those days the law officers, Attorney-General, Solicitor-General, were paid by fees marked on their briefs. A lot of their work was court work and on each brief, in each case, they would have a fee marked. They were very senior members of the Bar, so they got pretty senior fees.

RD What would have been your earnings, say, in your years as Attorney-General, if the old traditional system had been continued from 1945 onwards?

SHAWCROSS Well, I did some very big cases, you see, the Nuremberg case, the treason cases, that case that you just talked about, the Lynskey Tribunal case. Oh, I suppose around £50,000, something of that order –

RD In a year.

SHAWCROSS Yes.

RD And you instead insisted on taking a salary, much lower.

SHAWCROSS Yes, we reduced it, rather to the annoyance of the Bar, I think, who thought it was improper, to a salary of £10,000.

RD And do you think that was right, in retrospect?

SHAWCROSS Yes, I think it was. I think it was a system which was impossible to justify and which also I think had a – a bad result in this sense that if the Attorney-General was not a man of complete integrity he would perhaps multiply the number of briefs he accepted and diminish the other work –

RD In Parliament?

SHAWCROSS – parliamentary work. That would be a danger.

RD Turning to perhaps the most famous aspect of your work as Attorney-General, the Nuremberg War Crimes Tribunal where the Nazi leaders were tried and sentenced – some of them to death. Now, you were one of the leading prosecutors there. Looking back on your part, what do you recall as most impressed on your mind at that extraordinary court with English, Russian and American Judges?

SHAWCROSS Yes. Of course it was a unique occasion. We were all rather starry-eyed then, I suppose, and when the idea was first promoted of having a trial of this kind, and that was done at the very beginning of the war, we hoped that we would be laying down the law for the future, and that we would make it quite clear that the treaties which had already been concluded long before the war, against aggressive war, would be implemented and enforced and that we should be laying down principles of conduct for statesmen which in the future history of the world statesmen would observe. I'm afraid we've been somewhat disappointed by the course of events but still I think we did lay down some important principles and that justice was done.

RD Looking back though, do you think it was right, legally and historically, for the victors to set up a military court to try the vanquished?

SHAWCROSS Yes, I think so. Historically, I think it was certainly justified in the sense that it wrote the history of some terrible things in connection with the war and its preparation that would never have been written without such a trial. One must remember that when the war started, it was immediately stated that when we won the war – and we said when not if – when we won the war, the men who were committing these terrible atrocities and who had brought the world to this frightful war, would be tried and condemned for the wicked things that they were doing. So they were warned from the beginning that this would happen. When the trial did take place, it is true it was constituted as a military tribunal by the victors, but it was conducted with great fairness. Everybody who was condemned to death in that tribunal had committed murder. Not just a single murder but murder, ordinary murder, but on a vast scale. And although they were convicted of other offences which were new to the law, like the offence of waging an aggressive war, genocide, that kind of thing, these were new offences, I am sure that if the death penalty is justified at all, it was justified in those cases.

RD Of which Nazi leader at that Nuremberg trial do you have the most vivid recollection?

SHAWCROSS Oh, certainly Goering. He was the outstanding figure there. I think Mr Justice Birkett, who was one of the Judges, said in his memoirs that he could have dominated the court if he had tried to. Curiously enough, he never did try but one felt that he was a dominating personality. Indeed he sat at the corner of the front row of the dock, and I remember that sometimes in the course of the trial, something would go wrong, a witness would be asked a question to which the answer was Yes, the expected answer, and the witness would say No. And Goering would look across, usually at the British – I don't know quite why – but he would shake his head sadly and raise an eyebrow. And one had to be terribly careful not to catch his eye and smile. He had some agreeable qualities although no doubt he was a very evil man but he was undoubtedly the most able and the strongest personality amongst those people we prosecuted.

RD One of the Nazi leaders who was not sentenced to death was of course Rudolf Hess, who is still a solitary prisoner of Spandau Jail in Berlin. Should he be released?

SHAWCROSS Certainly he should be released. I've said so publicly for a great many years now. I go further. I was surprised that he was convicted. He appeared to me to be mad. His offences pale into insignificance compared with some of the others. I thought that he'd come over to us –

RD Half-way through the war.

SHAWCROSS – in a misguided hope of securing a peace. The Russians, you see, take a literal view about a life sentence. They say when a man is sentenced to imprisonment for life it means what it says. No civilized country in the world takes that view. But the Russians do and they can insist on applying their view to Hess in this prison which is conducted by the Four Powers in Berlin.

RD Which of the other cases of a capital character do you particularly remember from your career? You didn't do many murder cases as Attorney-General, did you?

SHAWCROSS No. The Attorney-General very rarely did a murder case. He was supposed to prosecute in all cases of treason and in poison cases. Poison is the worst form of murder because very often I think it's never discovered at all.

RD Why did you prosecute the Acid Bath Murderer, Haigh? He wasn't a poisoner, was he?

SHAWCROSS I thought in a way that I'd not been doing any work in the Criminal Courts and that it was a good thing for the Attorney-General occasionally to appear in the Criminal Courts. This was not a case of poisoning but it was a very very bad case of murder. He admitted to murdering at least eight people and dissolving their bodies in sulphuric acid. And he murdered seven people with success, disposing of the bodies in that way. It was a very grave case and I thought it was an appropriate case in which the Attorney-General should intervene.

RD Did you find that criminal cases, particularly those involving the death penalty, involved you in extra strain in view of your feeling against the death penalty, as an individual?

SHAWCROSS Well I suppose they did involve – the defence of them certainly involved a certain extra strain because one knew that if the man was found guilty, the result was inevitable and could never be corrected so in that sense certainly it involved an extra strain. In prosecuting, and often as not I was prosecuting in these cases, I think not. I was opposed to the death penalty but it was the law and it was the duty of barristers to administer the law as it stood, not to alter it.

RD Lord Shawcross, towards the end of your career at the Bar you were involved in a famous libel action, which didn't in fact come to trial, which Winston Churchill brought against the *Daily Mirror*.

SHAWCROSS Yes.

RD That was about the 1951 election, wasn't it?

SHAWCROSS Whose finger on the trigger, I think it was. I believe the *Daily Mirror* had a headline to that effect just before the poll, and Winston brought a libel action about it.

RD What was he saying the sting of the libel was?

SHAWCROSS Well, it was suggested that he was an irresponsible person who if returned as Prime Minister would lead the country immediately into war, because he would pull the trigger in circumstances in which that wasn't necessary.

RD And you were briefed by the *Daily Mirror*.

SHAWCROSS It was a curious experience. When I got into Chambers at nine o'clock in the Temple, at half past nine a retainer came along from the *Daily Mirror*, and a retainer which is accompanied by a cheque, in those days for £3 5s 6d, ties you to the particular client who sends it. Half an hour later another retainer came along from Winston Churchill, he wanted me to act for him. Well, eventually the case was settled. I think my clients, the *Daily Mirror* people, took a very responsible view and thought that it would be unfortunate to have a Prime Minister – not only a Prime Minister, after all, Winston was a great world statesman, in the witness box, cross examined by me as if he was a criminal and that it might not only be undignified but produce very unhappy results, and the case was settled.

RD But you say the *Daily Mirror* were responsible. What would have been your view as Counsel? Would you have been prepared to cross examine Sir Winston on the basis of a plea of justification that – or fair comment – that he was in fact an irresponsible warmonger?

SHAWCROSS ... That really introduces something which has become rather topical recently: the whole problem of the responsibility of Counsel. No, I think the answer to that is that I would not, unless I had been convinced that there was some substance in that charge. I don't think this question entered into the reasons for our settlement but I – and I don't think that I would have been instructed to do it by the *Daily Mirror* on reflection, but I think I'd have had great difficulty in doing it if the case had gone on.

RD On the point you've just raised about the duty of barristers in court, could you as a former Attorney-General and former Chairman of the Bar summarize for us how far a barrister is entitled to go in defending the interests of his client in court?

SHAWCROSS Well, it's a very difficult ethical problem for barristers. It's been said by some great judge that their paramount retainer is to truth and justice, and I think that's true, but they are, after all, as some other judge called them, ministers of justice. They're supposed to be assisting in the administration of justice and so, for instance, if they know that their client is guilty, they mustn't put him in the witness box to say he isn't guilty. And they mustn't suggest that somebody else might be guilty. All they're entitled to do, and this only arises in criminal cases really, is to make the prosecution prove the case.

RD When you say they mustn't suggest that someone else is guilty, to take a very famous case, the case of Timothy Evans, who was hanged for the murder of his child, part of the essential defence in that case, if you remember, was that Christie, who was one of the witnesses in that case and was later involved in his own murder charges, was the man who did it –

SHAWCROSS Ah yes –

RD – because he kept telling his Counsel, Christie did it.

SHAWCROSS Yes. That's quite different. You see, if Evans had said, 'I did it but you suggest that Christie did it,' that would have been absolutely wrong. It may happen but that would be absolutely wrong, but Evans in fact said, 'I didn't do it. Christie did,' and no doubt the barristers concerned in that case had a little more material than that to go on. Some circumstantial indication that Christie might have done it. And then, of course, they were entitled to make the suggestion, but they aren't entitled to invent another guilty person.

RD When you say it's a difficult matter for Counsel and members of the Bar, is it as difficult as all that if you are an honest member of the Bar? In your long career as a barrister, do you recall any real difficulty in deciding where your duty lay and how far you should go?

SHAWCROSS Well that sounds awfully pompous, I think, to say – to answer in those terms, Robin, really. But the answer is no, I don't think I ever had any difficulty. Of course, what is said about a barrister is that he is a taxi on the rank. And this is true. He's got to accept the fare from anybody who asks to be defended by him.

RD Subject to a fee.

SHAWCROSS Subject to a fee.

RD The fee being of suitable size.

SHAWCROSS A reasonable fee in the circumstances. He mustn't, in order to avoid a case, say he's going to charge ten times what he would normally charge. But the point about a taxi on the rank, that analogy, is I think misleading because you can hire your taxi on the rank, but you can't tell the driver how he is to drive. You can't tell him, 'You must go through the red lights' or 'You must ignore the signals of the police', or 'You must ignore the Highway Code'. The barrister may be a taxi on the rank but he's got to pay attention to the Highway Code, that is, to the code of ethics which restrains improper conduct by the Bar.

RD You wrote a long letter which made quite a sensation, Lord Shawcross, last year, to *The Times* in which you spoke in rather guarded and, if I may say so, mysterious terms about certain matters of corruption which you had come across in your earlier career, and I think your point was that there was more of this going on than one knew of, and you told of one case which you had come across at the Bar. Can you tell us about that and what difficulties it created for you personally?

SHAWCROSS Yes. Well this was a case which was brought to me for advice after I'd been Attorney-General and returned to private practice at the Bar. It concerned a highly-placed official.

RD Official.

SHAWCROSS Yes, it was an official. Civil Servant. Highly placed. And the allegation made on behalf of an industrial company was that he had been paid very very substantial sums of money for showing favour to them in a matter which was within his control, and I immediately said that I would not advise on this, they must make a statutory declaration as to the facts which were disclosed in my instructions and then inform the police so that the criminal law could take its course. And my instructions were immediately withdrawn by the solicitors, whose clients didn't want to get involved because, after all, they would have been guilty of an offence as well in having corrupted this man and paid money to him. I then thought –

RD Your clients were the industrial company.

SHAWCROSS Yes. I then thought, well I'm a Privy Councillor and I used to have some responsibility in this sphere of activity. I must disclose this to the authorities myself. And I thought, well, I'd better make quite sure I'm entitled to, and I asked first of all the Bar Council, of which I was chairman at the time, and they said no, the legal privilege under which this information has been given to you completely debars you from saying anything more about it. You must forget it. I then asked the Lord Chief Justice of the day. He took exactly the same view.

RD Lord Goddard.

SHAWCROSS It was Lord Goddard, yes. And I asked the Benchers at my Inn of Court informally, and all the advice I got was the same. It's covered by legal privilege and you would break what is regarded as one of the most important, confidential relationships that exist in this country if you were to go and tell the authorities what had been told to you in your – in confidence as a legal adviser, so I had to forget about it. And that went very much against the grain.

RD In your letter, I think you said that that person continued without prosecution and –

SHAWCROSS He did. I think he's no longer with us but he continued for some time, perfectly ostensibly respectable career.

RD What I'm not clear about is why you should have been consulted about this if there was no prosecution being brought.

SHAWCROSS Oh, I think the reason, at the time, was that they were not getting the goods that they'd paid for.

RD Why on earth would they come to Counsel to say that we bribed somebody and we're not getting the fruits of our bribe.

SHAWCROSS They were very naïve about it and they wanted to see if there was any remedy available to them and the moment I pointed out the significance of what had happened, they naturally got cold feet and scuttled away.

RD Coming back to one point which we were touching on earlier, Lord Shawcross, the death penalty. You've mentioned your opposition to that. Are you still opposed to the death penalty in this – in this violent age?

SHAWCROSS Well, I think so. I - I'm very worried about it. I've been opposed to it since I was a child almost. I hate the idea of it. I think I wouldn't want to execute somebody myself and that one shouldn't be prepared to do vicariously what you won't do yourself. But with the tremendous growth in crimes of violence, terrorist activities, hi-jacking, I begin to wonder whether the removal of the death penalty hasn't removed what was in effect a deterrent. I was never satisfied that the death penalty was a deterrent. I'm not convinced even now that it would be but I'm getting worried about it.

RD Bearing in mind the confusion which arose with the compromise legislation, the Homicide Act of 1957, I think it was, do you think that there would be any way of distinguishing between ordinary murders and terrorist murders by bomb outrage and hi-jacking and so on?

SHAWCROSS I think you could distinguish between that type of murder and other murders, but it's very difficult. I remember in the case of the compromise Bill, which I had to introduce as Attorney-General, having been in favour myself of total abolition, we did produce a Bill in which murder by poisoning was a capital offence, and other forms of murder were not. Winston Churchill, who made the speech in reply, said, 'If I murder my wife by giving her some poison which will enable her to go to sleep pleasantly dreaming in the night and never to wake up, I shall be hanged by the neck until I'm dead. But if I boil her alive in oil, I shall only be sent to prison for a few years,' and that is the difficulty – drawing any distinction between categories of murder. But hi-jacking, I think, and –

RD Kidnapping.

SHAWCROSS Kidnapping. Where do you stop? This is the difficulty in these days of arms and terror.

RD On the question of arms and terror, do you feel that the rule of law in this society, in Britain, is more in danger now, in every way, than it was when you were a young man, or do you think that this is exaggerated?

SHAWCROSS Oh no, I think it is much more in danger. When I was a young man, on the whole, we all had a considerable respect for the law. I don't think we obeyed the law because we would be frightened of being caught, so much as because we respected the law. And as a rule the law was not broken. Now I think we are – I really take a very gloomy view. I think we're moving towards an anarchical society in which power is the important thing rather than law.

RD Looking back at the Industrial Relations Act and the way that got swept away, whatever the merits of those measures, do you think that there is any practical basis for the use of law to control the activities of trade unions now?

SHAWCROSS Well, the one thing I would like to see, and I think it – which is practicable, and I think would make a tremendous difference to the orientation of the trade unions, is a compulsory ballot for election to the more important offices and on issues like strikes, and I would give them a postal ballot free, let the state pay for it and give them a postal ballot free. You see, the trouble with ballots nowadays is that they are generally taken in the local branch office. It's not only that pressure can be put upon people who go to the branch office to vote in the way that is desired, but that the great mass of the people don't want to go to the branch office after a full day's work, they want to look at the telly, perhaps they want to see you, or they want to go to the local. They don't want to go to the branch office, so they don't vote.

RD But what you've been saying means that on the whole, though, you're in favour of the postal ballot, compulsorily; does that mean that you don't on the whole think that the Industrial Relations Act and other measures which were also proposed by the Labour government are a good idea?

SHAWCROSS Well, I don't think any legislation is really workable unless you can be sure that the great mass of the population, particularly those affected by it, are going to accept it. The mistake of the Industrial Relations legislation of the Tory Party was, I think that they assumed, perhaps we all did, that the British people being very law-abiding would accept this legislation once it had been passed by a big majority in Parliament. Indeed in many ways it would have been beneficial to the unions, but in fact a great campaign was conducted against it. Trade unionists are extremely loyal to their leadership and they were not prepared to work it and without that co-operation, it was unworkable.

RD May I put to you some words of your own, Lord Shawcross, which you used in 1946 when you were Attorney-General –

SHAWCROSS I hope they don't contradict what I've just said.

RD You may be interested to hear them. You say: 'A principle of great and vital constitutional importance is that the respect for law in this country and the maintenance and strengthening of the rule of law, in a very large measure, depends on excluding from the Statute Book laws which are manifestly unenforceable and which would cause resentment on the part of a very large section of the population.' Now that is roughly what you've said now, you may be gratified to know, and also it's the very essence of the trade union case against Mr Heath's Industrial Relations Act.

SHAWCROSS Yes. Well, I think what I said then is substantially true although I think that Mr Heath may have been entitled to assume at that time that once Parliament had passed the law, the mass of the people who we hitherto have regarded as very law-abiding and loyal to Parliament, would abide by it. I think there has been – this is perhaps the view of an old and disillusioned man – I think there has been a marked diminution in the respect for Parliament and I think myself that this is understandable. I don't respect it so much myself.

RD Why is it different from what it was in your day?

SHAWCROSS Well, I think because of the development of a three-party system. I don't want to make a political speech, obviously I shouldn't, but you see, if you take the present situation, which is more exaggerated perhaps than it's been in the past, I get terribly irritated when I hear ministers saying, we have a mandate to do this, or we were elected to do that. Of course they weren't elected to do anything of the kind.

RD But this is precisely what you were saying in that very speech in 1946 when you were justifying bringing in that trade union Bill to repeal the Bill of 1927, the Act of 1927, and that's why you said we are the masters now – we've got the mandate.

SHAWCROSS Yes. In those days we did have the mandate. We had – the Liberal vote was very very small, we had a massive vote, but you see, you take the present Parliament, of the total electorate, they've got 28 to 29 per cent of the total electorate, 30 per cent didn't vote at all. The issues were, I suppose, basically, on the side of the Labour Party, on the whole anti-Common Market, in favour of public ownership. The Liberals and the Conservatives together got 39 per cent and the issues were the same, they were in favour of the Common Market and against public ownership, but the people who were running the country and who have the impertinence to say they were elected to do it are the people who only got 28 per cent.

RD But they were elected according to the Constitution and our parliamentary make-up has always been decided by the number of seats and not on a counting of electoral heads, otherwise we'd have a different system.

SHAWCROSS Well, this is excellent, but we'll have to have a different system now if it's to survive at all. This was excellent in the day of two parties, but you see, now we've got three parties, the Liberals and the Nationalists – I don't approve of this movement towards nationalism but it exists and it's entitled to make itself heard, the Liberals and the Nationalists and in a way the middle section of the population is quite unrepresented because they come second on the poll, in a vote of – for three candidates and the man who gets the bare majority gets elected.

RD When you say we've got to have a new system, do you mean electoral reform?

SHAWCROSS Yes.

RD Proportional representation or the alternative vote, or what?

SHAWCROSS I would say the alternative vote, but I think what the Conservative Party and the Liberals should do, and the Liberals are ready to do it, is to say that if they're returned to power, that means if the Tories are returned to power, they would have a Speaker's Conference to consider what is the best method of electoral reform but they would not only pledge themselves to that because that could easily be a confidence trick. They should say not only will we set up a Speaker's Conference but we will throw our political weight in favour of the introduction of a system which will give proper representation proportionately to the middle ground, the Liberals, the Nationalists, by means, I think, of an alternative vote in the existing constituencies. I think myself that the only way to protect this country from Communism in fifteen years perhaps will be some alteration of our electoral system which gives fair representation to all shades of opinion – significant shades of opinion.

RD Now that view will be interpreted by a number of people in the Labour Party and on the left as meaning, in other words, we've got to have electoral reform so as to stop the Labour Party from continuing to be in power.

SHAWCROSS Well – I don't mind if that interpretation is put upon it. I said, stop the Communists getting into power because I think before long the Labour Party will find itself largely dominated by Marxists. There's a very large proportion of them now.

RD There's no sign, there's no sign of Communists having political power through our present electoral system.

SHAWCROSS No. Not as Communists. Not as such.

RD Well, how are the Communists going to come in if we don't change it? What is your –

SHAWCROSS Well, I think the Labour Party is going steadily Marxist. A great many of them, even some members of the government are Marxist.

RD Do you think then that the Labour Party is likely to break up before long into what you call the Marxists and what are known as the Social Democrats?

SHAWCROSS I concede that there are men of integrity on both sides.

Indeed, this is the real strength of the Marxists that they really believe in Marxism as a religion; the rest of us perhaps don't believe in anything. So I would think that the philosophies being so conflicting, social democratic philosophy and the Marxist philosophy, that it's impossible to see them going on indefinitely together.

RD And do you think that that process would be initiated or achieved by the social democrats or the so-called right wing breaking away from the – what they would see as the – a left wing dominated party. Is that your scenario?

SHAWCROSS Well, it's difficult to draw up an exact scenario. So much depends on the course of events. But I think that particular one might well arise in the event of the economic situation becoming even worse, and heaven knows it's bad enough, than it is at present.

RD Do you really think that there are many Marxists in the real theological sense of that word, in the Labour Party?

SHAWCROSS Well, I think there are a considerable proportion of Marxists in the Parliamentary Labour Party and in the – activities in the local Labour parties. I think there's no doubt that the constituency Labour parties have been moving to the left, not in the sense that the numbers have greatly increased but in the sense, as happens in the trade unions, that the Marxists are the people who are active, who turn up at the branch meetings and who secure the adoption of candidates and so on. I think there are an increasing number of Marxists of that kind and also perhaps amongst a proportion of university students and young men.

RD May we move, Lord Shawcross, to your position as chairman of the Press Council, which you've had since last year. What is your view in that capacity of the legislation which the government wanted to bring in about the closed shop and the effect of this on the freedom of the press in general? Do you see the matter as dangerous or – ?

SHAWCROSS I see it as potentially very dangerous, yes. I think one has got to accept the general principle of the closed shop now in industry, although it is a clear breach of the universal declaration of human rights to which, when I was a member of the Attlee administration, the United Kingdom adhered. The point is that nobody may be forced to join, nobody must be forced to join any particular association. There are two human rights which are nowadays considered basic. That one is enshrined in the universal declaration; the other is the right to work and of course if you have a right to work but only if you join a particular association, you're in clear breach of what has hitherto been regarded as a fundamental human right. So I don't think one can –

RD Is that declaration upholdable in our courts like the European Convention?

SHAWCROSS No. No. It's not in the European Convention, I think, and it's not upholdable. It's supposed to be the superior document but it's not directly enforceable. What is directly enforceable is always something rather less than what is ideally desirable and I suppose the universal declaration goes rather further than what is immediately enforceable. I don't think one can deal with this particular problem on that basis perhaps, it's even – perhaps that's a little technical but I think it would be very dangerous if nobody could be an editor or contribute to a paper unless he was a member of the National Union of Journalists. That is admittedly not their objective at present. But one has seen unions becoming increasingly militant, indeed the National Union of Journalists has had a Communist in a very high position and it may be in future that they would wish to control editorial policy and wish to prevent anyone who is not a member of their union – and they are not the only union in the newspaper industry: there's another one, quite respectable, which they are seeking to replace –

RD The Institute of Journalists.

SHAWCROSS Yes.

RD But are you saying these things, Lord Shawcross, in your personal capacity or as chairman of the Press Council?

SHAWCROSS No I'm saying them in my personal capacity although the Press Council has submitted evidence to the Royal Commission on the Press expressing the view that the closed shop in journalism would be inimical to the freedom of the press.

RD What do you think are the main dangers to the free press at the moment, recalling your own experience as the chairman of a rather brief Royal Commission in the early 1960s. Can you just summarize the main points of your conclusion?

SHAWCROSS Well, the main point at that time was restrictive practices on the part of the trade unions resulting in gross overmanning and the continued use of obsolescent plant. That was the main economic factor which was making it very difficult to publish newspapers at a profit.

RD Is the position any different now?

SHAWCROSS No, I'm afraid, although I think the *Mirror* group of newspapers did manage to secure some reduction. That group of newspapers itself, by its chief executive, only the other day, said that gross
overmanning was bleeding their papers to death, that was the language
he used and that, after all, is a group publishing left-wing views in
their newspapers.

RD You've referred to the danger to press freedom from union action,
and related matters. A lot of people would say that some of the
dangers to press freedom have stemmed from the act of proprietors
who exercised their authority in ways which are not tolerable in a
more democratic age.

SHAWCROSS Yes, I think that in the past there has been some ground
for that view. Much less true today I think. Editors have become
much more powerful individualists with a high sense of integrity and
respectable editors nowadays are not prepared to have their policy
dictated to from day to day by proprietors. After all, you've also got
a tremendous diversity of view amongst the proprietors. The biggest
circulation newspapers in the country are the *Daily Mirror* group, 40
per cent of the Sunday circulation is in the *Daily Mirror* group.
Biggest single national daily, *Daily Mirror,* so there's great diversity
of opinion, even if you assumed that the proprietors were dictating
the opinion, which in fact they're not.

RD From your vantage point as chairman of the Press Council, and
in the City of London, do you have any forecast to make about
the number of newspapers we are going to have in, say, five years
time?

SHAWCROSS Well, I think the number will be less. We have a large
number, I think, is it nine national dailies now? Very large number
of weeklies of course and some very good local dailies, provincial
dailies. I should think the number of national dailies will be reduced.
I wouldn't like to make a guess at what it would be but it's quite
possible that there might be two or three going out of existence. I
hope that means will be found to overcome this. I am quite sure that
if we took a realistic view about the availability of modern techniques
of printing, you can — you can literally use computers for typesetting,
and you got down the manning standards, these papers would be
perfectly successful.

RD Lord Shawcross, may we move on to another point and that is to ask
you about your experience in the City because you have been involved
in this self-regulation, as it were, of City ethics. Now in America

they have a statutory system, don't they, where behaviour is laid down by law. Why don't we have that more in this country and something on those lines because there have been a lot of – if I may coin a phrase – unacceptable and unpleasant things heard from the City of London in recent years.

SHAWCROSS Yes. Well the Americans have a statutory system embodying what they call the Securities and Exchange Commission. I think one must recognize that they have rather different problems. We are a much smaller community, a much more tightly knit community in what they call the square mile in the City, and I think that our self-discipline is far more effective than any statutory system could be. I can certainly say that no one of any standing in the City would willingly break a regulation or a direction of the City Panel. If our rules were laid down in a statutory code, it would be perfectly legitimate for lawyers to say, well, this is forbidden, you mustn't do it, but you can get round it by doing that. There are always loopholes in a statutory code and lawyers will always point out what the loopholes are. That's perfectly legitimate. In the City Code, we say you must not only obey the rules that are put out, one by one, but you must obey the principles which are also set out as general propositions and not only that, you must obey the spirit of it, and so it's very difficult to get round the Code.

RD On a broader view upon your position in the City, how do you see the financial and economic state of this country? Do you view it with a sense of foreboding generally? Are we going to survive this crisis?

SHAWCROSS Foreboding would be an understatement. I've never been more frightened about the position of this country even in the very darkest days of the war. I think if we have inflation running at the present level, 25 per cent during the last six months, for another two years, this country will be in a state of complete economic collapse.

RD And perhaps political collapse?

SHAWCROSS Which will lead to anarchy and then be followed by some form of totalitarian regime. That appears to be the only way in which we shall get to have some sort of restoration of economic order. I say if inflation goes on at this rate.

RD Your view that the Opposition should not crudely oppose for opposition's sake and the remark you made on those lines, from that should I conclude that you are coalition-minded? That you would like to see not merely Parliament change in atmosphere but you'd like to see government of a coalition character?

SHAWCROSS In a time of crisis like the present, I would have thought that this may well become desirable, yes. I think we've got to face the fact that on a great many matters there is a feeling in the country of consensus and that what has destroyed respect for Parliament is this constant party battle that takes place in such an undignified way in the House of Commons. I think the mass of the people really get very confused when they hear demagogues on one side saying this policy is the right one; demagogues on the other saying it's the wrong one. I think that there ought to be some getting together and finding the correct policy.

'I repeat – we've got to create the wealth before we spend it.'

JAMES
CALLAGHAN

1976

'OUR LAST CHANCE: Jim gives nation a stark warning.' So ran the *Daily Mirror*'s huge front-page headline the morning after this crisis interview by Prime Minister Callaghan. It was during the 1976 Labour Party Conference in Blackpool, at one of the blackest moments in the post-war history of the party.

Sterling had come under fierce pressure. A bout of nerves had hit the foreign exchange markets in anticipation of the annual gathering of the IMF, due to take place in Manila at the same time as the Labour Party Conference in Blackpool. On the Tuesday the pound was plummeting, and Chancellor Healey had to turn back to London from Heathrow instead of going to the Far East to the IMF meeting. Healey could not risk being out of touch with London on the seventeen-hour flight. Callaghan records in his memoirs that as soon as the City learned that Healey had not gone to the Far East, 'Hysterical panic set in for forty-eight hours. The markets behaved with all the restraint of a screaming crowd of schoolgirls at a rock concert.'

Callaghan agreed with Healey that they should apply to the IMF for a loan. This would mean that management of the British economy would be under IMF surveillance. Healey's announcement of Britain's loan application had a steadying effect. He flew up to Blackpool to make his case to the Labour Party Conference. His fighting speech ('I do not come with a Treasury view, I come from the battlefield') was booed.

That night, the Thursday of Conference week, Callaghan went on television in grim mood, determined to calm nerves and raise morale. He had been Prime Minister for only seven months. Already he was giving the Labour government stronger leadership than it sometimes had under Harold Wilson. His courageous speech earlier

151

in that Conference week was the most memorable he ever made. The speech was partly written by his son-in-law, Peter Jay, an able economist. Callaghan records that it was the following Jay paragraph which 'made the fur fly':

> We used to think that you could spend your way out of a recession and increase employment by cutting taxes and boosting Government spending. I tell you in all candour that that option no longer exists, and that insofar as it ever did exist, it only worked on each occasion since the war by injecting a bigger dose of inflation into the economy, followed by a higher level of unemployment as the next step.

Thus did Callaghan, as a Labour Prime Minister, sound retreat from the Keynesian consensus which had dominated British economic policy for so long.

My first question began with a reference to the Prime Minister's warning speech, and to the huge IMF loan which the government had had to seek 'cap in hand', as the Tory gibe went. Also in my mind was the *Daily Mail* front-page story that the loan would mean tighter money, higher prices, higher mortgages, higher rates, higher VAT to curb spending, and higher unemployment because of spending cuts. Was this a scare story to demoralize the Labour Party, or was it the brutal truth? Either way, it was surely a question with which 'Big Jim' would wish to deal. But he brushed it aside as 'speculation'.

This was the first time I had interviewed Callaghan since he had become Prime Minister. And it was his first TV interview as Prime Minister. So it was something of a special occasion, apart from the sterling crisis. The atmosphere was not relaxed or chatty. The Prime Minister was in his no-nonsense mood. As was his custom on television, there was no Christian name chumminess. He called me *Mr* Day (this was long before the knighthood) and he seemed to emphasize the Mister as if to underline the seriousness of the occasion.

Michael Cockerell, in his book *Live from Number 10,* claims that Callaghan had carefully considered 'what his relationship as Prime Minister should be on the screen with Robin Day, who had interviewed him many times during the previous twenty years'. Unlike Harold Wilson, Jim Callaghan did not want an interview with the Prime Minister to be cosy. What Jim Callaghan himself said was this: 'I don't care for too much mateyness on the television between interviewer and interviewee. Otherwise the viewer will get the impression it is a set-up job.' He wanted, I think, an interview to be dignified and businesslike, dealing appropriately with serious facts. The facts we were dealing with in Blackpool on the night of Thursday 30 September 1976 were certainly serious.

The Rt Hon. James Callaghan MP, Prime Minister

Interviewed in BBC Tonight *programme*
at the Labour Party Conference in Blackpool
30 September 1976

ROBIN DAY Prime Minister, when you warned the Conference and the nation on Tuesday, in a speech which was much praised, that we could not go on borrowing as we have been, did you expect that the very next day we would be asking for a loan to the tune of £2,300 million?

RT HON. JAMES CALLAGHAN MP, PRIME MINISTER Yes, I thought it was quite likely. We'd talked about it for a matter of a month or two. Indeed it's been well discussed in the press, as you know, that with the special facilities that were given in the summer, expiring in December, that they would expect we would have to go to the IMF.

RD Why did we wait twenty-four hours and let sterling sink? Why didn't you announce it just then?

CALLAGHAN Oh, sterling sinks in twenty seconds, not twenty-four hours, I mean literally during the time in which you and I may be speaking dealers are picking up their phones, and they can push it up or push it down. Now it's very interesting this week. It's gone down from Tuesday, 1.67 to 1.62. It's now bounced back to 1.67 again. You see – especially when there's not a great deal of buying or selling.

RD What conditions do you expect, if any, will be imposed on the loan?

CALLAGHAN I doubt it, I don't think there will be any, you know, because the policies that the government are following have commanded a great deal of acceptance abroad. There's no doubt that overseas governments, and indeed those who are responsible for lending us the money are impressed by the way in which the British people are facing this situation. I'm sure there'll be discussion about particular matters, like, what shall we say, the amount of monetary expansion and that sort of thing.

RD But that's rather important isn't it?

CALLAGHAN I said there would be discussion about it, that will mean very important discussions ...

RD Well, that will mean that you'll have to give some undertakings.

CALLAGHAN It doesn't necessarily mean that, because I'm sure you do remember that the Chancellor's already indicated the guide lines that he is following. I think those sort of things will be discussed.

RD None the less is it fair to assume that the IMF will expect something more than what *The Times* describes today as – quote – a nice letter from Jim?

CALLAGHAN That was Pierre Paul Schweitzer who said that, about ten years or more ago, I think ten or eleven years ago, when I was Chancellor. I think – I don't know what they're going to say, that the policies that we're following are the only policies that are going to get Britain through, and then we shall have to see what they say in response to that. But as there are day to day contacts on these sort of things – or month to month contacts, indeed we have a permanent representative there, I think we've got a pretty good indication of what their general attitude is – about our policies, just as we know pretty well the kind of things that they think.

RD Despite what you've claimed for your policies so far, Prime Minister, doesn't the fact that we've had to get this loan, and the fact that sterling has been crashing a bit in the last few days, doesn't it indicate that the government has failed to restore confidence?

CALLAGHAN Yes, I think it does. Whether the government has failed to restore confidence in the foreign exchange markets is a different thing from whether it's failed to get confidence for its policies.

RD That's what I meant –

CALLAGHAN – with overseas governments.

RD That's what I meant.

CALLAGHAN Whenever I talk to overseas governments, and those who are responsible for their financial affairs, there is no doubt that they think this government is – I don't wish to be immodest about it – they think that our government is really facing these problems, and trying to handle them, in a way that any government could. But on the sterling markets, restoring confidence is a very difficult operation. Confidence is a slow-growing plant. I don't know when it will come, but I would say, that sterling is not at its proper value now. When I was in the Midlands last week I was told by a group of Midlands manufacturers that they were able to get a price, when they export, of 2.20 for their exports, whereas the official rate is 1.60 or 1.65 – 1.67 now.

RD Do you and the Chancellor agree with the statement by the NEC, Labour's National Executive Committee, which says that the government should resist any loan conditions which would mean imposing any further cuts on public expenditure?

CALLAGHAN I don't think there's any need for that at the present time.

RD But does that mean you rule out further cuts in public spending?

CALLAGHAN I don't think we shall be asked for it, and I don't think there's any need for it.

RD Could I come to something which is perhaps more interesting than the economic technicalities, Prime Minister, what will result from this crisis and this loan, so far as the standard of living of the people is concerned?

CALLAGHAN The loan won't make any difference to the standard of living, because we shall be using it, as we are using it now, to finance a great deal of investment – the North Sea investment, and that sort of thing. The standard of life of our people is not being fully earned, and hasn't been for some years. They are now, I think, coming up to the crunch on this, but it won't make any difference to the projects and plans that the Chancellor's already set out, which did involve a fall in the standard of life – that's one of the reasons why the protests are taking place.

RD I ask you the question, Prime Minister, because it has been suggested this morning that as a result of the loan, and tighter money which may result, people should be prepared for higher prices, higher mortgage payments, higher rates, higher VAT to curb spending perhaps, higher unemployment because of spending curbs, now is this possible?

CALLAGHAN You're saying – when you say what's said this morning, do you mean at Conference?

RD No, no, no. In the press, in the press.

CALLAGHAN Or did you mean on the front page of a daily newspaper?

RD Particularly on the front page of the *Daily Mail*, but also in other papers.

CALLAGHAN That's right. Yes, yes, yes, yes, yes. I saw that, but that is, I think, pure newspaper speculation.

RD And no truth in it at all?

CALLAGHAN Speculation.

RD Is there any truth in it?

CALLAGHAN Speculation.

RD Is there a possibility of it?

CALLAGHAN Look, I've said already, the only – the only certainty in life is death. There will be a Budget next April. What will happen I don't know. And I think it could help a great deal if the press were not to speculate so much about all the worst things that could possibly happen.

RD No, I was only asking you, Prime Minister, because –

CALLAGHAN No, and I'm not attacking you, Mr Day, on this.

RD I certainly wasn't attacking you, Prime Minister.

CALLAGHAN I know, I know, I understand.

RD It's not my job to do that, but I know you appreciate that what the people want to know at the moment is the brutal truth.

CALLAGHAN Well I do, and I'm giving the brutal truth. But there are some questions that I simply cannot answer. And I think you understand that, when I see a front page of a newspaper saying this is what will happen, they have no more idea than you do or I do, frankly, about that sort of thing.

RD How are you going to make sure, Prime Minister, that this loan is used, not for spending more than we can earn by production, which you've said is wrong, but for building industrial recovery, and building economic strength?

CALLAGHAN You can't make 100 per cent sure of that. But you see at the present time we're following a very difficult path politically, because we're holding back domestic consumption, and this is one of the reasons why, in the Conference this week, there's been a lot of criticism of the government. We are trying to make the resources that exist available for exports, available for regeneration. Now it is in that way that we're, as it were, cramping things into this particular area, and that is the way in which I hope it will be used.

RD Is the Labour government's ability to govern in the national interest being hampered now by the increasing conflict between government and National Executive, and by feeling in the party also?

CALLAGHAN I don't think there's a conflict in that sense. I mean what the party has said to me this week, very clearly, is 'we want more money spent on education, on schools, on houses, on hospitals, on pensions, on children's benefits'. That's what conferences, with respect, are for. And I don't say that in any denigratory way. They are there to state the aspirations of the Movement, and I respond to those aspirations. What the Chancellor has to do, and I back him up in this, is to say when we can meet those particular aspirations. I think you'll find (although there is a group of people who say the economic strategy is wrong, but they never produce one that's going to be any more attractive than ours) I think you'll find that the major criticism of the government, this week, has been, 'Look, we want more money spent on all these social benefits.'

RD But isn't the problem –

CALLAGHAN That's what all the resolutions have wanted.

RD Understood, but isn't the problem that the party, and certainly many members of the National Executive – that their feelings seem to be deeper with regard to these aspirations, which you share, than do their feelings for the practicability of paying for them? That's the difficulty.

CALLAGHAN Well I don't know. I think conferences obviously tend to show that side of it. But what we rest on is this bedrock agreement with the Trade Union Movement, through the Social Contract, which says that we place the needs of manufacturing industry first over the next two or three years. Now, that is the more important thing that we've got to do. I repeat – I don't like repeating what I've already said – we've got to create the wealth before we spend it.

RD Now why should – this is a question being asked by your opponents – why should the country have confidence in you? Because looking at what has happened in two and a half years of Labour government – the cost of living has gone up over 50 per cent, production is lower than the three-day week, they say, unemployment doubled, the pound down by 20 per cent. Now is that a record, whatever else you may say, which should give confidence in your administration?

CALLAGHAN I don't think that it should either give confidence or detract from confidence, because a number of these phenomena that you quote follow from the policies of a long, long period. That is to say you have the highest rate of pumping money into the system, you then get the highest rate of inflation. I have always taken the view, and I spoke to Conference about this, that higher inflation is always followed by high unemployment. Let's take some of the other sides of the coin. We have reduced inflation by one half. We've made our exports competitive now. We've got a basic agreement with the Trade Unions for the regeneration of British industry. I think the difference now, and certainly the difference as far as I'm concerned, is that we've got to take a long-term view of what we're doing. It's no use expecting a gimmick to cure it in six months. That is why I think that if we stick to this with resolution, the country can look forward, not to an immediate easement – not to an easement next year, I'm not undertaking that – but we can enter the 1980s, I think, with a powerful economy. I say that with the more confidence, because on the shop floor there's a growing realization of what needs to be done, and we've got this bonus of oil. Now, as you know, I don't rest everything on the oil, but by golly it is a bonus. It's going to be worth – what is it? Ten billion dollars a year or something – eight to ten billion dollars a year to us. Now that's an awful lot of money that will come in the 1980s. We've got to get people through the next two or three years, not in a convalescent state, but in the state of preparing themselves to be a really powerful economy.

RD Would you agree with the suggestion that if we don't succeed in conquering inflation, increasing our industrial base, that our system of democracy will then be in danger of collapse, and that is the gravity of the situation facing us? We may be threatened with totalitarianism from the left or right if we don't do it wisely, in the democratic way?

CALLAGHAN I think you're right, Mr Day. I think that this is the responsibility that falls on our government. I think you cannot govern against the Trade Unions today, because they are made up of a great mass of articulate and well-informed people, you've got to get the co-operation of industry. I think if we were to fail, and I don't want to make party points here particularly, I don't think another government could succeed. That I don't think leads you into a national government, or anything like that. I fear it would lead you either to totalitarianism of the left or of the right. That is why I want, and am going to fight so hard, to make sure we succeed.

RD One little personal point, Prime Minister, when you became Chancellor you had a sterling crisis, and you resigned as Chancellor because of devaluation. No sooner have you become Prime Minister than you're in another crisis. You haven't always been 'Lucky Jim', have you?

CALLAGHAN No, but I – you know it's a great advantage to have lived through this before, I tell you – I've seen a lot of these sort of things before, and therefore I can take, perhaps, a slightly more detached view than some of them, who are seeing it for the first time. And by that I certainly don't mean our Chancellor [Healey] who is being one of the most robust people, as we saw in Conference this afternoon, that I've ever met.

RD Thank you, Prime Minister.

CALLAGHAN Thank you.

'Do we really want the kind of dictatorship which enables one quarter of the electorate to elect an omnipotent Parliament?'

LORD HAILSHAM

Lord Hailsham of St Marylebone, when he gave me this interview in January 1979, was speaking as a former Lord Chancellor. He became Lord Chancellor a second time three months later under Mrs Thatcher.

Lord Hailsham has been a charismatic and controversial figure in our public and political life for well over half a century. Not since the great Lord Birkenhead has there been such a colourful and brilliant Lord Chancellor.

Our subject was constitutional and parliamentary reform, a subject on which Lord Hailsham had memorably focused attention in his 1976 Dimbleby Lecture for the BBC. He attacked the 'elective dictatorship' of the Commons majority. He called for a radical overhaul of the British Constitution. Lord Hailsham, hitherto thought to be a staunch traditionalist, advocated a completely new Constitution for the United Kingdom – a written Constitution under which the elected Parliament would no longer be unfettered.

Because of these extremely radical proposals I took the mischievous liberty of introducing this elder statesman of the Tory Party as a revolutionary. His outspoken attack on our fundamental doctrine of parliamentary supremacy was thought to come rather oddly from a lifelong Conservative, and even more oddly from a former Lord Chancellor who, when in office, had happily served as a principal operator of the very Constitution whose radical overhaul he was now demanding.

Lord Hailsham is steeped in parliamentary, constitutional and legal learning. He has had a long and unique career as a parliamentarian with some memorable ups and downs. For twelve years from 1938 he was Quintin Hogg MP. In 1950 he became the 2nd Viscount Hailsham after his father's death. Then in 1963 he became Quintin Hogg again after renouncing his inherited vis-countcy. In 1970 he was back in the Lords as a Life Peer when Ted Heath made him Lord Chancellor. And a few months after this interview in 1979, Margaret Thatcher made him Lord Chancellor again.

He was not only a splendid parliamentarian on both the red and the green benches, but a magnificent performer on television. Quintin Hailsham never gave a dull broadcast on TV or radio in his life. In this interview about constitutional reform he lightens what, for some, could be a heavy theme, with the brilliant luminosity of his powerful brain, and the mischievous sparkle of his boyish humour. The prospect of an interview with Lord Hailsham always filled me with excitement and enthusiasm. This one in particular. I was not disappointed.

The Rt Hon. Lord Hailsham of St Marylebone CH

Interviewed in BBC 2 series The Parliamentarians
28 January 1979

ROBIN DAY Lord Hailsham, I took the liberty of introducing you as a revolutionary because of your extremely radical proposals for replacing our present parliamentary system by a completely new Constitution. Would you accept the description therefore of a revolutionary?

RT HON. LORD HAILSHAM OF ST MARYLEBONE I think I'd prefer the adjective radical rather than revolutionary. You see, I would keep Queen, Lords and Commons or rather Queen, Upper Chamber and Commons in any system that I approve.

RD May I suggest that in advocating these radical changes, if you prefer the word, you are concerned not so much about the way Parliament works – although I'm sure you are concerned about that – but rather more with what governments do and what governments can do by virtue of the – what you have called the 'elective dictatorship' of the Commons?

HAILSHAM I think this is part of the truth but I am concerned with the efficiency of structures and our parliamentary system was designed – it's like a boiler which was designed for a different pressure to what it's being subjected to now and so it's bursting at the seams.

RD But your proposals, which we can discuss in more detail in a moment, are really, aren't they, essentially to stop governments doing things by virtue of the all-powerful majority in Parliament, if in fact they have one at any one time, to stop them doing things, governments from doing things which are contrary to your political philosophy?

HAILSHAM No, I think that my objective is to try and make them do less and to rearrange the functions, the existing functions of government between more sources of power.

RD But don't we have a paradox here, because you are saying that Parliament, or rather the elected majority in the Commons, is much too powerful, whereas many people are worried about the fact that Parliament and the government which may control it is not powerful enough and cannot enforce its will and cannot uphold the rule of law and cannot stand up to challenges from outside groups?

HAILSHAM But isn't this just the other side of the coin. You see, we are trying to do too much at the centre and isn't the effect of trying to do too much that in fact, that you do it badly and so lose your moral authority?

RD Without going into too much detail, could you give us an idea of the kind of fundamental rights and principles which you would like to see safeguarded in your written Constitution? Do you refer only to civil rights or do you want to safeguard certain social and economic rights as well?

HAILSHAM Well, there are two quite separate sides to this. One is my belief that we must come to terms with federalism – forget that for a moment, but that is one of them.

RD The division of the country into regional Parliament and subordinate Parliaments?

HAILSHAM Yes. Now forget that – then we've only got one option and that is the European Convention on Human Rights as it stands and as it may be amended, because although it may be arguable whether you have a Bill of Rights or not, it's obvious that you can't have two.

RD But do you want to include in your safeguarded fundamental rights certain economic and industrial rights? For instance do you want to safeguard the right to pay for education or the right not to lose your job because of the closed shop? Do you want to do that kind of thing?

HAILSHAM I think that would be covered by the European Convention but only in so far, because I keep on saying and it must be true, that you can't have two sets of entrenched rights. We are committed to the European Convention on Human Rights, which of course has nothing to do with the Common Market, and being committed to it and having it enforced against us we can neither go outside it nor go less far; we've got to take it as it stands until it's amended.

RD What fundamental rights of any kind, either those covered by the European Convention or other ones you might wish to add, are threatened or could be threatened in your lifetime or mine by a government in this country?

HAILSHAM Well, let us take the very simple cases of what has been happening in the last few weeks. The right to a job can be threatened by the closed shop. Now I believe myself that that is contrary to the European Convention – if it isn't it ought to be.

RD But once you get into discussing which rights of that kind should be in a fundamental Constitution, is it going to be possible to get any kind of general agreement? Because things like the closed shop, as we very well know, the right to pay for education and other social rights or privileges, these are at the very heart of political argument.

HAILSHAM Well, they're not, you know, because the European Convention is something by which this country is bound.

RD Well, if the closed shop is contrary to the European Convention why is it going on?

HAILSHAM Well, that is what we want to know, but there is litigation going on. You see, the European Convention has its own enforcement machinery and that you've got to accept, but you can't go outside it – I mean if in fact it's upheld by the European courts at Strasbourg and so on, then we can't go outside it except by ordinary Act of Parliament.

RD And am I right in assuming that if you did have such a Constitution as you advocate, that the judges would have power to say that a piece of legislation was contrary to the constitution and fundamental rights set out in it and therefore was invalid or could not be applied?

HAILSHAM Yes, they would have the same powers as the judges at Strasbourg, neither more nor less, and the same powers as the EEC Judges have got, neither more nor less.

RD And you're not worried as a long time parliamentarian ... about devaluing Parliament by making it subject to non-elected judges who would be taking essentially political decisions?

HAILSHAM Well, we are subject to non-elected judges, only they happen to be at Brussels and Strasbourg. Are we to say that our own judiciary is either too stupid or too biased politically to do what they're already doing for us?

RD Well, there may be those who say that just because we happen to have got a bit of this system by virtue of the European Community that that's no argument for extending it.

HAILSHAM But I don't think we are extending it.

RD It would be under your system.

HAILSHAM Not at all. All we would be doing would be to say that the British judicial system would be able to enforce that which is already enforced against us by foreign judges. And I would trust a British judge rather than a foreign judge any day of the week.

RD But are you – is it not indeed revolutionary to suggest that a British judge or a British court would have the power to say this Act of Parliament is invalid and need not be obeyed?

HAILSHAM It would be a change which I would accept, the word radical change, but it is a change which has already been made – the only difference is that we've given the power to foreign judges.

RD But have we had a case, or do you seriously foresee a case when a British court will say this Act of Parliament approved by the Queen and passed by Lords and Commons is not valid and shall not be obeyed?

HAILSHAM Well, I think you've got to look at the European Communities Act because it can happen under that and it's only a matter of time before it does.

RD May I suggest that you might achieve something of what you are after without such a radical change in the Constitution if Parliament were to pass an Act which would say that in future no Bill, including any amending or appealing Bill, dealing with certain fundamental rights which you wished to protect, should be presented to the Royal Assent unless, for instance, it had been approved first by, say, two–thirds majority of the people in a referendum?

HAILSHAM You see, that would be to give the judges a much greater power than I was suggesting because it would enable the judges to do what they've never been able to do and never ought to be able to do, and that is to look at the internal workings of Parliament.

RD But that could be effected by a reformed Second Chamber?

HAILSHAM It could be effected up to a point by a reformed Second Chamber, which is part of my proposal. And I am bound to tell you that I regard the civil rights part of it as the least important of my proposals.

RD Would not the process of a convention to work out the terms of such a new Constitution be very slow and very complicated and really too slow to deal with what you obviously believe is a very urgent problem?

HAILSHAM I think it would be too slow to deal with the Second Chamber problem because the Labour Party is now committed to the abolition of the House of Lords and therefore I think that a Conservative government ought to try and deal with the Second Chamber problem in priority to the others.

RD That's precisely what I wanted to ask you about because it does seem to me that if you regard this problem of rights and safeguarding them as fundamental and checking the power of the elected majority in the Commons, that the swiftest and simplest way to achieve this is to have a Second Chamber with a credible and elected membership with slightly greater powers.

HAILSHAM This is exactly what I want, only I wouldn't say slightly greater powers, I mean greater powers. The point about a Second Chamber to my mind under our present system – and I am only trying to modify our present system – is that it ought to reflect the will of the people by being elected but on a different system to the House of Commons. I think the House of Commons ought to determine the colour of the executive and control finance, but that both Chambers ought to be equivalent to one another in matters of legislation of a general character.

RD And you would have them say, perhaps, elected on proportional representation, this Senate, would you?

HAILSHAM Yes, I would. I'd have constituencies the size of Scotland, Wales, the Midlands and so on and I would have some form of what I broadly call proportional representation.

RD And they would be what – elected a third every three or four years or something of that nature?

HAILSHAM Well, I think that could be discussed. My own proposal is to have them elected at a General Election so that you have one Chamber elected on first past the post, so that the largest organized minority governs, and the other Chamber elected on proportional representation so that the people can control the character of legislation.

RD Coming back to the point which led us into the Second Chamber, could you not have such a Second Chamber saying that if a Bill is contrary to the Fundamental Rights Act, which, let us say is on the Statute Book, this has got to go to the people for a two–thirds majority referendum? Wouldn't that be a much simpler way than your great elaborate new Constitution?

HAILSHAM No, it wouldn't because it wouldn't work at all. There are two factors you would have to take into account, there is the possibility that Parliament might repeal the whole of the arrangements you suggest. The fundamental doctrine which I am trying to say is that only the people should be able to modify the Constitution and that should involve (a) an Act of Parliament and (b) a referendum confirming it.

RD I remember you saying to me on a radio programme on these very matters almost ten years ago, Lord Hailsham: 'I do not think it is constitutionally possible to insert in an Act of Parliament in any form a provision that that Act cannot be repealed, because you cannot fetter Parliament. That,' you said, 'is one of the dogmas and axioms of our Constitution.' If that is so, how can you possibly set up the kind of written constitution which would replace our present parliamentary system with the supremacy of Parliament embedded in it?

HAILSHAM Well, that is a logical problem but I don't think it's insoluble if you have an elective Second Chamber because I don't want less democracy, I want more democracy. I don't want the Second Chamber to be a Court of Appeal either from the House of Commons or from the people: I want it to reflect the will of the people. In the end no form of Constitution, whether it's a modification of our own or some invented form, will be able to stand against popular opinion so long as we remain a democratic country.

RD But you say that the point I made was a logical problem but not insuperable: let's say you set up your Constitution with a reformed Second Chamber, what is to prevent the doctrine of – or the axiom, as you put it, of parliamentary supremacy being invoked should both Houses of Parliament at that time have the will to pass an Act of Parliament?

HAILSHAM Well, you see, you'd have abolished the House of Lords. The doctrine to which I referred ten years ago does involve the existence of the House of Lords. Once you've abolished the House of Lords and put another Chamber with limited powers in its place so that the House of Lords can never be reconvened, the dogma would only become a reality if some government under proclamation from the Queen was to reassemble the old type Parliament in order to repeal the Act.

RD Supposing you did have a new Upper House, a Senate, formed and constituted as you suggest, would that not be a recipe for rivalry between two elected Houses which would make for constitutional friction?

HAILSHAM Not if you keep from it the power of executive government and the power of finance, which in my view is part of executive government. What happened in Australia in 1975 mustn't be allowed to happen here.

RD In other words, that was when the Senate claimed power of supply, to deny supply to the Lower House?

HAILSHAM Well, it had the power to deny supply and used it.

RD It had never actually used it before, had it?

HAILSHAM Not to that extent.

RD Supposing your Constitution were to be established, may I put it to you that we would have lost several of the great virtues of our present system. First of all would we not have lost the flexibility of our present system, the freedom, as you once put it, of Parliament to act in a moment of crisis which you have said you want to preserve.

HAILSHAM Well, that is quite true and what I have said must be contingent upon the continuance of peace. If you had a third world war then you'd have to go back to omnipotence of Parliament – we would never have won against Hitler if we hadn't an omnipotent Parliament.

RD Leaving war aside, nowadays there are plenty of other situations, we all know only too well, the possibility of violent revolutions, upheavals, industrial chaos and so on, where we want government in Parliament to be able to act in the national interest and they might well be inhibited by some legalistic constitution.

HAILSHAM Look – bless you, every country in the world has a written Constitution except ourselves, New Zealand and Israel. The question is whether we are out of step or they're out of step. But I don't notice that the Swiss are noticeably badly governed when I go there, and Germany, since they've had their modern Constitution, has gone right ahead, so has Japan, so has France, so has the Netherlands, so have Belgium. Are we really – do we have a double dose of original sin or something or are we a separate race of primates?

RD I thought we had a triple dose of national excellence.

HAILSHAM Well then, don't worry.

RD In the sense that we had built up a Constitution which was notable for its simplicity, six unwritten words, the Queen in Parliament is supreme – yet you want a Constitution which would be a paradise for lawyers and something much more complicated.

HAILSHAM I can't think why you call it a paradise for lawyers, though lawyers are entitled to their paradise no less than ordinary men. But in fact there would be much less litigation in some ways under what I propose than what there is now. I mean, consider the confusion of the law at the moment: consider the 3000 pages of legislation being churned out without discussion by the House of Commons at the moment; consider the 10,000 pages of subordinate legislation and ask yourself, wouldn't it be better to have subordinate legislatures and so on like other countries of our size?

RD Subordinate legislatures is a different point. When I hear you remind me of the vast amount of legislation and regulations we have, this seems to me an additional case for not adding to the amount of statutory law which has to be interpreted and argued about by creating a new Constitution.

HAILSHAM But surely what I am suggesting is not to add to the quantity of statutory law but to reduce the flow of it. I am turning off the tap a bit so that in different parts of the country local governments, which are closer to the people and composed more of amateurs and less of bureaucrats, will be under the control of the people. I don't think it's a different point – I think it's part of the same point. Parliament is over-centralized, we're trying to use a boiler which was designed for 30 lb pressure per square inch and putting 3000 lb pressure per square inch into it.

RD Let me come back on the point about flexibility. You see, I asked Lord Denning the other night on his eightieth birthday whether he agreed to the idea of a written Constitution such as you and indeed Lord Scarman have also advocated. He said he didn't like the idea. He believed in the flexibility and also he thought that a written Constitution would be much more rigid and offer opportunity for the taking of technical points and so on.

HAILSHAM Lord Denning is one of the most lovable creatures in the world and one of the most lovable things about him is that his complaint about proposals like mine and Lord Scarman's would bring the judges into politics. Is Saul also among the prophets?

RD Another virtue which in my submission we would lose if we went to your system would be that we would lose the characteristic of familiarity. For all its faults everyone understands that Parliament is supreme and people go to the ballot-box, they know they are electing a Parliament; they're not electing a Parliament which is going to be in your words policed by the judges. Haven't we had enough – I put this to you in your capacity as a Conservative – don't you think we've had enough institutional upheaval to be going on with? Do we want another reorganization of our government?

HAILSHAM Well, I would reply with another question: do we really want the kind of dictatorship which enables one-quarter of the electorate to elect an omnipotent Parliament and to impose against the will of the people one set of laws after another which undermine their fundamental rights and liberties? If you want to go on like that by all means do so because you'll live longer than me and have to live under the system.

RD But if I may say so, that is a slightly loaded question and it's not for me to answer it, but if I may put another question in return. You say a government based on a minority of only 29 per cent of the vote – but when such a thing has occurred have our fundamental rights been destroyed and taken away? Things may have happened which you don't agree with but have our fundamental liberties been undermined?

HAILSHAM I would have said that they have been – the will of the people has been disregarded in almost every nationalization measure, but just look what's been happening in the last few weeks. Look at the combination of the closed shop on the legislation of 1974, 1975 and 1976 of industrial relations. It is destroying fundamental liberties and, what is more, people are now becoming afraid to speak their minds. They're afraid of being blacked, they're afraid of having their card taken away, they're afraid of being turned into bankruptcy, as a result of legislation passed by this Parliament which is totally unrepresentative of the people.

RD Some people watching you, Lord Hailsham, may say this: you are proposing constitutional changes when during your lifetime you haven't advocated them before, you are proposing constitutional changes designed to block measures of a Labour government which you do not happen to approve of.

HAILSHAM But just look at it the other way. It isn't only Labour governments that impose their will on the people. Look at Idi Amin, look at Hitler and Mussolini, consider the National Front, consider the movement – the ideas of Enoch Powell, these are all people who could capture the 'elective dictatorship' with a minority. Do you really want to be ruled by any of them? Are my remarks the remarks of a senile Conservative being hostile to Socialism, or are they the remarks of an old-fashioned liberal that want the people and right to govern this country instead of extremists?

RD But if extremists of the kind you are concerned about were to come to power, intent on destroying fundamental rights much more than they have been up to now, wouldn't we be in a situation where no law, no constitution is going to be any good? It would be a question of the tanks outside Broadcasting House.

HAILSHAM Well, if they come to power by the will of the people no one in the whole world can stop them staying in power by the will of the people, but if they come into power by the will of a quarter of the people, then I say that a Constitution can stop them. You've got to remember that Hitler got in constitutionally and he passed his laws constitutionally by an omnipotent Reichstag, and if he hadn't done it, and if the law had stood up to him, he wouldn't have been able to do it.

RD Are you saying that if there had been your kind of constitution in Germany in 1935 and 1936, that this would have made the slightest difference to the stormtroopers and the brown shirts?

HAILSHAM I am saying that if it had happened in 1933, which is the right year, it wouldn't have happened, but what happened was that Hitler got in through a chink in the Weimar Constitution and then he used the power of an elective dictatorship to destroy the freedom of the German people.

RD But you want to check the power of people who are in power – that's why I chose 1935 and 1936, because once someone gets the power democratically, as we've seen in various countries, they can use the apparatus of government to stay in power – to hell with courts and Constitutions.

HAILSHAM But do you call it democracy that you have a first past the post system of voting with no effective Second Chamber, a party caucus selecting the candidates and the party caucus in the constituencies infiltrated by extremists? This is what you're defending.

RD No, I am asking whether this system for all its faults merits replacement by a totally different system.

HAILSHAM I would say not – if it were not for the fact that it is manifestly breaking down.

RD Suppose the Constitution had been changed as you want to see it, with Parliament subject to the review by the courts and so on, would you have been so enthusiastic as you were as a young man in 1938 to enter the House of Commons if you thought you were going to be not a member of a sovereign body but a member of a subordinate body to be policed by non-elected judges?

HAILSHAM I don't see less enthusiasm in Canada or in Australia where they have the kind of Constitution I am suggesting, and I don't therefore see why I should have been less enthusiastic then, when I was young, than I would have been if I'd been a young Canadian, a young American or a young Australian.

RD But would not the office of MP – office is perhaps not the right word – but the career of a Member of Parliament perhaps seem less attractive than, say, a career leading to be one of your judges striking down legislation?

HAILSHAM I should have thought it was much more attractive. The one thing which is certain about the modern MP is that he has got too much to do. He has to spend all night sitting in that ghastly Chamber, traipsing through the lobbies as lobby fodder instead of living a family life – as they always used to. When Gladstone was Prime Minister Parliament sat for five months in the year and Gladstone as Prime Minister spent most of his time in North Wales. Now that was a gentleman's life.

RD Parliament did so much less in those days.

HAILSHAM Well, I know – that's what I'm suggesting it should do now.

RD If a Conservative government is elected this year, Lord Hailsham, and if you are on the Woolsack, do you think you will be able to persuade your colleagues to move us towards this sort of system and to reform the Second Chamber?

HAILSHAM Broadly the answer is no, I don't. The British are too conservative.

RD But will you try to persuade them?

HAILSHAM Oh, yes, of course I will. I keep on dripping away like a contentious woman on an extremely rainy day.

RD Thank you, Lord Hailsham, and people heard you use the word senile – I hope you'll agree that it was not I who used that of you and never would.

'In peace as in war, it is the great, the ultimate question for any nation: if we still are a nation. So really I am inviting the British people, and have been these many years, to say whether they intend still to be a nation.'

ENOCH
POWELL

1979

On no subject has Enoch Powell spoken with greater passion and conviction than on Parliament and its sovereignty. That was our subject for this 1979 interview. In my introduction I quoted some stirring words of his own: 'Take Parliament out of the history of England and that history itself becomes meaningless. The British nation could not imagine itself except with and through its Parliament.'

Enoch Powell has consistently argued that the sovereignty of Parliament is something other for us than are the assemblies of other nations for them. As we enter the 1990s this belief has been echoed by Margaret Thatcher in her campaign to prevent the European Community becoming a federal super-state.

This 1979 interview was done at the end of the decade in which Britain had joined the EEC, and had confirmed its membership by referendum. In it we can now see a vintage discussion of the sovereignty issue which has surfaced again in the 1990s. In 1979 Enoch Powell commanded little support. As he himself admits, 'I may be a general without an army, I may be a guerrilla chieftain in the hills ...'

At the time of this interview Enoch Powell was Ulster Unionist MP for Down South. In the General Election of February 1974 he had refused to stand as a Conservative and, in a sensational campaign intervention, advised the electors to vote Labour as the only way to get Britain out of the EEC. From a man who had once stood for the leadership of the Conservative Party this was seen as an act of desertion. But to Enoch Powell it was Edward Heath and the Common Marketeers who had deserted true Toryism.

The fascination of Enoch Powell's oratory, or indeed of his conversation, is his compulsive gift of presenting his opinions as if they were logically unassailable. This is partly due to the force and intensity with which the opinions are uttered, and partly to the grandiloquent structure of the language he employs. Enoch Powell has never stooped to use telly chat.

As shown here, he always liked to engage in dialogue – the more vigorous the better. But woe betide the interviewer who was ignorant or ill-prepared. An interview with Mr Powell was therefore an event to be approached with trepidation lest one's research and preparatory thinking had been less than perfect.

The Rt Hon. J. Enoch Powell MBE, MP

Interviewed in BBC 2 series The Parliamentarians
4 February 1979

ROBIN DAY Mr Powell, would it be right, broadly speaking, to say that
you're less interested in the reform of the way Parliament works than
in the need to uphold the sovereignty of Parliament and to protect
it against erosion and surrender?

RT HON. ENOCH POWELL MP You don't have to worry about the reform
of Parliament because Parliament or the House of Commons keeps
on reforming – it would only be a slight exaggeration to say that
almost every day it reforms itself. Its procedure, its conventions and
so on are a living, changing body from generation to generation. So
reform is – the use of the term reform in the sense of organic change
or deliberate change is a misconception of the creature with which
we are dealing. But power, sovereignty, the fact that the ultimate
power is there in that Chamber, that's of the essence. Everything
else – the institution, the rules, the customs, the unique combination
of intimacy and solemnity which is the House of Commons, that
would be worth nothing if power did not ultimately reside there. It's
about the exercise of power, it's the unique form of the exercise of
power, the self-conscious exercise of power by a nation.

RD On this question of ultimate power, there are those like Lord
Hailsham, who argued recently that the ultimate power of Parliament,
the sovereignty of Parliament, had become nothing less than 'an
elective dictatorship' of the Commons majority and that we should
have a new Constitution to safeguard our fundamental rights against
the power of a temporary Commons majority. Now what is your
answer to that?

POWELL Heaven help us – for Conservatives who go around peddling
new Constitutions. He was a little unkind to me, I don't see why I
shouldn't be a little unkind to him, you know, tit for tat. Well, he
wants in the last resort, ultimately, that's the word, rule by judges.
He wants the great issues of politics to turn upon the interpretation
by judges of a written piece of paper – a written fixed piece of paper
in which the only change can be introduced by the interpretations of
judges or the interpretation by them of whether the rules for changing

it are being complied with. Now don't get me wrong – I've no disrespect for Her Majesty's judges. They too, though a subordinate, are still an expression of the royal power of sovereignty. But I don't want to be governed by judges – I want to be governed by my peers in Parliament, I want to be governed through the self-expression of the British people as it occurs Parliament after Parliament. And as for safeguards, we have stronger safeguards than any built in guarantees.

RD You say we have stronger safeguards than any built-in guarantees. But what safeguards are there against our present parliamentary system being used by a government which happens to have (let us say) a Commons majority which may only perhaps have the voting support of less than a third of the electorate pushing through major constitutional changes, abolishing fundamental liberties? For instance, such a Commons majority could abolish the Second Chamber without any safeguard against it doing so.

POWELL I don't think so – and I think this can be disproved in practice. For example –

RD What *constitutional* safeguard?

POWELL One can play with the word constitutional but let's look at the way in which Parliament actually behaves. Now this question of abolishing the Second Chamber, the House of Lords, has featured several times in the programme of the Labour Party. I understand it may feature again. But I was fascinated by something which happened in the course of the debates which go on in the course of a formulation of the policy of the Labour Party. They said, 'Oh, but if we are to propose that, we shall have to put in some safeguard; we shall have to tell people that there will be an equally effective, if not a more effective, check upon what any one House of Commons could do.' Now why did they say that? They were misrepresented, the thing was reported against them? But that was what they were really saying. Why did they say that? Because the House of Commons knows and political parties know that they come from the people and they go back to the people and the people are going to be their ultimate judges. And they said to themselves, unless we can show that what we propose is going to give at least as good safeguards as are enjoyed in Parliament as it is at present, we shan't carry it. We shall be laughed or hissed out of court.

RD But the point still remains that a Commons majority which may only command the support of a minority of the electorate under our present system, could – and this is the point – could constitutionally abolish the House of Lords or even – and let me come on to another point perhaps even more serious – could prolong its own life indefinitely if it was so determined and not have an election.

POWELL But it is as unrealistic to use that word 'could' in that context as to say that Her Majesty 'could' refuse her Royal Assent to a Bill passed by both Houses. Constitutionally, and equally constitutionally, she 'could' – but we know that she won't. And for the same reasons we know that the House of Commons will not prolong its own life because that is something so contrary to the nature of the House of Commons, so contrary to its unwritten but all the more real compact with the electorate that it couldn't get around to doing it. Now I will give another example from the case of the House of Lords which you mentioned. A few years ago there was a consensus between the two front benches to reform the House of Lords – actually to reform the House of Lords so as to give it more power and so as to give the executive more control over it. Now there was a majority on second reading for that measure – the two front benches were hand in glove, you might say. Of course Parliament *could* do this, the House of Commons *could* do this. Why didn't it do it? It didn't do it because when it was – the proposition was got on to the floor of the House and picked over and looked at and debated, when the Commons did its thing on the proposal, then the House of Commons itself began to see this is ridiculous, this is indefensible.

RD You have in fact picked validly but very conveniently a proposal which was shot through with criticism from all points of the compass.

POWELL But so could a proposal for the House of Commons to prolong its own life.

RD Yes, but what we're talking about in discussing the nature of parliamentary government is what could happen and what people are proposing to prevent it happening – but I take your point. And may I move from that to ask you why you take the view, if you do take the view, because I am not sure if you do, that our parliamentary sovereignty has been diminished by or has been surrendered by reason of our membership of the European Community?

POWELL Of course it has because in so many terms the House of Commons enacted that laws should be valid in this country which it had not made, that taxes should be levied which it had not imposed and that judgments should be delivered on the interpretation of its laws otherwise than by the judges of the Crown. I don't know how more comprehensively any Parliament could get around to destroying its sovereignty than that.

RD But how can you possibly argue that, because you have quoted, with great relish and enthusiasm and eloquence on a number of occasions, the government's own statement on the subject (which is engraven, I thought, on your heart) – 'our membership of the Community in the future depends on the continuing assent of Parliament'. In other words, what Parliament has done it can undo.

POWELL That's true.

RD So the sovereignty of Parliament is undiminished.

POWELL But you're still playing, Robin, with this unreal concept of could or can. Now it is true that at present and for a time to come the House of Commons can repeal – and I believe one day it will repeal or radically amend, which comes to the same thing – yes. But the referendum, from the context of which you quoted those words, did not by those very words settle the question. It left it still to Parliament.

RD Exactly. Because Parliament is supreme.

POWELL I repeat: Parliament can still for a time to come undo or radically modify what has been done. But a time will come when with a directly re-elected Parliament (they will call it) in Europe, with one step after another which binds the United Kingdom more and more as a province into a new state, when that 'could' becomes as unreal as the 'could' in the sentence 'The Queen "could" refuse her Assent to Bills passed by both Houses'. In other words, what is practicable changes – changes with the real world and there comes a time – I'm not going to predict when it is and I shall die fighting however long – but I cannot deny that there could be a time when the repeal of the 1972 Act or the amendment of it would be as unreal as the refusal of the Royal Assent.

RD But you said our sovereignty – that Parliament had destroyed its sovereignty. Would you accept on reflection –

POWELL You offered me the alternatives of destroyed or diminished and –

RD Surrendered was the word I used.

POWELL Surrendered or –

RD You used the word destroyed.

POWELL Yes. Well, it destroyed it pro tem and it destroyed it in so far as any one Parliament could. But it remains in practice a revocable Act, but whether it is revocable depends – and again I come back to my underlying theme – upon what those who make and unmake Parliament want. And that is why on this subject I address myself not primarily to the House of Commons but to its makers in the country.

RD But I put it to you this is not just an academic argument. I put it to you that for the foreseeable future unless we were to join some – the European Federation of a formal kind, for the foreseeable future that is nothing to prevent the British Parliament deciding at the will of the British people that they should come out of the European Community if there were some overwhelming mass public opinion demanding it.

POWELL Well, you say that and I say that, but the supporters of British membership at the referendum and since have constantly spoken of it as a thing inherently inconceivable, that what they call the Treaty should be broken, as a subject which is closed and finished once for all. So this is a matter on which two views exist.

RD Is it your view, Mr Powell, that our system of parliamentary government would be improved or not improved by the current proposals for legislative devolution to Scotland and Wales?

POWELL Legislative devolution inside the United Kingdom is unworkable and will destroy one or the other of the poles. It will either destroy the union or it will destroy itself. It will either be seen to be an impracticable form of organization in Scotland – and surely much sooner in Wales – or else it will be seen to be a denial of the union itself and open the path to the separation of Scotland from the parliamentary union into which it was joined in 1707.

RD Do you think it will take away from the sovereignty of the Westminster Parliament?

POWELL Yes, it is bound to do so in so far as the Westminster Parliament attempts to live with a subordinate Parliament which it has created. Now we have a little experience of this, a very tragic experience, in that in 1920, having devolved legislative as well as administrative power to a Home Rule Parliament in Northern Ireland, although in the Act in which it did it the House of Commons claimed to retain complete sovereignty over all persons and things whatsoever in Northern Ireland, it turned its back on that part of the United Kingdom and wanted to know nothing about it for fifty years. I suppose that that was not so much a diminution of sovereignty, it was a betrayal of sovereignty and of its duty as the sovereign assembly of this country and very harshly the people concerned have had to pay.

RD But of course that illustrates the basic point that –

POWELL The incompatibility.

RD – the sovereignty of Parliament remained unimpaired by that piece of legislative devolution because Stormont has been abolished.

POWELL Well, it also illustrates how after the lapse of time there comes an ever-increasing gulf between practicably exercisable sovereignty and sovereignty which has become moribund or has become self-renounced. I think it's a lesson which both in terms of Scotland and of Northern Ireland we ought to learn.

RD Do you think that the sovereignty of Parliament would be better exercised by the Commons if it were elected on a system – I won't use the word reform because that's a loaded phrase – an electoral system which was changed to be more proportionately representative of public opinion?

POWELL No, sir. Because the House of Commons is not a photograph of public opinion at a moment of time – a picture which we know very well from the opinion polls to be as shifting as the shifting sands. It is a delegation from the nation, place by place, of authority to assent or to withhold assent to the proposals and the acts of government. It is a representation in local terms, place by place of the nation, but it is a representation for the purpose of saying yea or nay. It is not an attempt to find out the exact shadings of opinion across the whole spectrum. It is a means of arriving at valid, sustainable decisions. And it does so by a method which indeed is rough and ready, which one might say is harsh and peremptory, but which, for its validity, rests upon its acceptance. Despite all these apparent arithmetical contradictions and imperfections people accept what the House of Commons votes until they secure a change in what the House of Commons has voted.

RD There are increasing signs of a number of people *not* accepting what the House of Commons votes –

POWELL Well, not on that ground.

RD Well, one of the arguments of course for proportional representation is that this would give Parliament greater moral authority.

POWELL I must say that you need to be pretty credulous to suppose that if this present House of Commons – if this Parliament had been elected on some form of proportional representation what's going on at the moment would not be going on in similar terms. The difference would be that lacking though the majority may be in accepted authority, the government would then lack all credibility, since it would be a government which existed by the tolerance of those elected to represent opposite or differing points of view.

RD But of course those who advocate electoral reform, as it is called, do so on the grounds that they say this would be another stage in the continuing development of the electoral system that we've seen over the last 150 years, for instance – the Reform Bill, universal suffrage, votes for women at thirty, then votes for women at twenty-one, then votes for people at eighteen. Next, they say, we've got to make it an even fairer system.

POWELL To change the franchise has nothing to do with changing the electoral system. The implications of the single representative of a single constituency entitled on behalf of that constituency as a whole to say yea or nay are just the same whether it is a restricted franchise, a pot-walloper franchise of the early nineteenth century in some places, or whether it is the universal franchise of today. But you alter something radical when you say that the House of Commons is intended to be a mathematical representation of the spectrum of opinion, and we will only have a government which can obtain a majority, draw a majority, from that represented spectrum. That would be a different constitution altogether.

RD What do you say to the view which is quite commonly held nowadays that the parliamentary system that we have at the moment is to blame to a very great degree for our economic and industrial problems and the decline of our nation in some ways, particularly because, it is said, of the adversary system which dominates our present parliamentary atmosphere. Indeed it is supported by the very physical layout of the Chamber.

POWELL Well, if I had to attribute blame for the mess we are in, it would be to a lack of the use of the adversary system. It is that both sides of the House over so many years have connived in fictions which, as politicians, workers in the same trade, they found convenient, but which increasingly they knew to be false and yet the falsity of which they have not been able to renounce. But then in the last resort that is a reflection – I fear a rather truthful reflection – of the makers of Parliament out of doors. They wanted to be deceived. They wanted to be told that you can have public expenditure and not finance it by taxation. They wanted all these tales to be told to them and so the House of Commons, which is their creature and their reflection, told them the tales they wanted. And only when the people say 'We're sick of that tale', only when the people turn on those who told them the tales as they sometimes unfairly do, will we be freed to face our difficulties and to deal with them.

RD So it is not the parliamentary system which has failed the nation, but it is the nation and the MPs it elects who have failed the parliamentary system.

POWELL No, but I never claimed more for the House of Commons than that it was the most authentic expression of the British people.

RD How important in the scale of issues confronting the British people at the coming General Election do you place the dangers to the sovereignty of Parliament and our system of government?

POWELL I will place them as high as I possibly can, since however long a time one may have still realistically to change, we can repeal, can amend, the 1972 Act.

RD The European Communities Act?

POWELL – The European Communities Act. However long or short a time we may have, that must be the question which subtends all others. What Parliament can do must be more important than the particular way in which, Parliament by Parliament, Parliament exercises its powers.

RD So you would say, would you – I hope I am not misrepresenting you – that the question of parliamentary sovereignty and national sovereignty as affected by our membership of the EEC, is the issue on which you would like to see most people have as their reason for voting one way or the other?

POWELL Yes. For – in peace as in war, it is the great, the ultimate, question for any nation: if we still are a nation. So really I am inviting the British people, and have been these many years, to say whether they intend still to be a nation.

RD Now if you regard it as an issue of that importance, which in your hope would determine how people should vote, which government, Labour or Conservative, would you think is most likely now to prevent or to reverse the surrender of sovereignty which you see as a result of being members of the European Community?

POWELL I may be a general without an army, I may be a guerrilla chieftain in the hills, but at least I don't make the elementary tactical mistake of deciding on the deployment of my forces, such as they are, until I have the full intelligence of the enemy's dispositions.

RD That means, in simpler language – ?

POWELL I shall wait and see where and when and how the opportunities best present themselves. And work towards the end of restoring to the British nation both the consciousness and the reality of being a self-governing nation.

RD But as you see the political parties at the moment, Conservative and Labour, which of them do you think looks more likely to – to reverse the decision or make that decision less serious, the decision to join the – and remain in – the EEC?

POWELL I see a Labour Party of which the majority inside the House and in the country is hostile to our membership of the Common Market, instinctively, probably on the same grounds as I am myself. I see a Conservative Party of which the soggy centre is lukewarm on the subject but will go the way that fortune beckons. I see a leadership which is imprisoned in past events and doesn't know how to break out of that prison. And I see a gallant, and not diminishing, maybe slightly increasing, but small, minority, which carries on the struggle from within. That is the picture which, to continue my metaphor, from my eyrie in the hills I see below me on the plains. But there is a factor which is always present in my mind. This thing must be done with the maximum assent or consent. We have seen too much in recent years of steps which were taken without full-hearted consent. I want to pull the nation together. I want to pull Parliament together. It has been a minor consolation of my declining years that justice was done to Northern Ireland by the almost universal consent of the House of Commons and not as an act of one side or the other.

RD May I contradict your suggestion that you are in your declining years?

POWELL Well, that's generous – thank you. But I want to see nationhood reasserted, wholeheartedly, and I shall use whatever forces I command or can persuade with a view to that. So when I told you that the tactical picture is still developing, I was not merely putting you off. After all, you know I never put you off.

RD But I still would like to know whether you think nationhood can be reasserted and parliamentary sovereignty restored as you see it, that is, more likely to be achieved under a Labour government or a Conservative government? As you see them at the moment, having had your description.

POWELL The predicament of the parties, the electoral chances, the electoral context even, at a specific moment, can wonderfully sharpen the apprehension of principles on the part of all concerned. I haven't yet seen the battle lines drawn up. One thought they were drawn up last September but it turned out that they weren't. Then one thought they were drawn up next month, but then maybe they are not. And there's a lot can happen in six months.

RD Mr Powell, thank you very much for giving us your views on Parliament and other matters.

'It's the kind of clubby atmosphere of the place ... it's the only working place I know where there's a pub or several pubs open from early morning to the end of the night.'

DENNIS SKINNER

Dennis Skinner, the left-wing Labour Member of Parliament for Bolsover since 1970, has never been a minister or a front-bencher, and is unlikely ever to be one. He sits on the front bench, but below the gangway. He is one of nature's back-benchers.

Why is there a place in this assorted selection for an interview with the Beast of Bolsover? Because he is a brilliant parliamentary character. I do not use that word in the derogatory sense. Skinner is not a character in the sense of being eccentric or flamboyant or a crank. After only a few years in the House he became a parliamentary character by skill and persistence. He has made his mark, and has kept his mark, as the most aggressive back-bencher in the Commons. He is a fierce and uncompromising challenger of what he sees as humbug and hypocrisy, corruption and consensus politics, and of time-wasting ritual.

But aggressiveness and being radical and anti-establishment are not enough to make a parliamentarian. Skinner has the parliamentary skills – procedural know-how, assiduity in attendance, timing, and humour. And he does his homework. His interventions, savage or sarcastic, abusive or absurd, are well thought out in advance.

It would be wrong to characterize him as a mere performer. He has strong principles – some would say too strong, too pig-headed. He is a left-wing socialist, and was a coal-miner for twenty years before entering Parliament. He believes in the old-fashioned red-flag socialism of Clause 4 and class war which the Labour Party has been steadily discarding in the last few years.

Though admired as a parliamentary performer, Dennis Skinner is not taken seriously in the House as a political thinker. But his well-practised invective and full-throated presence make him a formidable trouble-maker. Call him a parliamentary personality, call him (as Churchill called Bevan) a squalid nuisance, Skinner is his own man.

Skinner deals here in characteristic style with criticism of his attitudes – his refusal to have a pair, his contempt for compromise, his frequent defiance of the Speaker, his scorn for office-holding, and (what Healey accused him of) 'his proletarian humbug'. Here is a star of the Westminster stage, yet one who professes contempt for the cult of personality and for the parliamentary atmosphere in which he flourishes.

Dennis Skinner MP

Interviewed in BBC 2 series The Parliamentarians
11 February 1979

ROBIN DAY Mr Skinner, in your opinion, is there a lot wrong with Parliament as an institution, apart from the fact that it hasn't got a majority of Members who believe in your kind of socialism?

DENNIS SKINNER MP Yes, there's a lot wrong with Parliament. It's a club, you see, as well as being a place to pass Bills and to enact legislation. And so there is this sort of overriding thing that means that when governments come into office there's a tendency – and here I'm talking specifically really about Labour governments, I don't know too much about the Tories – there's a tendency for it to consume what is known as the national interest over and above the interest or the mandate that it got from the people in terms of its manifesto.

RD But is that anything to do with Parliament as an institution? Or is it a characteristic of Labour governments?

SKINNER No – except that it is a characteristic of Labour governments, that's true, most of them, not all – I think the Attlee government for several years gave the impression that it was trying to enact the legislation that it had put before the people.

RD But why does Parliament as an institution tend to have that effect on Labour governments? And indeed, if I may say so, some Tories would say that Tory governments become less Tory when they get in office.

SKINNER Yes. The thing about the club is – this all-party embrace. For instance, when you go into Parliament – mind you, it's rather strange about when you go into Parliament because you're never told to attend, you know. I was waiting after the election to try and see on what day I got this all-important call in 1970. But it never turned up and I went to work – I went down the pit again the following Monday.

RD You didn't know that your pay started from the moment you were elected?

SKINNER Well, that was the main point. I couldn't really afford not to be in work and in actual fact the only time that you're told is by the Chief Whip and he tells you to attend in order to ensure that, come the division on the all-important Queen's Speech, you'll be there to vote for the party perhaps. So you're not even notified and it's the kind of clubby atmosphere of the place, the smoke rooms and the bars, it's the only working place I know where there's a pub or several pubs open from early morning to the end of the night.

RD None the less, for all its faults, Mr Skinner, has not Parliament, this ancient institution, has it not provided you with a wonderful sounding board as it has for others in the past? And hasn't it given you many opportunities, which you have seized, to fight for what you believe in?

SKINNER Yes, it gives me that opportunity, although not as much as I would like, obviously. The problem, you see, is that I believe that the Labour government, when it gets into power, should be more concerned with its own interests – the ones that it has obviously got elected on – rather than this sort of fairies-at-the-bottom-of-the-garden national interests. And that's why in my view we can't get – or perhaps more importantly, why people are more sceptical about politicians and about governments and so on.

RD I remember Aneurin Bevan once saying to me that Parliament was both a workshop and a theatre – workshop in the sense of making legislation and a theatre with a stage for protest and so on. Which do you see it mainly as? A theatre?

SKINNER There's too much of that. The sort of yah-boo politics that we get – for instance when the BBC now have their radio broadcasts on Prime Minister's Question Time, I think it shows pretty clearly that there's a lot of sort of this kind of animal bleating and so on. I try to get a few remarks in now and again when the bleating's stopped but I get pulled up for it. I think it's unfair. But yes, it's got that kind of theatre and there are lots of people on both sides that want to applaud their leader; the development of the personality cult is there all the time. They're all anti-democratic, all these things, in my view and so I want Parliament to be an institution which is so well oiled that it allows a Labour government to come in and to get its legislation through so that it can satisfy those demands.

RD You talk about a personality cult and so on, but doesn't it occur to you that your success as a back-bencher has made you something of a parliamentary personality, a kind of star performer on the Westminster stage? Can you escape the charge of personality cult? I don't criticize you in any way because Members of Parliament are there to make use of the procedure.

SKINNER Yes, there is a problem with the Labour Party and it is because of the fact that some go to Parliament and generally speaking they tend to be looked upon as a little bit better than the ordinary fellow – and that comes back to the democratic accountability, you see. And so yes, it is a problem that I have to face. I try to fight against it, make no mistake about that.

RD May I suggest that you perhaps should not fight against it? Because you talk about parliamentary tradition but may I suggest that you are part of a parliamentary tradition of very long standing, that in every parliamentary generation there are a few Members who stand out against the prevailing wisdom, and make themselves rather unpopular; clash with the Speaker from time to time, clash with Prime Ministers of their own party. Aneurin Bevan attacking Churchill during the war – Churchill called him 'a squalid nuisance'; Shinwell, Maxton before the war, Emrys Hughes. What's wrong with that tradition?

SKINNER There's nothing wrong with the tradition, but you see, I want to see more than that accomplished. It's not sufficient for me, certainly not satisfying for me, to think, 'Well, I've had another clash with the Speaker, there's another story in the newspapers tomorrow morning,' it's like dog bites man story, it's old news. No, I would much rather be able to see headlines that said that the Labour government were able to carry through certain of these things and be more able to carry them through, in my view, if Parliament sort of changed from being the kind of club that it is and became an institution for getting through legislation. Now that means a lot of changes.

RD But a lot of people would say, Mr Skinner, that far from being merely a club where people drink and talk and say yah-boo, it not only produces a great deal of legislation, by the yard, but also a bit too much for some people's liking.

SKINNER The problem with some of the legislation is that it tends to be this kind of consensus stuff – it comes from the soft underbelly of politics, the part that I don't like, because I believe that we make progress in this world based upon the conflict of ideas – and sometimes even industrial conflict has to emerge in order to project those ideas even further.

RD Do you regard as hypocritical, Mr Skinner, the parliamentary tradition that some Members develop friendship, and even affection, for their political opponents? An example of which, for instance, when you came back to the House after a long illness you were welcomed back by Tory Members, apparently sincerely.

SKINNER Yes – you said apparently sincerely.

RD I choose my words carefully.

SKINNER I suppose that they were demonstrating once again that here we are, we're part of the club, someone's had a slight heart attack, he's come back to – not work, as such, not work in the sense of the kind that I used to do before I went to Parliament – and therefore they try to sort of get me into their embrace.

RD The Tories rather like you, Mr Skinner, don't they? Because they rather enjoy the way you embarrass your own colleagues and ministers on the Labour front bench by accusing them of not practising what they preach.

SKINNER Yes, that must be helpful to them in some circumstances. But it has to be done. The fact that it might satisfy Tories is neither here nor there.

RD Do you feel any personal respect or admiration for certain Tories?

SKINNER Well, I've got so much on my mind and so little time in which to do it that I can't spend too much time worrying about them, quite frankly.

RD I'm not asking you to spend time – but do you think it's wrong, for instance, say for Michael Foot to have, as he does, a profound respect for Enoch Powell, with whom he differs on a great many issues as a parliamentarian. Is that foreign to your thinking?

SKINNER Yes, it is really. Because I refuse to join any of the all-party groups in Parliament and I refuse to take part in any of those systems which means that I have to sort of go along with a Tory.

RD Do you admire Enoch Powell as a parliamentarian?

SKINNER As a man who can sort of put a speech together and there you can see the general tenet of his argument and all the branches setting out – yes, he can do that quite well. He's had a lot of practice at it, of course.

RD A lot of people have had a lot of practice but don't do it very well.

SKINNER Well, yes, and some of them get to high office.

RD Do you ever discuss parliamentary technique and tactics with Enoch Powell?

SKINNER Not really. I mean there is a great divide, isn't there? In terms of politics.

RD Yes, but that answer means that sometimes you do?

SKINNER No, sometimes I don't. Obviously you hear odd things now and again.

RD Why do you never accept a pair, the system by which members of opposite parties pair themselves off and don't vote because they have some outside engagement?

SKINNER Well, largely because I think it's playing truant. When I first went to Parliament, when I'd received my writ from Bob Mellish, the Chief Whip, then the next question was: 'Well, you have to have a pair, Dennis.' And I said what's one of these? And they told me and explained it was to enable somebody to go to the Ascot Races while somebody was doing an important engagement –

RD But it's also to enable someone to go perhaps and give a political speech or go and address some students or attend some perfectly legitimate parliamentary function. Because Members of Parliament aren't supposed to be locked in Westminster twenty-four hours a day, are they?

SKINNER Yes, but you see, I take the view that if you are going to retain any integrity at all as a politician – you've nothing else to sell, remember. A politician has got nothing, only the fact that he can point to consistency and integrity. If that's gone, there's nothing else left in my view. And therefore when I am condemning Tories, or anybody else for that matter, for attacking workers outside – because I must relate to them all the time – say for being absent from work or being on strike, I want to be able to point to those – say twenty or thirty – remaining in the Chamber, many of whom have gone to these very important engagements, and I want to be able to turn to them and say that you've some need to talk about workers when there's only 120 voting out of 165.

RD But on a relatively minor –

SKINNER Now I can't do that if I take part in that sort of system.

RD But on a relatively minor division – I'm not talking about a crucial three-line Whip vote on which the fate of the government depends because they don't have pairs generally for that occasion, unless it's sickness or something. But is there anything really wrong with an MP who may have a genuine engagement of an important public character pairing off with somebody? Why is that wrong? It's been done for many, many years.

SKINNER Yes, let me explain this. If, say, for instance, there's a minister going to a very important engagement somewhere in which lives could be lost and lives could be saved, of course that's got to be dealt with. But what I'm trying to explain is that there are hordes of MPs who take part in this exercise every week and as soon as the Whip is declared – on both sides of the House – then they're already marking their diary and finding those engagements. So I'm not against people doing very important jobs outside – I'm not against that. But what I am against is all these fictitious arrangements that are made.

RD You give the impression, Mr Skinner, and tell me if this is unfair, that any kind of compromise by politicians is a betrayal of principle and a betrayal of those who elected him. Is that roughly right?

SKINNER Yes, roughly right, yes.

RD Let me ask you this: without compromise, how would Parliament work? How would the Labour Party work? Indeed, how would any human organization work without compromise, which is a pompous word for give and take?

SKINNER In a democratic structure, starting from the bottom, there will be all sorts of ideas, conflict will take place, something else will emerge, that's a compromise. It goes up to a higher level in the structures like, say, the Labour Party through its organization, compromise is being effected all the time – till it gets to the top. Then that is put to the people. Now in my view that's the end of the compromise. You have said to the people: 'Here we have a document which has been batted around, has been put before you in order for you to vote on.' Once that is there, in my view that should be taken to Parliament and then that should be pushed through. Now there are lots of reasons why it's not.

RD But are you not compromising with your integrity? And are you not perhaps betraying your principles every time you go into the division lobby to vote for a government which you disapprove of in many ways and regard as having sold out, or for having defied party policy or something. Why, is that not a compromise? I wouldn't criticize you for that compromise, but it is one.

SKINNER Yes, except that I'm pretty selective about when I walk through those lobbies. I think you will find, say, on fundamental questions like the Common Market, I have always voted against the Common Market legislation in all its aspects. On matters such as incomes policy, it doesn't really matter to me which government is in power, we were elected in 1974 on a manifesto that said an irreversible shift towards working-class people and their families and collective bargaining. Not free collective bargaining, because there's no such thing as free collective bargaining. No trade union shop steward has ever had the freedom to get what he wanted. But we were elected on that, and on fundamentals like that then I think you haven't got to shift, in my view. Of course there would be –

RD But none the less you have supported this government throughout its pay policy, and on other matters, and you have done so because you –

SKINNER No, I voted against it on its pay policy.

RD Well, yes, but you've supported it despite its pay policy.

SKINNER That's right, yes.

RD And you've supported it because, I suggest and this is quite understandable, that you prefer a Labour government to a Tory government. But that is a compromise.

SKINNER Exactly. The point I think that has escaped you is the fact that I tried to indicate to you that if you put a programme before the people then you've got to try in all various ways to get the fundamental things of that manifesto through.

RD I understand that.

SKINNER If you fail, then you've got to be prepared to go back to the people and explain why.

RD If you put integrity first – and many people would respect you for that – whom do you detest most? A socialist hypocrite, who has betrayed his principles, or a Conservative who sincerely believes in and practices Toryism and capitalism?

SKINNER Well, of course, in the case of the socialist hypocrite I would have hoped that through any democratic procedures you would have been able to get rid of him. I could give some examples. You will not want me to, I know. But there are many. There are quite a number of them now writing in the various newspapers of our time, condemning workers who are trying to get a little bit more in order to live – the same people getting paid a lot of money for doing that. Many of whom were quite glad to have union support in their time.

RD But if you put integrity first, should not your admiration come more for your opponents, providing they are honest, rather than your colleagues, if they are hypocritical, that is the point I am trying to get at.

SKINNER Yes, I understand the point. And I think in all fairness that I would have to acknowledge that the fellow that stood by his principles – let's say, for instance, that there is a Tory on the benches now who voted against the Common Market – not for the same reason as I but voted against it through thick and thin. Had a lot of stick from his constituency party –

RD Neil Marten.

SKINNER That's the man in question. Yet he's still managed to pursue this line. Yes, one has to have some sort of admiration for a man taking that line on that issue.

RD May I put it to you, Mr Skinner, turning to another aspect of Parliament, that the House of Commons would become a shambles if every MP were as disobedient or as disrespectful to the Speaker as you are sometimes. Only a day or two ago the Speaker threatened to throw you out if you went on doing what he said you oughtn't to do.

SKINNER Well, it is a boring story, isn't it? I mean, the Speaker does this about once a month. I'm the sort of hit man. He needs to be able to demonstrate to the rest of the Members of the House of Commons that he's got control of affairs, so if I happen to say something which he doesn't like, sometimes he doesn't hear – I'm not too sure that he is the one that you are referring to now – none of the parliamentary correspondents seem to know what I said. But he needs, when –

RD I don't think it was what you said, because I was in the gallery, and couldn't hear it. I don't think it was what you said, but it was the fact that you were shouting from a sitting position and making the speech impossible.

SKINNER Yes. After a horde of others had done the same. And the point I am trying to demonstrate is that he needs a target man. The thing was getting out of control. Who better than to pick on me?

RD Yes, but none the less, Mr Skinner, you have to have a Speaker and he is elected, and what I am saying is that if you or any other backbencher feels the Speaker is carrying out his duties wrongly, you have the option of putting down a motion of censure, which other members may support if they wish, rather than constantly clashing with him.

SKINNER Well, that wouldn't do any good. Because in order to get a motion debated, I would have thought, of that kind, there would have to be a lot of signatures on it. And the following day, in the aftermath of what went before, I can't see many Members of Parliament wanting to upset the Speaker and signing my motion.

RD That's democracy.

SKINNER Because they are concerned about getting in the following week. They're concerned perhaps about getting to the Speaker's tea parties.

RD Well, if you can't get support for your motion, that's too bad, isn't it? That's democracy.

SKINNER Yes. But – I suppose you might call that democracy. I would call it perhaps grovelling, or wanting to obtain some favours. Which brings us back to the same old argument about Parliament – the club.

RD Now by a happy coincidence, Mr Skinner, this programme is going out on your forty-seventh birthday. By the time your fifty-seventh birthday comes round, do you think you will have held office?

SKINNER No. No. Not unless we had a procedure which enabled MPs, back-bench MPs, to be elected to governmental posts. I strongly believe in that. That's another part of the democratic scene.

RD Have you ever been offered a job?

SKINNER Oh no. No. Not in so many words. There have been sort of little things floated around. Naturally a Prime Minister who is in the business for hiring and firing, which I abhor, I think it should be obviously changed, he is not going to risk the rebuff, if he can help it.

RD But do you, by sitting on the sidelines and not accepting responsibility –

SKINNER Not on the sidelines, no –

RD No, but by not accepting responsibility are you living up to your own beliefs really, in the way people should behave? Because if I may say so, it takes courage to accept political responsibility. It takes courage to face up to the compromises which that sort of job entails.

SKINNER Yes, but I've done all that, you see. Not in parliamentary terms.

RD No, but in parliamentary terms.

SKINNER I think what you are attempting to suggest to the viewer is that I am not prepared to take on responsibility. I am prepared to take it on –

RD You've just said you aren't, unless it's under a system you approve of.

SKINNER Ah, no, not a system that I necessarily approve of, but a democratic system. Like, for instance, being elected to the National Executive. I stood for office there. I've had to take on some responsibility. We've just been discussing the Common Market, a thing which I detest. We've produced a document which is a compromise.

RD But given the system which we have, what would have happened if no Labour back-benchers had ever been willing to accept government office? People like Ernest Bevin, who came in from the trade unions. Ernest Bevin, and Nye Bevan and Jim Griffiths, another coal miner.

It would have been a poorer country if men like that hadn't been in office, wouldn't it?

SKINNER No, I'll tell you what would have happened. I'll tell you what would happen if all these people who take, share my view, in this, in believing that it should be a democratic system instead of having a Prime Minister hiring and firing 100 government ministers when he chooses, we would have that system that I want in much quicker.

RD Are you in favour of specialist committees, as has been recommended by the Select Committee on Procedure, as watchdog committees over all the departments? The idea being to make Parliament a more effective scrutiny, give it, make it a more effective scrutiny of the executive?

SKINNER I think that is likely to come about, but I don't agree with it. I think there are a lot of Members of Parliament that are going to push that through. You see, there is – because people believe that Parliament ought to be changed in some way, and because they are not prepared to take the steps that I want to take, to get rid of the unelected House of Lords, and to – to have an elected Cabinet, to politicize the departments so that back-bench MPs are formulating decisions as distinct from having to follow them when ministers put them forward. Because they are not prepared to take those adventurous steps, my guess is that Parliament might well take those other steps which you have described.

RD Why do you object to them? A lot of people might think, irrespective of party, that it was a good idea to have closer scrutiny of government and ministerial actions by these experts, committees with expert assistance.

SKINNER Yes, I've no doubt that they might be able to. Mind, in my view they'd have to be staffed separately. There would have to be political secretariats on both sides. So that we don't have this kind of consensus coming through all the time.

RD So you want the Labour members having specialist experts who shared their views?

SKINNER Yes, that's right.

RD I understand.

SKINNER To produce the conflict of ideas, yes.

RD You say that you want to abolish the hereditary House of Lords and a lot of people would share that view. But do you want to replace it by nothing?

SKINNER Yes, I don't think there's any need for it – for a Second

Chamber, that is. Under my system – if I ever had the chance – I would rather tend to the view that since we've got a lot of lawyers in Parliament – in fact they're very much over-represented – then some of them, because under that same system Members of Parliament would be full-time – then these lawyers, or some of them, could act as a revision committee. All you really need –

RD I wouldn't leave revising to lawyers.

SKINNER Well, in the terms – I don't think you've fully understood what I'm trying to say. What I'm saying is that when the Bill has been dealt with, in the partisan way that it would be in the House of Commons in all its various forms, in all its various stages, then we need a committee to look at it purely from the point of view of making sure that it can in fact be interpreted in the proper way. Not to do anything in a political fashion.

RD This is the, as it were, new committee of the House after third reading which the NEC have suggested – roughly like that?

SKINNER They have suggested something roughly like that – although the discussion is still continuing.

RD Do you know of any major democracy, Mr Skinner, where there is a single chamber government?

SKINNER Yes, I think New Zealand has one – and one in Sweden.

RD That's right, Sweden and New Zealand. But they don't quite rank as major democracies, do they? But I take your point.

SKINNER They've probably not had as many crises that we've had.

RD You said, Mr Skinner, when you entered Parliament that you were determined – first you were determined to speak for your own constituents, second to speak for working-class people in general, and third to speak your mind on all occasions. All admirable aims but do they not conflict one with another?

SKINNER Oh, many times. Yes, that's one of the judgments that we have to make.

RD One of the compromises?

SKINNER One of the compromises – but it's all done through a democratic system in the sense that I'm elected by the people and therefore I'm able to judge these on the basis that I've got to go back, that at the end of the day, or end of the four or five years or whatever it is, you've got to go back and answer them. Now I can say that on many of these very important issues in my next election manifesto, when we put it out, whatever the Labour Party do, they'll put out their general manifesto, but I'll put mine – I'll be able to say that on certain fundamental matters I've been able to carry forward those views consistently right throughout Parliament.

RD But which do you put first? You see, when you're speaking your mind, and in view of your belief in integrity you must do that, how do you justify not speaking for your own constituents, which according to that list of priorities which I read out, you put first?

SKINNER Yes – except that you mustn't get the impression, as some people do, that you can speak for all your constituents at the same time. I and many MPs saying that we represent everybody in their constituency. Now, it's impossible. There are different interests in a constituency – an employer might be sacking 1000 workers, whose side are you on? Are you on the employer's or the workers'? I know whose side I'm on. And therefore all the time, whilst you're representing your constituents you're representing them in a way in which you believe that that's the group that want lifting over the stile.

RD Mr Healey accused you on one occasion in the National Executive of the Labour Party, accused you of 'proletarian humbug'. And he said – and I quote Mr Healey: 'You don't carry a certificate to speak for the working class any more than I do.' That was Denis Healey speaking. What's your answer to that?

SKINNER I think he's right in the sense that I don't hold a certificate – hold a certificate any more than he does. The only point that I was making is that in those circumstances of having put the bank rate up massively, what he was doing was not acting on behalf of the working-class interest. Because he had said – and others, the whole government had said – that the reason why we had the IMF package and the reason why they wouldn't adopt the alternative strategy is because they were going to have a strong pound, they were going to have strong reserves and so on, so we could withstand all these short-term fluctuations. And my point was the first time that we got some short-term fluctuations on the foreign exchanges the bank rate shot up, and with a result of it a credit squeeze, people being thrown out of work and so on. So it was in that context.

RD Forgive me, as they say in Parliament, if I don't follow you on those interesting points because we've come to the end of the programme. Can I just ask you this: for all you have said about Parliament and its club atmosphere and the privilege and everything else, are you proud of being a Member of Parliament?

SKINNER I'm proud to represent people who thought, way back in about

1970, that I ought to be the man for the job. Because throughout the whole of my industrial life in terms of the trade union activities, in terms of local government, when I've been elected to these positions, I think that it's an honour to be able to represent working-class people, to try and do, in a small way perhaps, advance their well being. Yes, I'm proud of it in that sense.

RD Mr Skinner, thank you very much indeed for appearing in this series with me.

'Would you please quote, Mr Day? Would you please quote what you are saying?'

MARGARET THATCHER

1983

This *Panorama* interview is remembered by some people for an utterly trivial and irrelevant happening. As I said to her immediately afterwards, 'It's not important, it does not matter to me, but the viewers will notice.' I was referring to the fact that she had addressed me as *Mr* Day throughout. Gordon Reece, her TV adviser, came over to her and said, 'Prime Minister, you seem to have stripped Sir Robin of his knighthood.' But it did not bother me in the slightest. The knighthood was very recent. I was still frequently addressed as Mr Day.

Some Tory viewers were outraged at what they thought was discourtesy by the Prime Minister. Others wondered if she had been delivering a snub. But of course her slip was accidental. She had simply addressed me as she had been accustomed to address me in all the previous ten years or so. And in our interview she was concentrating on matters like mass unemployment and nuclear weapons.

This interview was done during the 1983 campaign, the second of three elections in which she triumphed. Mrs Thatcher's first government, formed in 1979, had had a troubled start. Unemployment and inflation had risen. Her determined pursuit of monetarism, with government spending cuts, provoked almost open Cabinet revolt. By the end of 1981, according to the opinion polls, Britain's first woman Prime Minister was also the most unpopular Prime Minister on record. By the spring of 1982 the parties (including the Alliance of Liberals with the new SDP) were level-pegging. Then the political scene was transformed by the Falklands War. By June 1982, when the Falkland Islands were recaptured, the Conservatives had soared into a comfortable lead, which they were to keep for some years. In the Falklands War was heard the resounding smack of firm leadership from Margaret Thatcher.

There was another bonus for her in the 1983 campaign. The Labour Party had elected Michael Foot as leader to succeed Jim Callaghan. Labour's manifesto was later described by Gerald Kaufman as 'the longest suicide note in history'. It promised to scrap nuclear weapons, to leave the European Community, to nationalize more industries.

My interview with Mrs Thatcher ten days before polling day was for one of the three election editions of *Panorama*. According to the opinion polls, the question that night was not whether the Tories would win, but by how much. There was concern (and not only in the opposition parties) about what the effect of a massive Tory majority would be. Some Tory 'moderates' or 'wets' were worried that if there was a Thatcher landslide the vague language of the Tory manifesto might turn into a blank cheque for unspecified Thatcherite extremism.

But though the opinion polls pointed to a Tory victory the campaign arguments offered much to ask the Prime Minister – about mass unemployment, about her autocratic style of government, about her intentions for the NHS, about why Britain needed an independent nuclear deterrent. Unfortunately my interview was marred by an unedifying wrangle about the cost of having three million unemployed. The figure put to her by me was an authoritative and widely-quoted estimate, but the Prime Minister insisted that this was 'false, phoney and distorted'. Her estimated cost and the figure I had quoted were both arguable. But you could not have an argument about statistics in a TV interview. When I asked about the high cost of mass unemployment, there was no need for me to have quoted a particular figure which she would challenge.

Reaction to this 'bruising encounter' (as the press called it) was mixed. My own immediate feeling was that I had handled it badly. I said as much to the press. To *The Times*, I doubted if it was useful to the people for the Prime Minister and an interviewer to have a wrangle about statistics. The responsibility was mine.

But Mrs Thatcher had certainly come determined to beat down her interrogator. She came in carrying a huge array of papers and reference material ready for use – and she used them. No Prime Minister had ever before come to an interview with me thus armed. I was pleasantly relieved to read the *Guardian* account by the veteran Ian Aitken. He described it as 'a devastating forty-minute interview on BBC *Panorama*, the most courageous of a long and abrasive career'. Perhaps I was a bit too apologetic in my own reaction.

This memorable interview, though acrimonious and heavy in parts, was not without its sparkle. I shall long cherish the memory of one piece of dialogue which the reader will find here in its full context. I ask if the less Thatcherite Cabinet Ministers would be sacked if there were a Thatcher victory. She answers that all Prime Ministers want all views in Cabinet. Then we continue:

RD So Mr Pym, and Mr Prior, and Mr Whitelaw and Mr Walker are not necessarily going to go?

THATCHER You are going further than I wish to go.

RD Well, naturally. That's part of my job, Prime Minister.

THATCHER Yes, indeed. It's part of my job to try to stop you.

Ten days later she won an overall majority of 144. Her Foreign Secretary, Francis Pym, who had warned that massive landslides did not produce successful governments, was promptly sacked. The Thatcher ascendancy was here – to stay for another seven years.

The Rt Hon. Margaret Thatcher,
Prime Minister

Interviewed for BBC Election Panorama *from Downing Street*
31 May 1983

SIR ROBIN DAY Prime Minister, do you understand why some people, including some of your own Tory people, are worried at the thought of you getting too big a majority?

RT HON. MARGARET THATCHER, PRIME MINISTER No, I don't, because there's only one way to be certain that Conservatives get a majority at all and that is to support the Conservative candidate in each and every constituency. Otherwise some people might say, 'Well, they're going to get a big majority, we'll not vote for them here,' and the result could be that we got no majority at all but that Labour does get a majority, and that would not, I believe, correspond with the wishes of the majority of our people.

RD But what do you say to the thought which must worry some people that the elective dictatorship of a huge Commons majority should not be in the hand of someone so dogmatic and strongwilled as yourself?

THATCHER I believe in certain things. I believe in them very strongly. Those things I place before the people openly in the manifesto. We did last time, they now had not only our last time's manifesto but our performance, they have this time's manifesto and the majority does not alter what is in the manifesto in any way. The policies, whether it is a majority of twenty, forty, or 200, are precisely the same. What it does change is the authority with which you're viewed abroad. If you get a really good majority then they know that you have the authority for the policies you're putting forward.

RD None the less, if you get a majority of 150 instead of a majority of fifteen that would raise your morale and would encourage you to go forward with – perhaps this is the view – policies which are perhaps a little more Thatcherite than some of those in the manifesto?

THATCHER No, I shall carry on in exactly the same way as I have in the last four years. I believe certain things very strongly. We follow those things, we persist in those things. But we're always ready to help to cushion some of the harsh effects of some of the world recession.

And, indeed, you know, I have. People were quite surprised that we went on supporting British Leyland. I did because I knew the devastating effect on the West Midlands and on other places if we didn't. But we didn't just say, 'Look, here's the taxpayers' money.' We said: 'Look, you've got to earn it. You've got to perform better. You've got to stop your striking.' And so we achieved two things: we helped them to a better performance, but we helped many many people through difficult times.

RD A serious charge is being levelled at you in the middle of this campaign, Prime Minister, and that is that you're trying to con the electorate with what appears to be a relatively moderate manifesto and you're concealing your real intentions. This is the charge. What do you say to it?

THATCHER It is an absurd charge. I believe most people know that I've been absolutely honest about what we're going to do and why we're going to do it. But there's one other thing. At the beginning of this campaign, I was warning that this would happen. The reason is because the same thing happened during the last campaign. Let me read you an example, it came up at the Press Conference this morning, so I'm ready for it. During the last campaign the Labour Party then ran a scare story – several scare stories – first to recut pensions. Secondly, that we would abandon the National Health Service. This is what Mr Hattersley actually said on 19 April 1979. He said there can be no doubt that when Mrs Thatcher talks about Tory cuts in public expenditure, the future levels of pensions is an item high on her list. That was his last time's scare. Note the similarity with this time's. Let me look what was our performance. Let me give you our performance. The retirement pension was £19 for a single person, £19.50 when we took over. It's now £32.85. For a married couple, when we took over, it was £31.20. It's now £52.55. That was our performance. It's over and above the increase in prices. The scare was cruel, callous and designed to make frightened the very people whom we all wish to protect. There's another one on the National Health Service, but you carry on with your questions and I'll try to supply the answers.

RD If I may, Prime Minister, because –

THATCHER They must not heed those scares. They're cold, callous and ruthless. And they make frightened the very people we should be protecting.

RD If we go back to 19 April 1979, that happens to be the same date on which you said you'd had no intention of putting up prescription charges?

THATCHER Would you please quote, Mr Day? Would you please quote what you are saying?

RD Yes.

THATCHER Would you please quote precisely?

RD Yes, I can because I heard you say it at the Press Conference this morning, and I know what you're going to tell me, but you said, 'no government could possibly give a commitment to say they wouldn't go up.'

THATCHER Let me give you whole –

RD You did say you had no intention ... Let's not get involved in too many detailed quotations, Prime Minister ... you did say you had no intention of putting up prescription charges?

THATCHER Let me give you the question and the answer. Not interpretations, but what came from the actual Press Conference in the last election. The question: Accepting the pledge you've made that you'll continue to spend the same amount on the Health Service, not reduce it. But can you make a specific statement that you would not increase prescription charges, and that you would not charge for visits to the doctor or for hospital stays? Answer: I cannot make specific statements. I don't think there'll be any question of charging for visits to a doctor. I doubt very much whether any responsible government could say that over a period of five years, regardless of what happened to the value of money, they would not put up prescription charges. I doubt whether they could.

RD But did you not also say you had no intention of putting them up at that time?

THATCHER They went on questioning me and I said it is not my intention to raise these charges –

RD That is what I said.

THATCHER Yes, indeed. But what was quoted this morning was that I had given an undertaking not to put up prescription charges.

RD I didn't –

THATCHER One moment, Mr Day –

RD I didn't accuse you of giving an undertaking. I said that you had said that you had no intention of so doing and yet a few weeks afterwards you did increase them.

THATCHER Indeed, yes, we had to. Don't forget that when we got into office and looked at the books Labour had left us with a debt of twenty-two billion dollars. We've now, in spite of world recession, paid off ten billion of that, the rest is still round our necks and round the necks of our children, if we don't manage to pay it off. I was quite clear that no government could give that undertaking. I could not give that undertaking now, and do not. I gave two undertakings then. One was that I would not put, or not institute charges for stays in hospitals nor for going to the doctor. I repeat those pledges. Those are ones that we can give. What I cannot take is totally and utter selective quoting designed to deceive, and it was designed to deceive. In the meantime, may I point out that we have spent far more on the National Health Service than ever Labour did. We have more doctors, we have more nurses, and our performance on the National Health Service excels anything which they were able to achieve.

RD Can I now come to the substance of the matter and to ask you whether there is any intention at all on your part, if you're returned to power, of privatizing the National Health Service in some way or other or changing the basis on which it is funded?

THATCHER We already co-operate between the National Health Service and the private sector, and it makes sense for both to do so. For example, many beds in the National Health Service are taken up by geriatric patients who have nowhere to go, therefore they have to be looked after. Honestly, it doesn't make sense to have them in hospital beds when they really need looking after rather than medical attention. And we already co-operate. Some of them go out under contract with the National Health Service to private nursing homes where they're looked after. That is to the benefit of the National Health Service and to the benefit of those who run private nursing homes, and it's a very very good thing. We have no intention of changing the finance of the National Health Service. As you know Sir Alec Merrison looked at this and had a major report upon it, and it's very interesting. But we have no intention of changing it, it will continue to be financed by taxation.

RD Do you stand by your statement of last October (and I quote), Prime Minister: 'The National Health Service is safe with us. The principle that adequate health care should be provided for all regardless of ability to pay must be the foundation of any arrangements for financing the National Health Service.'

THATCHER Yes, Mr Day –

RD Then why isn't that in the manifesto?

THATCHER Because no one had ever thought that there would again be a charge of the kind we had in the last election that we would dismantle the National Health Service. It was proved to be false, bogus and phoney last time.

RD But you made the statement twice. Once at the Tory Conference, once in the House of Commons –

THATCHER Please may I answer? It is false, bogus, phoney and calculated to deceive this time. The National Health Service is safe with us. Our performance in the National Health Service is better than that of the last Labour government, and I would no more think of dismantling the National Health Service than I would think of dismantling our defence forces.

RD If you do get a big majority, Prime Minister, would you see that as a clear mandate for continuing your policy of high unemployment?

THATCHER I have not a policy of high unemployment. I have a policy for securing a better standard of living for all of our people and a policy for procuring jobs in the longer run. That has to be done on a sound financial basis, not on borrowing from the IMF, money which the Labour Party couldn't possibly repay. Not of having a false boom which goes to a bust, but steady, continuous, sound financial policies. Steady rise in industrial efficiency. Steady policies of pleasing the customer and then you win the jobs. Those policies are the right ones. And I think people in their hearts and minds know that. The whole world has been hit by the world recession. Twenty-six million people are out of work ...

RD Are you saying that the increase of unemployment is entirely due to the world recession?

THATCHER Not entirely, no. I think there are four reasons. One is the world recession, another is that at the same time we've got all the newly industrialized countries of the Far East producing the goods which we used to produce and marketing them here and overseas. That is new competition. Thirdly, we've got new technologies coming. The first effect of those new technologies is, as you know, to take away unskilled and semi-skilled jobs. The next effect is to create more jobs, and more jobs are being created now, because it makes possible all sorts of products that we never thought of before. The fourth one in this country is that we were hit harder because we had never dealt with certain things in the past – overmanning, restrictive practices. For the whole decade of the seventies our inflation was at a higher rate than that of our competitors. And one of the worst things of all, people regarded themselves as having an absolute right to increases in pay regardless of output, and regardless of industrial performance. Those things were worse here. And we had to tackle those as well.

RD Do you say that your government has had no responsibility whatever for the increase in unemployment since 1979?

THATCHER In putting inflation top priority to get it down it meant that in the short run we'd have a bigger increase in unemployment. It means in the longer run – and the longer run is that which will happen in the next Parliament – in the longer run our jobs will be better and more secure and have better prospects for the future.

RD So you do accept responsibility –

THATCHER I accept that I had to take a decision as between the short run which would have meant you could have phoney short-run jobs which would have come out in higher longer-term unemployment. I think it's better to pursue a policy which gives our young people better prospects for good jobs which they can keep, and therefore they can begin to plan their future around something that is much more built on rock than the sandy, phoney, high-inflation, boom or bust policies.

RD Does your policy of continuing to reduce inflation require a further increase in unemployment?

THATCHER No, it does not. What is more, the policy of reducing inflation now is protecting the jobs of the twenty-three and a half million people in work. And if we ever went to a higher – policy of high inflation, many many of those twenty-three and a half million people in work would be very very fearful indeed. A lot of them are in work for exports, a lot of them have to compete with imports into this country and a much bigger proportion of those twenty-three and a half million jobs would be at risk. And it would be at risk now if I hadn't pursued the policies I have. And I think we're coming to the time when the rate of unemployment would have been higher in this country had Labour pursued their policies, and in the future it'll be much higher. To go back to a policy of high inflation would put twenty-three and a half million jobs at risk. And to come out of Europe would put a lot more as well.

RD When do you think unemployment will start to come down, Prime Minister?

THATCHER I am very wary of predicting when. I know the opportunities are there. I go round and see companies – new companies starting, and in the last two years there's been a net increase of 20,000 more companies which have started. I go round to the new technologies as

I did all day Friday. There were marvellous success stories there. But some of the older industries are still in difficulty – some of the steel and the coal and there's still overmanning on the railways. And those are still coming down while the others are going up. But the new jobs are coming. I'm wary of when the cross-over point will come, but I believe that within a reasonable time – if you ask me just precisely what is a reasonable time, I can't really put a time on it – that there are more opportunities and that there'll be a good chance if those opportunities are taken. And if people give us a fair chance then unemployment will come down.

RD Do you promise that unemployment will come down in your next term of office, if you get one?

THATCHER I believe it will. I cannot promise it. I cannot. One moment, I'll tell you why. I could not foretell that people in good jobs in Halewood on Merseyside would go on strike and let the world know that when they've got good jobs and they've got good prospects they nevertheless put them in jeopardy by striking. I could not foretell that people in British Leyland, just when the taxpayer's given them money to produce two excellent cars – the Metro and Maestro – they'd tell the world that Britain is unreliable as a deliverer of cars if they went on strike. It depends on people. Democracy depends upon people, exercising their own responsibilities. We in government will exercise ours and give them every chance and every opportunity.

RD None the less, the tradition since the war has been accepted by all governments, from Churchill through to Heath, that governments have a responsibility to maintain full employment. Have you turned back on that principle?

THATCHER No. I have not. This is a question that frequently comes up. I have carried this employment policy White Paper with me for many years –

RD So I've heard, Prime Minister.

THATCHER So you've heard. It's even got my maiden name on top – Margaret Roberts. Let's look at what that says –

RD Don't read too much of it, will you?

THATCHER No, it's on my side. I'll gladly read you the whole lot. But let's have a look at one of those which is right at the beginning, and I've quoted it before, but not on television.

RD Yes, paragraph 56?

THATCHER No, right at the end of the foreword. I'll quote you paragraph

56 too, if you'd like. It says this: The success of the policy outlined in this paper will ultimately depend on the understanding and support of the community as a whole, and specially on the efforts of employers and workers in industry, for without a rising standard of industrial efficiency we cannot achieve a high level of employment combined with a rising standard of living. Mr Day, that's pure Thatcherism. Now do you want paragraph 56?

RD Well, it might help if you like, because it says something about private enterprise – letting people stand on their own feet?

THATCHER No, it says: For if an expansion of total expenditure were applied to cure unemployment of a type due not to absence of jobs but to failure of workers to move to places and occupations where they were needed, the policy of the government would be frustrated and a dangerous rise in prices might follow. I think what you really meant was paragraph 54?

RD That's right.

THATCHER Workers must examine their trade practices and customs to ensure that they do not constitute a serious impediment to an expansionist economy and so defeat the object of a full employment programme. There are a lot more paragraphs ... I think you might like to ask another question. But you see that policy for full employment is the policy which I am pursuing.

RD Well, then, what do you say to what Mr Prior said the other day, Prime Minister. He said this, and I quote: 'You can't tell people the whole time that they must take the medicine unless it is going to result in something better for them afterwards.'

THATCHER Yes, but I believe that there are already signs of recovery. And I answer it in that way. And if you look today at the CBI survey you'll find that they too have said that improvements in the economy continue. So there are signs. Also, don't forget inflation down itself – down to 4 per cent – is enormously good news for everyone who saves; everyone who's got savings in building societies, in National Savings – that's a lot of people. Every old age pensioner who's saved, everyone who wants to invest in industry. They know that if inflation is down they won't suddenly find the cost of their investment running ahead of their resources. Everyone who wants to rebuild stocks, everyone who wants to invest in housing and the construction of housing. That itself is good news for those people, and good news for jobs. Productivity up 14 per cent. That's good news for everyone who works in industry. It means we can hold up our heads and

compete. It means that we're rising to the challenge of the times. It
means that Britain has a new self-confidence –

RD But is not the challenge of the times, particularly for the Western
world, mass unemployment? And you did not put, as I understand
it, any proposals forward at the Williamsburg summit for joint
concerted – for expansion and growth to deal with unemployment
such as, for instance, Mr Heath has argued for and many others ...
and Mr Jenkins?

THATCHER The whole of the Williamsburg communiqué and the whole
of our discussions were about trying to get a better standard of living,
and that is a quotation from the document, if you've got it there. A
better standard of living and more jobs. The methods were set out
there. Again, if I might say so, the viewpoint of the seven industrialized
nations, their leaders, their finance ministers, their advisers, is to
endorse the policies I am pursuing. Let me go over it, it is in the
communiqué itself. If you want me to quote from it I will. It is: Get
inflation down. Get interest rates down. Get deficits down. We've
done all of those things – and keep a firm control on expenditure.
Try to persuade people that they must accept new technology because
in the end it will produce more jobs. That's what we're doing and
we're giving grants for new products and new technology to try and
get them on to the market. Try to stop protectionism, because in fact
if we get an expansion of world trade it helps industries – it helps
countries that export. In the meantime, you must help those people
who are unemployed and particularly help the young and have massive
training schemes. We have the biggest ones ever started in this
country. The most exciting go-ahead one starting in September. But
we don't wait for that. We also have £1000 million being spent to
help the unemployed on special measures. Every single one of those
things which they endorse. And they say we have to do these things
together, because that's the way in which to get an expansion –

RD Was not the Williamsburg summit, however, a failure from the point
of view of those who wanted to see those great industrial nations
commit themselves, as they did at a previous summit, to a certain
degree of growth – to expand their economies?

THATCHER They are referring back to the Bonn summit which urged
those countries which in fact had been very wise and prudent in
financial policies and had got inflation down. They asked them to
reflate by 1 per cent. In other words they urged those who'd run
prudent policies to run imprudent ones. Germany did it and her

inflation went up and ultimately her unemployment went up, and she will never do it again. They were asking them to run unsound policies. They tried it once and they won't again. Look at what happened to running those unsound policies. We ran into the worst bout of unemployment we've known in the post-war period.

RD Why does the government prefer to spend £15 billion or more, Prime Minister, a year to keep people doing nothing rather than spend some at least of that to encourage them to do something less wasteful and more constructive?

THATCHER I don't know where you get the £15 billion pounds from –

RD Well, can I tell you?

THATCHER Yes, it's a totally inaccurate figure, and it's based on not getting income tax in, which we would get if people were in work. The precise figure of spending on people who are unemployed I will give to you. It's been given in the House of Commons many times. It is five and a half billion. Of that 1.8 billion comes out of the National Insurance Fund for unemployment benefit for which people are insured. The difference between 1.8 billion and five and a half billion is because most people who are unemployed are on social security payments which tops up their unemployment, and the actual figure paid out to help those who're unemployed to have a reasonable standard of living is five and a half billion. Some of them go out and do part-time work, they can do a certain amount. That's the actual figure. We also spend one billion on special employment measures, including temporary part-time working compensation, including community programmes to help the long-term unemployed and added to that we're spending an extra billion on the training programmes. I can't stand false, phoney, distorted figures . . .

RD Well, they're neither false, phoney nor distorted, Prime Minister, and you know that I wouldn't put them to you if they were. The figure of £15 billion, now estimated at £16 billion or £17 billion, that is the amount used in the large number of expert documents, including the All-Party House of Lords Select Committee on Unemployment and it quotes that figure. But anyway whatever the figure is –

THATCHER No, no, no, I have not finished –

RD Whatever the figure is, why do we spend money on keeping people unemployed rather than giving them constructive work to do which a lot of people suggest would be more sensible?

THATCHER I'm coming back to that figure. I have given you the precise sums which are paid out –

RD But that's one way of looking at the figures, Prime Minister, we can't have an argument about statistics. I can't contradict you, and I've quoted that one in good faith.

THATCHER Mr Day, you raised the statistic. That statistic –

RD But it's the one in common use in discussions.

THATCHER I'm very sorry. What I'm saying is that it is the wrong one. The actual figure paid out on unemployment is five and a half billion. The figure you have calculated is what they might be paid on average earnings and the tax they pay which is lost, because we have unemployment. But it's nothing to do with the amount paid out for unemployment. I've indicated we pay out five and a half billion. We're perfectly right to do so. I've indicated we've got two billion on special employment measures to help the unemployed. If half of those people who talk about unemployment knew how to go about and build and start and create new business, employ people and expand and really create genuine jobs in future, I'm mystified why they don't stop talking and do so.

RD So every time Roy Jenkins or any other person of responsible expertise talks about £15 billion being spent on keeping people unemployed in one way or another that's a lot of nonsense, is it?

THATCHER I give you the precise figures and I urge you to go and look at the calculation of that other which is based upon assuming that everyone has a job. Assuming that they're paid average wages and then calculating income that will be lost. If everyone had a job, that would be absolutely marvellous, but those people who talk about it are not those people who have any idea how to create and build up an industry for themselves.

RD Could we turn to the subject of defence, Prime Minister, because one can't spend the whole time on these extremely interesting economic questions. Were you able to get at the Williamsburg summit in your private talks with President Reagan any satisfaction on the question of dual key control of the Cruise missiles expected in this country?

THATCHER Dual key did not come up in the summit because we had already dealt with it before ... we had already dealt with the problem of joint decision. The argument was that the joint decision had not been reviewed in the light of the deployment of Cruise missiles either on or off base. Joint decision, as you know, is the formula that has stood from the time of Mr Attlee with Mr Truman through all Prime Ministers, Conservative or Labour, with the American Presidents. We reviewed that, and it does apply to both Cruise missiles on base and off base, and you'll have seen that President Reagan gave an interview on it. And asked if that meant that we had a veto, he said: 'Yes, of course, it does.'

RD Did you ask for at any time, either this weekend or before, for dual control, or dual key control, as Dr Owen says?

THATCHER No, we have not because we were offered it right at the beginning if we should purchase the missiles. It did not seem to me the best use of money to purchase those missiles. What the Americans were doing was offering those to us and to everyone else who stations them, for our own protection, for our own deterrence against the Soviet Union. When you're offered that, you do not in fact say: 'All right, I will pay for it.' We have other things to do with our money, and it's very generous of them to offer them to us free. And so we said: 'Right, the joint decision will continue to apply,' and now that has been published.

RD Do you understand that many British people, including many of your own supporters, would be happier if they knew that the British Prime Minister had a finger on the Cruise safety-catch.

THATCHER What I think they're saying is that they distrust our staunchest allies. I do not. And if they tackle it in that way, what they're doing is undermining the whole of the NATO – the trust of the NATO alliance, which is that if one is attacked we are all attacked. What they're doing is saying that what has been all right and satisfactory for every Labour Prime Minister, every Conservative Prime Minister until now is no longer satisfactory because they mistrust. I do not mistrust. Even a veto doesn't quite accurately express it, because it's deeper than that. Yes, we do have a veto. But should the commander-in-chief – should war start and the commander-in-chief come on and wished to use nuclear forces it isn't that America decides and then asks us if we agree. We're all in it together – we're in the thing consulting the whole time as to whether a decision should begin to form. If you cannot trust your staunchest ally who has done so much for the defence of Europe, which has 350,000 of her soldiers stationed in Europe and their families, which in fact had the Marshall Plan for Europe, which is taking the role of policeman all over to keep peace with freedom and justice, then you are fundamentally undermining, and wilfully undermining the whole of our defence strategy.

RD What are the circumstances, Prime Minister, in which you or any other British Prime Minister would have to use or would have to be ready to use the British strategic deterrent – Polaris or Trident – independently of America or NATO?

THATCHER The British independent deterrent is total last resort deterrent, if we ourselves were threatened by the Soviet Union. Our Polaris strategic missiles are only $2\frac{1}{2}$ per cent of what the Soviet Union has – we face something like 2600 –

RD Why do we actually need it. Why can't we trust our American allies?

THATCHER Because I cannot in the end rely upon not being threatened separately. After all we had to stand alone last time, and this is a total last resort.

RD May I put to you on that point what a former Chief of the Defence Staff said – Field Marshal Lord Carver – and I had better quote his words accurately: 'I can conceive of no circumstances in which it would be right, responsible or realistic for the Prime Minister of the United Kingdom to authorize the use of British nuclear weapons when the President of the United States was not prepared to authorize the use of any US nuclear weapons.'

THATCHER But with all due respect to him, his views are not shared by other Chiefs of Staff, and with all due respect to him, he's missed the point. The point about nuclear weapons is not use: it is to deter other people from the use either of nuclear weapons, chemical weapons, biological weapons, conventional weapons, because that's what they've got. And do you know bullies go for people who are weak. They do not go for people who can deter. This is a deterrent weapon. It has worked not only to stop nuclear war, but to stop any other kind of conventional war, and even conventional is terrible.

RD But it only deters if the Russians believe that it will be used?

THATCHER Of course, that is a deterrent. If they believed that someone was just sitting there and saying, 'Well, we've got them, but don't worry anyone in Moscow, don't worry you lot in the Kremlin, of course we'd never use it,' it wouldn't be a deterrent and you'd be liable to have either theirs used or they'd start a conventional war and could sweep across Europe and sweep across us as well. It is a deterrent. It has kept the peace in Europe for thirty-eight years. That is to be the greatest price of all.

RD Is Polaris a deterrent against conventional attack only or only against nuclear attack?

THATCHER It is a deterrent against a major war starting in Europe. Now if you had no nuclear deterrent, I thought the point was put very well. I think it was Group Captain Cheshire ... who said, 'Look, if you haven't got nuclear weapons you then just couldn't fight anyone who had. There wouldn't be any point in starting to fight them with conventional. Right, you fight with conventional, we use nuclear.' The only alternative to nuclear deterrent is surrender or capitulation. Surrender or capitulation for Britain? Never.

RD Let me move to another form of deterrent, if I may, Prime Minister, that involved in our own problem of law and order. If a House of Commons under a large Tory majority were by a free vote to vote to bring back capital punishment for murder would the government under you feel obliged to introduce a Bill to give effect to that wish?

THATCHER Yes, of course we should. I have always voted for capital punishment. I believe – and it is an individual belief and I speak now as a Conservative candidate because each person has a free vote on this. I'm speaking not as leader of a party, but as a Conservative candidate. I believe that there are some people who'll be deterred if they knew that should they murder someone else they would suffer the final penalty. So if we got a majority then, and as Willie Whitelaw said in our press conference the other day, we should honour that majority and bring in a Bill to restore capital punishment.

RD For what?

THATCHER Well, for murder –

RD All murders as before?

THATCHER Well, indeed. You have to decide what is murder, what is manslaughter, what is first degree murder, what is second degree murder, what are the defence. And as you know there was a very very complicated law before, but you'd have to bring in capital punishment as 'a punishment' for murder, not as the only punishment. You know there was a time when for murder capital punishment was the 'only punishment'. At the moment capital punishment is not available as a sentence. It will be available as one sentence for murder, and of course the rest will be up to the Judge as to which sentence he imposed.

RD But are you sure that you want capital punishment for terrorist murders, bearing in mind that one type of murderer who may not be deterred is the fanatical, political terrorist. Indeed, why have we abolished capital punishment by a Conservative government in Northern Ireland?

THATCHER Capital punishment, as you know, has been abolished really by a free vote of the House of Commons. I think it was back in 1956. It was before I was in the House, and I think it was abolished then. I believe that capital punishment should be available, and I believe there are some acts of terrorism which are so hideous, so callous, so cold-blooded and so cruel that it would be as well if the sentence of capital punishment were available for that. The precise detail of a Bill would have to go through the House of Commons. First we'd have to get a vote to bring it back. Then a Bill would have to go through all its stages. So I stress I am talking on this subject as a Conservative candidate, as a person –

RD Yes, yes, but your government would obey the wish of the House of Commons and bring in a Bill and advise Parliament on how it should be done?

THATCHER Government is accountable to the House of Commons. It is a pride of our democratic system that we are.

RD Could we just come towards the end of this interview, Prime Minister? May I ask you this, and if the voters (coming back to the General Election campaign), are the voters not entitled to ask you, if you are elected again, whether you will have a Cabinet consisting solely of hard-line Thatcherites or whether those who are known to be less strongly Thatcherite in their opinions will be ditched – sacked?

THATCHER I'm not going to form my Cabinet again before I've won an election. But let me just say this. I think all Prime Ministers have all views of their party reflected in their Cabinet.

RD So Mr Pym and Mr Prior and Mr Whitelaw and Mr Walker are not necessarily going to go?

THATCHER You're going further than I wish to go.

RD Well, naturally, that's part of my job, Prime Minister.

THATCHER Yes, indeed. It's part of my job to try to stop you. All Prime Ministers have various views in their party reflected in their Cabinet because you have still to keep your party together. And it is not just stones coming down and handed out to people. We are a party. We believe strongly in certain things. We discuss them among one another. We even talk to one another in the Conservative Party and discuss together, and we form those policies. We set out our broad direction, and I have a Cabinet which has carried out our broad direction and carried it out very well. We keep the whole party together and we've done it very well.

RD I asked you that question, Prime Minister, not simply to be mis-chievous but because many voters who might be deciding whether to vote for the Alliance might worry, well if she wins a whacking great majority she's going to get rid of all those 'wets' and she's just going to go on on her own line but ...

THATCHER Perhaps you've been very kind and given me the opportunity to indicate my views, but may I also point out no Cabinet Minister has resigned of his own accord from my Cabinet save John Nott who went because he was not going to stand again, and not on any matter of policy.

RD As we enter these last few days of the campaign, Prime Minister, are you afraid that people who might otherwise have voted for you to prevent a left-wing Labour government will now feel free to vote Alliance because they don't see any chance of a left-wing Labour government, any danger of one, and that you've got a huge lead?

THATCHER There is always a chance of a Labour government getting into power on polling day, which is the only poll that counts, unless more Conservative members are returned to Parliament on that day, and to think that you have some latitude is totally and utterly wrong. The exercise of that latitude could lead in fact to the return of a Labour government even though the people do not want that. And so there's only one way to ensure that a Labour government is not returned and does not carry out that very extreme manifesto, and I believe that indicates the truth of what they would do, and that is to ensure that we have a good Conservative majority. Only one way, and don't look at the polls – no poll matters – until the one on polling day. And that's the way you actually vote . . .

RD Finally, Prime Minister, why have you refused an invitation to take part in direct debate with the other two party leaders. Wouldn't that be better than bandying statistics with interviewers and so on?

THATCHER No, I believe you get more thorough chance to question me in the way in which you are doing it now. The others, and I've seen some of them, they start to shout at one another, they talk over one another. I've had it every Tuesday and Thursday in Parliament for four years. It is not conducive to getting the true policies and good debate. It is clash, it is hurling insults, it is making false allegations. This is much better, this is considered, it is studied, I give you considered replies and I believe you get much better idea of the true manifesto and the true policies this way.

RD Prime Minister, may I apologize to you for having interrupted you occasionally. I had to make the same apology to Mr Jenkins last week. I did so simply out of enthusiasm for the subject and the interest of the viewer.

THATCHER That's all right, I can cope with you.

'I decide with others the way we're going, then I bend every single effort to getting that through, overcoming all obstacles. It isn't arrogance, in my view. It is determination and resolve.'

MARGARET THATCHER

She had now won two general elections and had been in power for eight years. If she won again in this 1987 election, she would be the first British Prime Minister to have been elected to three consecutive terms of office since Lord Liverpool, over 150 years ago.

Strong claims could be made for Margaret Thatcher's leadership. Had she not rolled back the state, curbed the trade unions, defeated Scargill, Galtieri and Ken Livingstone, and defied terrorism? She had narrowly escaped assassination in the Brighton bomb atrocity.

Inflation had stayed in the 4–5 per cent range. The pound was strong. The economy was growing. But the second Thatcher government had seen some rough weather. There was the violence during the prolonged miners' strike, and in the printers' dispute at Wapping. There was the Westland helicopter affair, when normal Cabinet government disintegrated. Heseltine walked out of the Cabinet and Thatcher came perilously near to falling from power. There was certainly no shortage of ammunition for critics of Thatcherism in the 1987 campaign.

Labour, with its media skills, and a brilliant film boosting its new leader, Neil Kinnock, was widely held to have won the campaign. But it lost the election.

Mrs Thatcher herself had developed her formidable bull-dozing technique in television interviews. Two university research psychologists analysed this interview. They made the following solemn comment on my reference to the need for the interviewer to ask questions: 'The fact that such an experienced and eminent interviewer as Sir Robin Day should need to justify his role in this way is a very striking example of the way in which Margaret Thatcher's tactics put the interviewer on the defensive.'*

Many viewers may have felt that such tactics by a party leader seeking election are for the voters to judge. What did it matter if a TV interviewer is brushed aside or put in his place? As Mr Roy Hattersley (a shrewd if not impartial critic) wrote: 'Mrs Thatcher's appeal is to the viewer who observes "Say what you like, she doesn't stand any nonsense. They don't push her around." '

To be fair, Mr Heath as Prime Minister was also a dominating and wordy interviewee, but he did not brush aside his questioner.

I make no complaint whatever for myself. In fact I enjoyed the uphill battle to interject the necessary questions. But I could not help feeling that a healthy principle of British television was being destroyed, namely the principle that if a politician agrees to an interview on television there should be reasonable opportunity to put critical questions. This, after all, was the distinction between an interview and a party political broadcast.

Whether I am right or wrong, the text of this memorable performance by Margaret Thatcher is now offered for the reader's cool judgment. It should be added that her television style did not prevent her from winning another huge majority of 102, not as huge as in 1983, but another three-figure landslide none the less.

This 1987 election was a triumph for what had come to be called Thatcherism. Few people, if any (certainly not I), then thought that this three-times victor, this invincible vote-getter, this woman so admired around the world, would soon be forced out of office. Yet three years later, in 1990, that is what happened to Margaret Thatcher. For the first time ever in peacetime, a British Prime Minister in good health, commanding a majority in the Commons, was kicked out of office.

This interview of June 1987 includes a classic definition of Thatcherism from the horse's mouth. It is the gospel according to Margaret. She is on her top form, in full flow, almost unstoppable. In content and style, this is vintage Thatcher. My attempts to

---

* Peter Bull and Kate Meyer, *Journal of Language and Social Psychology*, vol. 7, no. 1, 1988.

interject were frequently cut short and did not always win viewer approval. At one point I am driven to suggest that we were 'not having a party political broadcast but an interview, which must depend on me asking some questions occasionally'. According to Richard Last, the admirable TV critic of the *Daily Telegraph*, I was 'crushed with the effortlessness of a beautifully coiffured steamroller flattening a blancmange'.

The Rt Hon. Margaret Thatcher, Prime Minister

Interviewed for BBC Election Panorama from Downing Street 8 June 1987

SIR ROBIN DAY Prime Minister, if you win this election you'll be the first British Prime Minister to have been elected to three consecutive terms of office for well over a hundred years. Now why should the British people give to Margaret Thatcher that prize which they denied to Gladstone, to Disraeli, to Salisbury, even to Churchill?

RT HON. MARGARET THATCHER, PRIME MINISTER I wonder why you put the re-election of a Conservative government so much on my name. There has been a third Conservative government re-elected, and in my first time in Parliament in 1959 was one such. We were elected in 1951, we were returned in 1955 and we were returned again in 1959. It was Conservative policies that were re-elected. And as I hope this Thursday it will be Conservative policies that are re-elected. The fact that I am the leader does not seem to me to be the most material thing. It is the policies that people are voting for and when it comes to decide you have to look at those policies and consider what the alternatives are.

RD But you have stamped your image on the Tory Party like no other leader ever has before. We never heard of Macmillanism, we never heard of Heathism, we never heard of Churchillism. We now hear of Thatcherism. What is it – for the help of the undecided – what is it that Thatcherism means?

THATCHER Sir Robin, it is not a name that I created in the sense of calling it an 'ism'. Let me tell you what it stands for. It stands for sound finance and government running the affairs of the nation, a sound financial way. It stands for honest money, not inflation; it stands for living within your means; it stands for incentives, because we know full well that the growth and economic strength of a nation comes from the efforts of its people, and its people need incentives to work as hard as they possibly can. All of that has produced economic growth. It stands for something else. It stands for the wider and wider spread of ownership of property, of houses, of shares, of savings. It stands for being strong in defence; a reliable ally and a

233

trusted friend. People have called those things 'Thatcherism'. They are in fact fundamental common sense and having faith in the enterprise and abilities of the people. It is my task to try and release those; they were always there. They've always been there in the British people, but they couldn't flourish under socialism; they've now been released. That's all that Thatcherism is.

RD Can you tell us that if there's four or five more years of Thatcherism, whether you can promise, or at least hope to achieve, any of the following things: for instance, will unemployment be brought down below two million?

THATCHER I cannot promise you a specific figure. I think you must have asked me that question at the time of the last election, possibly in this room in 1983. I could not forecast then that there would have been by now one million more jobs created, over a million, but there have, in fact, been. I wouldn't give a forecast then, and now unemployment is falling. It will depend upon many things. It will depend upon world trade, that is one reason why I wanted to go to Venice; it will depend upon the world economy; it will also depend upon how far thousands and thousands of companies, whether in manufacturing, extraction or service, respond to the markets of the world. Our strength, our economic strength, our standard of living depends upon our companies producing goods that people will buy at the price of the quality. They are responding magnificently at the moment. For years I wondered if we released the controls, if we gave incentives, whether the spirit of enterprise would come back. It is back! And young people are doing fantastically well; they are creating new businesses; it is happening.

RD If you are re-elected for another four or five years will inflation be brought down to zero?

THATCHER It will be our aim to bring down inflation further. We shall run our financial policies in that way. I wish I could promise that it would be brought down to zero – I can't. We want it down further and we will continue to try, endeavouring every way to get it down.

RD Will the standard rate of income tax come down to 20 per cent?

THATCHER Mr Day, I think you're asking me – I think you're inviting – I'm so sorry, I made that mistake last time, I won't do it again. Sir Robin. I think you're inviting me to try to tie any future government up in promises that it couldn't be sure it would deliver. You know I will never do that. It isn't my way, it isn't my way personally, it isn't my party's way, which is much, much more important –

RD Let me ask you –

THATCHER No, please, let me go on. Yes, I do want income tax further down. That will depend upon how successful our companies and businesses are. The more wealth they produce the more income tax can come down and the more resources we'll have to put to social services. We shall endeavour to get income tax further down. Just as in the last eight years we got it down from 33p, the basic rate in the pound to 27p. Just as we got the top rate down from 83 per cent on earnings to 60 per cent, so we shall strive to get it down by running the economy in such a way that we get this fundamental partnership between government doing good housekeeping and people responding with using their talents and abilities to create more wealth.

RD Can you promise anything about the increase in crime? Will that have been slowed down, if not halted, within four or five years?

THATCHER I can promise you that we shall continue to increase the numbers of police. They will have more numbers, they will have the equipment; we have given them rather more powers, and we will continue to strive to do every single thing we can to get more co-operation with the public, because people can do so much to make their homes more secure. They can do so much to keep a watch in their neighbourhood, and many of those neighbourhood watch schemes, 29,000, are working quite brilliantly. But in the end, let's face it, government isn't a dictator. We're a free country. Everyone has freedom of choice, and everyone has personal responsibility for their actions. Yes, there's good and evil in everyone, and what we have to do is to have a legal system such that those who take the course of crime have strong sentences – we've had that – the right framework of law – we're doing that – a police force which co-operates with the public. All of that we shall do. And I wish, perhaps above all, that one could wave a magic wand and get crime down. In an ideal world one would wish there were no crime. A man is given freedom of choice, and I'm afraid the same thing that gives us power to do good, is that same freedom that gives some the power to do evil. And we have to deter that, and we do.

RD Prime Minister, what do you say to those who say – and they are not only your political opponents – who say that you are autocratic, domineering and intolerant of dissent?

THATCHER Well, they should come to some of our Cabinet meetings and listen to the very, very vigorous discussion that we have, and we've always had. Yes, because we do believe in coming to our conclusions by very vigorous discussion. Good heavens! You know you've seen some of it, not in Cabinet meetings, but I've never been unwilling to get involved in the clash of debate and argument, and I'm not now. It is because we have that that I believe we thoroughly thrash out our problems. I think what you're accusing me of –

RD No, I'm not accusing you. I'm inviting you to answer criticisms frequently made of you, Prime Minister.

THATCHER I'm so sorry. I don't see how one can be accused of being arrogant when one has in fact tried throughout the whole of the eight years I've been in office to give more power back to the people. We've abolished many controls, because government ought not to have had them, we've taken away –

RD This is a personal question, this is a personal question.

THATCHER You're asking me a personal question, then I'm afraid I must leave other people to judge. I don't think –

RD All right.

THATCHER Please may I just finish. I don't think oneself is perhaps the best judge of one's qualities. Yes, when I believe in things very strongly, it is then I bend everything to getting that policy through. I go to the House, I explain it, sometimes there's a combative way, yes. I decide with others the way we're going, then I bend every single effort to getting that through, overcoming all obstacles. It isn't arrogance, in my view. It is determination and resolve.

RD You've referred to your Cabinet meetings, Prime Minister, which I haven't had the opportunity of attending, but Mr Francis Pym is one of those who have and who was sacked by you. He said any dissent, any dissent, even the admittance of doubt, is treachery and treason. And he went on, 'after nine years as party leader, five as Prime Minister, Margaret Thatcher still asks people the question: "Are you one of us?"'

THATCHER Look. I think you are insulting many in my Cabinet. The Cabinet is made up of people of a wide variety of views within the party, of a wide variety of people geographically and of a number of different age groups. And I don't think any of them would say that they weren't invited from time to time to give their views. There are twenty. Frequently we go around the Cabinet table – 'What are your views?' – and if you are saying that every single person in that Cabinet is a 'yes' man, then I think you are delivering a totally unjustifiable insult. Yes, I do put my views combatively. I hold them combatively; I'm in politics because I want to get them put into practice. And putting them into practice, Sir Robin, has given economic strength, strong defence, a strong standard of living, better than ever before, and a better standard of care. But it isn't easy. I don't say it is.

RD But isn't it very significant – this is something people have commented on – that many of the Tory Cabinet Ministers whom you have sacked have been those who believed in the tradition of Toryism which is known as 'one nation Toryism', started by Disraeli, followed on by Butler, Macmillan and others. But under Thatcherism, and this is what your critics say, the nation is not one nation but a divided nation.

THATCHER Let me answer that very deeply, because I feel very strongly about it. The greatest divisions this nation has ever seen were the conflicts of trade unions towards the end of the Labour government, terrible conflicts. That trade unions movement then was under the dictate of trade union bosses, some of whom are still there. They use their power against their members. They made them come out on strike when they didn't want to; they loved secondary picketing; they went and demonstrated outside companies where there was no dispute whatsoever, and sometimes closed them down. They were acting, as they were later in the coal strike before my whole trade union laws went through this government, they were out to use their power to hold the nation to ransom, to stop power from getting to the whole of manufacturing industry, to damage people's jobs; to stop power from getting to every house in the country, power, heat and light to every housewife, every child, every school, every pensioner. You want division, you want conflict, you want hatred, there it was! It was that which Thatcherism, if you call it that, tried to stop.

RD But –

THATCHER One moment! Not by arrogance. But by giving power to the ordinary, decent, honourable trade union member who didn't want to go on strike; by giving power to him over the Scargills of this world, all those laws went through when we had the coal strike. That is one conflict, that is gone. Now another one. I believe passionately that people have a right, by their own efforts, to benefit their own families. So we've taken down taxation. It doesn't matter to me who you are or what your background is. If you want to use your own efforts to work harder, yes I'm with you, all the way! Whether it's unskilled effort, whether it's skilled. And so we've taken the income tax down. And the third thing: all my predecessors, yes, I read Disraeli, yes, Harold Macmillan; I would say I am right in their tradition. It was Disraeli One Nation. We've had an increase in home ownership, the heart of the family –

RD Can I get in this question please Prime Minister because –

THATCHER You asked me the most fundamental thing. I must beg of you –

RD I know, but we're not having a party political broadcast, we're having an interview, which must depend on me asking some questions occasionally.

THATCHER Yes indeed. You asked what I know you call 'the gut question'. Right, it's gone to the gut, it's gone to the jugular. Let me finish it. More home ownership, far more share ownership; far more savings in building society accounts; this is what is building 'one nation', as every earner becomes a shareholder, as more and more people own their homes. No, we are getting rid of the divisions. We are replacing conflict with co-operation. We are building one nation through wider property-owning democracy, by . . .

RD Prime Minister –

THATCHER Please go ahead, I'm sorry, but it was a pretty fundamental question.

RD Thank you, and indeed, the next one is equally. Do you not, though, see a nation, despite all your attack on what happened in 1978 and 1979 under the Labour government, do you not see a nation divided deeply now between north and south, between the prosperous suburbs and the inner cities, between the employed and the unemployed; between the poverty-stricken millions and the whizz-kids of the big-bang in the City?

THATCHER I do not see a nation divided in anything like the terms which you say, or even divided in that way. Yes, there are some parts all over the country which were reliant on industries like coal, like steel, like heavy engineering, like ship-building. And when modern methods came in, when new technology came in, when other countries began to build ships, build steel, yes, those industries have suffered. And where they are they have suffered grievously, take Consett, yes it was closed down. Take Shotton, yes it was closed down. In Shotton, which I visited the other day, new industries are springing up. Yes, there are more of them in the north. But there are fantastic numbers of highly prosperous areas, businesses, people in the north and they are growing. I visited many of them. There are also parts in the south where heaven knows some of us have experience of it, a particular industry closed down. But Mr – Sir Robin – you simply, you cannot stop change. You cannot stop technological change; you cannot stop Third World countries from building up their own industries and therefore not getting goods from us. And we are doing as much as we can to alleviate that change. Take Corby as an example.

RD No, I don't want to take Corby. I want to follow up your point about denying that it is a divided country, because –

THATCHER Right. No, I do not see the divisions in the way in which you depict it.

RD Well let me point you a division which you have yourself seen, because you've expressed great concern about the City salaries and you've said 'it causes me great concern; I understand the resentment,' you said. And you said: 'If I feel strongly – ' (this was last year) 'if I feel strongly about what they are taking in the City, compared to what Cabinet Ministers are taking, then look at how the people who are struggling to get work feel.' Now that shows that you understand there *is* a resentment to these disparities.

THATCHER Of course, we live daily by the City. We're just on the fringes and we lose some of our best people to the City. Yes, we do, and I know what happens. People come in and say, 'Well they're getting those salaries, why shouldn't we?' And I know full well that there is no way in which a government can just hand out money like that. Equally, I have to remember this: the City is becoming the foremost financial international centre of the world, foremost! More foremost than New York, better than Tokyo because it is cosmopolitan. That the City, in fact, earns for everyone in the United Kingdom for our balance of payment, a net seven and a half billion a year. Without that we wouldn't be in surplus as we are, and it must go on gathering strength. And I tell you, one of the troubles, you know, is that the City has to compete with salaries with other people who take them away. I think part of it –

RD Yes –

THATCHER Can I just finish; I think part of it was the transition the City went through, the so-called 'big bang', when I think there was a lot of competition for getting the best people. Yes I do find that some of the salaries there, I find, I feel just exactly as you said. That makes me know how other people feel. But it is not Cabinet Ministers. We choose to come into politics and we must take the salaries, and they are very good.

RD If the economy is so strong under Thatcherism as we are continually told during this campaign, why do we still have three million unemployed?

THATCHER First because – I will give you a number of reasons, will you give me time? First, because when we took over there was a massive amount of overmanning and hidden unemployment. That was one of the troubles of our industry. There was a massive amount of restrictive practices; those had to go. Secondly, we'd had, in common with the rest of Europe, which also suffers from unemployment, a great technological revolution. We can and are producing a lot more with fewer people employed in certain manufacturing industries. We can't resist that change. We have to accept it, but we have in fact to have an economic policy that tries to create more businesses and more jobs. Thirdly, we have gone through a period of ten years during which there have been far more school-leavers than people retiring. So the population of working age has been getting bigger for ten years, and therefore a million new jobs did not reduce it on the unemployment register. But equally, when we came into power the spirit of enterprise had gone, it was shackled; it is now returning and the new jobs are being created and unemployment is going down. Unemployment is going down faster in this country while it is still rising in Germany and France. So I think we have got the answer. One further point. There is no government in the free world that can guarantee everyone a job. And I want to make that absolutely clear. Yes, you could guarantee everyone a job in a Soviet society by total direction of labour, you do what you're told to do and you don't have a chance of anything else, and you go where you're told to go and you don't have a chance to go anywhere else; and you haven't got any human rights, and so on and so forth. It's in that society you can have a guarantee to everyone a job; it wouldn't be the sort of society worth living in. We are going about it the right way; we got inflation down, we got enterprise up, we're getting jobs up, we're getting unemployment down.

RD Let me –

THATCHER And I hope very much that will go on.

RD Let me put –

THATCHER Because jobs come from successful business.

RD Let me put a question which was put to you and other politicians, but specifically to you, by the Bishops of the Church of England, and I quote: 'What do you consider to be an acceptable level of unemployment?'

THATCHER There isn't an acceptable level of unemployment. The Church
   Commissioners know this full well, and so do the Bishops. The
   Church Commissioners do a lot of investment. I saw an excellent
   investment of theirs the other day in the north country. It happened
   to create a lot of jobs; it was the biggest shopping centre in Europe
   at Gateshead. They know full well. They too have had problems with
   redundancies; they've had problems with redundant churches; they
   know full well there's no such thing as an acceptable level of
   unemployment. You do everything you possibly can to get industry,
   manufacturing and services in a fit condition, everything the government can do, then you enter into a partnership with people in
   industry, whether it's managers or employers, of tax incentives, of
   the right trade union law, of the right framework and the new
   jobs are being created. And you don't stop there. Because in this
   technological world there are going to be more and more jobs for the
   skilled and fewer jobs for the unskilled, so you have the biggest
   training problem, the biggest training scheme we've ever had. And
   we're tackling that, and we're tackling it vigorously and half Europe
   comes to see how we're doing it, because we're leading in that
   sphere.
RD But –
THATCHER The Bishops have had problems in the Church, they know
   that.
RD Let me come now to what might be called 'the jewel in your crown'.
THATCHER I haven't got a crown to have a jewel in.
RD I was speaking metaphorically, as you will see if you wait for a
   moment, Prime Minister, and I was referring to your record in cutting
   inflation which we are reminded of in advertisements in the papers
   this weekend. That it is the lowest for nearly twenty years and so
   on. But isn't it still regrettable that the inflation rate in Britain is still
   above the average of our industrial competitors, higher than America,
   higher than Germany, higher than Japan. And therefore we're not
   really properly competitive yet.
THATCHER Oh, we are getting very, very competitive indeed. Germany
   has always had a very, very different view from us and you know
   why. Germany actually suffered from rampant, galloping hyper-
   inflation between the wars. It destroyed all what were called 'the
   middle classes of Germany'. It destroyed all the people who saved,
   because that's what Lenin said: 'If you want to destroy a society you
   debauch its currency.' It did. And Germany has always known that

if ever you get a government that spends, spends, spends and spends again, the value of the money will be worthless if it is spending by printing money. And Germany has always gone about reducing her unemployment although even she has a lot at the moment. Never by saying you spend money you haven't got, but by saying it is effort and the right goods and services. Japan – neither Japan nor the United States spend as big a proportion of their national income as we do and that's –

RD And aren't wages here running too high?

THATCHER Wages here, yes, are still running too high in proportion to what we produce. Although the CBI did say, and I think they have some reason to say it, that unit wage costs are not rising now as fast as our competitors; you know what that means. That at last the fantastic investment they've put in is increasing productivity. It means, of course, that we still have a problem with unemployment. But CBI did say recently, and it is good news as far as competing is concerned, that our unit wage costs are rising more slowly. But we have had one thing in this country I think others didn't have. You know during the period of prices and income policy people got used, almost as a right, to an annual increase regardless of whether it had been earned. And we are still suffering from that, because really you ought to have to earn your increases if you are to keep the value of your money absolutely steady.

RD Now, you explained the other day, Prime Minister, that you used private medical care so that you could go to the hospital on the day you want, at the time you wanted and with the doctor you wanted. That, for you, you said, is absolutely vital. Many people may have understood your case for doing that, but did you not, at the same time, lay yourself wide open to the charge, politically and to a lot of ordinary people, of seeming insensitive to the needs of ordinary people who are not so fortunate?

THATCHER Well, I hope not. It wasn't intended in that way at all. People didn't criticize Labour Cabinet Ministers if they used private health service. I think they would have criticized me had I done what some other people have done and said, 'Look I am very important, I'm in politics, I simply must come in the time I want and I must have a room on the National Health Service.' Do you know, had I done that, you'd have criticized me too. But no, along with five million other people, of whom I know many are in the media, in fact I have paid my way for private health, five million of us. But I've done something else, Sir Robin. I've seen to it that we have the best health service we ever had.

RD Well, I want to ask you about that because –

THATCHER Yes, the best health service we ever had and also – may I say something else – I pay three times. You accuse me of many things. May I now and then say a word in my own defence? I very rarely do. Yes, I pay my whack, in taxes, to the health service; we all do whether we use it or not. I pay my own thing personally to go to a doctor, and I also forgo 20 per cent of my salary, which falls back into the Treasury. So I hope that no one will ever accuse me of being thoughtless about the needs of other people.

RD Isn't it a fact though, Prime Minister, which is attested by the British Medical Association and other medical bodies, and by the Royal College of Nursing, that the National Health Service is falling steadily behind in its attempt to keep up with the growing demands on it?

THATCHER There will be increasing demands. Of course as we get medical science advances we get new operations, we get new treatments. Every new treatment does mean a new waiting list. And as we get a population which is growing older, we're growing older and as part of that growing older, of course, there will be increasing demands. It was in 1977 that Sir Alec Merrison who did a study of this under the Labour government said: 'We have no difficulty in believing that the entire national income could be spent on the National Health Service.' Well, of course it can't be. But it has never had as much more spent on it over a period of years than this government has spent on it. Everyone has to live within a budget. Doesn't matter whether you run a business, run a home or run a health service. But the day – we're in No. 12 Downing Street now – the day I walked in two doors down to No. 10 the taxpayer could afford, under a Labour government, to spend eight billion pounds on the Health Service, eight billion. Today, after eight years of Conservative government, the taxpayer is spending twenty-one billion pounds on the Health Service.

RD May I then –

THATCHER Now that is far more, and I want to get this over most strongly, the Health Service means a great deal to me. It must almost to anyone, we never know what might happen to us. We might be permanently ill. It means a great deal to me, it means a great deal to me that people can go there and that we have more doctors and nurses and more cases after eight years of the government I have been privileged to lead than ever before.

RD But I want to put a quotation to you which is not from Mr Michael Meacher or some critic of the government, or some opponent, but is from an independent medical expert, Sir George Godber, formerly Chief Medical Officer of Health to the DHSS.

THATCHER A very good Chief Medical Officer and I remember him well.

RD And loaded with every conceivable professional honour. He says – quote: 'Ministers endlessly relating a few selected statistics will not convince us that the NHS is safe in their hands.'

THATCHER Well, I am very sorry he said that, nevertheless you cannot ignore the tremendous extra resources that have been put in, the extra number of hospitals that have gone up, the extra nurses, the ordinary tax pays. But I sometimes do feel that every single case, and there are a million people employed in the Health Service, every single case of difficulty is brought to us. May I remind you of what actually happened under the alternative government, under Labour? These are headlines which eventually I took out, of what happened to the Health Service under Labour government. This is February 1979, 'Target for Today', 'Sick Children'. This is also under a Labour government, 'Have mercy on my Son', 'Bone Marrow Mothers plea to Hospital Strikers'. Here is another *Daily Mirror* one, 'Mum Dies in 999 No Go Row'. This is another one: 'Cancer Ward sent home under Labour Government'. This is another one: 'Hospital Chaos Spreads'. This is another one: '999 Ambulance men to Stop at Midnight, 999 Strike'. Another one: 'Troops on Ambulance Standby'. Another one: 'Don't let the Children Suffer' ...

RD But, Prime Minister, the expert I quoted said (and he wouldn't deny, I presume, your criticism of those events) that without extra resources, extra resources from central government, the future of the National Health Service looks grim.

THATCHER There have been extra resources, from eight billion, that was the general family of four, paid eleven pounds a week when I came into Number 10 towards the Health Service every week, whether they used it or not, through taxes. Now they are paying twenty-seven, twenty-eight pounds a week, every family of four, in taxes to the Health Service, that is a very considerable increase in resources. Resources don't come from governments, they come from the tax-payer. In addition to the Health Service they are also having to spend £55 a week, every family of four, on Social Security, in addition to that they are having to spend £23 every week in taxes to education. Money comes from the taxpayer. It is my firm contention that because of the economic strength, because of the higher growth that we have created, we have been able to increase the money to the Health Service, to Social Security in that way. Destroy that economic strength, and the Health Service would get far fewer resources, some of the hospitals we have built, the hospitals cancelled by the Labour government when it got into economic crisis. So yes, I would challenge anyone: no government has put as many resources into the Health Service as has happened under mine. Yes, there will still be more needed and there are plans steadily to increase it and it will go on demanding more, but it is the taxpayer who pays. We have in fact given priority to the Health Service, along with defence and law and order. My record will stand comparison with almost anyone else.

RD Does it surprise you or upset you when you see yourself or hear yourself described as 'a hard woman', 'uncaring' and 'out of touch with the feelings of ordinary folk'?

THATCHER It is usually a charge levelled at me by the left and often some ordinary Labour members who have that record on health, who had the record in coal strikes that I described, who brought this country low during their time of office, so low that no one would lend them a penny piece in borrowed money, no one would come into sterling, no one in charge of pension funds, or insurance funds would put a penny piece into gilts which should have been spent G-U-I-L-T under a Labour government. And they level that charge at me, to try to take away from our excellent record, they cannot level that charge at me and have it stick, whether in terms of our record in government, and certainly they would not level it at me personally because, as you know, both Denis and I spend a great deal of time working for our own favourite causes, my own the National Society for Prevention of Cruelty to Children, and I sometimes wish that instead of giving up 20 per cent of my salary I'd just let them have it. And Denis for Sports Aid Foundation, for Lords Taverners, yes, we all work for these causes. It is a ruse to take away attention from their record in government, which was a disgrace, from what they want to do on defence, and what they want to do on trade unions. Please may I say, the charge is cruel, it is intended to be, it is intended to upset me, it would but for one thing, I look at the people who make it and know what they are up to.

RD Mr Enoch Powell has made it clear today, Prime Minister, that people should vote Labour, in his opinion, or at least against you because of the faith, which is your faith, in the nuclear deterrent, and I quote him: 'The faith in the nuclear deterrent is a palpable and pernicious delusion.'

THATCHER Well you know Enoch has been saying that for twenty years, and you know you won't change Enoch. He turned against us when we went into the Common Market, and as you know he was a Conservative member. Within a few weeks of an election he just turned round and told the people who worked for him loyally for years that he was not going to stand and urged people to vote Labour and it must have hurt them deeply. It is very strange. May I say this for Enoch. Having said that against him, he is a remarkable politician, quite a remarkable person, a fantastic brain. I disagree with his judgment on many things, including that, but I somehow have always thought that politics would have been the poorer if it hadn't had people like Enoch in it. And I say this again for him, he is, I would always trust Enoch, he never hides his opinions and he is a totally honourable person. Although he says things against me, I disagree with him fundamentally on this. I would rather take Winston's view and I look at people who are against us, I look at the possible adversaries, I look at the terrorists who may one day get a nuclear device but I know we must keep the nuclear deterrent.

RD Let me quote you what this remarkable man with the tremendous brain, Mr Powell, says. In his latest utterance he says it 'almost defies belief that grown men and women should seriously propose so crazy a scenario', which he says is this: Russia invades Germany or northern Norway perhaps, the United States declines to commit suicide, so, he says, Britain fires the nuclear salvo at Moscow and Leningrad. And he asks the question, how barmy do you have to be to believe that or believe that the Kremlin believes that.

THATCHER Yes, but you see so many of Enoch's arguments stem from the starting place he chose, and the starting place he chose isn't the right one, this has always been one of Enoch's problems, the most fantastic logic, the most fantastic brain, but not the right judgments, you see Winston was right when he said and warned, and I have quoted him everywhere, including the United States Congress, never, never give up the nuclear deterrent before you are sure that you have got something as good or even better to deter war. The whole point of the nuclear deterrent is it has kept the peace in Europe for forty years. We know that conventional weapons are not enough to stop conventional war. We have been through it twice in Europe but this nuclear deterrent is so terrible that, yes, it would be barmy, to use Enoch's word, to really want to start a war. But if you got rid of them all and went to conventionals the race would be on as to who could get it first or who had stowed a few away, and it is etched on my heart, and probably on yours, and my mind too, and I am surprised it isn't on Enoch's that had Hitler got that nuclear weapon first and there had been no deterrent we should not be here talking now.

RD But I put to you another quotation of Mr Powell, and I only quote him because he expresses in vivid language what many people feel –

THATCHER – Oh, his language is outstanding.

RD – but many people who aren't necessarily your political opponents, let me put this to you which refers to events since Winston Churchill: the salutary event of Chernobyl strengthened and crystallized an already growing impulse to escape from a nightmare, the nightmare of peace being dependent on the contemplation of horrific and mutual carnage.

THATCHER It is fantastic language isn't it, but you see –

RD But what is the logic like?

THATCHER Well, I will tell you where my logic is. It starts from a different point. What Chernobyl proves is the significance of the nuclear deterrent because it shows that it would be even more damaging if anything nuclear were ever to be used if any war started, because if a war started even though you had no nuclear weapons at all, if a war started the race would be on to get the first nuclear, and who would stow them away somewhere. What Chernobyl says is the nuclear deterrent is even more of a deterrent than we thought. Even more of a deterrent.

RD In what circumstances, Prime Minister, would you be prepared to use either Polaris or Trident?

THATCHER The nuclear weapon is a deterrent. NATO has said that we are only a defensive organization, that we only use any of our weapons, we only use any of our weapons in response to an attack. If there is no attack there will be no war. If there is a nuclear deterrent I believe there will be no attack. I would not have that confidence if there were no nuclear deterrent. After all Europe was full of weapons when Hitler went to war. And if you looked on the side of the Allies there were probably more than Hitler had. Russia was full of weapons, actually, when Adolf Hitler attacked her. It did not stop a war. This nuclear deterrent has been so powerful it has stopped it and that is the argument.

RD If Labour wins, Prime Minister, and decommissions Polaris immediately, as Mr Kinnock has announced his intention of doing, what do you think is the duty of the Chiefs of Staff? To resign if they disagree with that order, or to obey the orders of the democratically elected Queen's first minister?

THATCHER The Chiefs of Staff have to make up their own mind. Each person is responsible for what he decides. It would be for the Chiefs of Staff to decide whether in their view, and it would certainly be mine, that the damage done to NATO, the damage done to liberty because Britain has always stood for liberty, the damage done to Britain's defences, would be so deep, so fundamental that they could no longer be responsible for carrying the burden of defence, or for being in charge of our armed forces without a nuclear weapon of any kind when those armed forces faced an adversary that had. And I know what I would do, I just could not be responsible for the men under me under those circumstances, it wouldn't be fair to put them in the field if the other people have nuclear weapons. I know what I would do, but they are free to make their decision, that is a fundamental part of the way of life in which I believe. But it would do untold – just let me get in this. Britain isn't just another country. We have never been just another country. We wouldn't have grown to an empire if we were just another European country of the size and strength that we were. It was Britain who stood when everyone else surrendered and if Britain pulls out of that commitment, it is as if one of the pillars of the temple has collapsed. Because we are one of the pillars of freedom. And hitherto everyone, including past Labour Prime Ministers, have known that Britain would stand and Britain had a nuclear weapon.

RD Do you think sometimes –

THATCHER What a fantastic decision, Sir Robin –

RD Do you think sometimes, as you look at this campaign, Prime Minister, that if Labour did not have a policy of unilateral nuclear disarmament, which you have just condemned with such force, if they did not have such a policy that you would probably lose the election because of your record on unemployment, on the National Health Service, on various other social matters?

THATCHER No, my record on the National Health Service, as I have indicated, compare mine with that, compare the resources we have put in with that. Our record on increasing the standard of living has been quite outstanding. Look at Labour's record, putting power in the hands of the trade union bosses, just at a time when all the left wing, being unable ever to stand in their true colours, worked for the trade union movement and worked through the Labour Party. Labour would put the power back into the hands of the trade union bosses, Labour would bring back many, many of the controls which we had to get rid of enterprise. Labour would bring back many, many industries into nationalization. I don't know many politicians who can run businesses.

RD Well, we are coming to the end of this interview and you have got to go to Venice –

THATCHER Well, I am sorry, I would love to go on –

RD You've got to get to Venice, Prime Minister –

THATCHER – and I would stay even a few more minutes to put it but you won't let me.

RD – and we have only got a moment or two longer. If I might ask you this: if you don't win an overall majority but you are the largest party, will you resign?

THATCHER Look, I don't think so, for the largest party. I do not see why I should resign.

RD Well, if you had a majority, which you have of 140 or so, and that is wiped out, as it would be in the hypothesis I was discussing, wouldn't you regard that as a defeat?

THATCHER I am not going to prophesy what will happen on Thursday and I am not going to be tempted along this route. I hope and believe we shall win, I hope and believe we shall win with a reasonable majority, and to be perfectly honest I tremble to think what would happen to Britain if we don't. That is my view. It is my privilege, the privilege of democracy to have been here, and submit ourselves to the judgment of the people. I am not going to tie myself as to what may happen under circumstances which I cannot predict. I shall leave myself totally free to decide when the time comes, in consultation with my colleagues, and ask them to put their views frankly and fearlessly.

RD So you do not rule out any Alliance, or deal with the Alliance in the event of a hung Parliament?

THATCHER I am used to that line of questioning, I shall consider what happens at the time. I had this line of questioning at this time during the last election campaign. And I said then, as I say now, I hope and believe we shall win with a resonable majority and I tremble to think what will happen to Britain if we don't.

RD But would you not think that if there is a hung Parliament, with you losing your majority, which you have got at the moment, don't you think that would indicate that the British people would expect some sort of co-operation and compromise between their politicians?

THATCHER No, not necessarily. I have worked too long, had to work too long on the international scene with coalitions, my goodness me. I guess some of them are pretty thankful that we have got in Britain a strong government that can take decisions which they shy away from. Do you know what it is like? You'll say what are you going to do with them on government. You will consult with them. Oh well, we have got to meet with our coalition partners. I say, well, you sit in the same government, you can meet every day. Oh no, we will take some time to meet and then they go behind closed doors. Do they decide on clear decisions? It is an argy-bargy between them. What are, what is the price you exact to keep you in the coalition? Can you imagine it? A major party with a mixture of the SDP and Liberals who are a miscellaneous group of views anyway, with the Scottish Nationalists, with the Welsh Nationalists, with several different Irish parties. Britain governed by that! No, I would rather take it in the largest minority party, lay my programme, our programme before Parliament and say deliver your judgment upon it.

RD Which would you regard as a greater evil, a coalition between Thatcherism and the Alliance and others, or letting in a Kinnock minority government committed to socialism and unilateral disarmament?

THATCHER I do not accept that that is the alternative.

RD Supposing it was?

THATCHER I think you have possibly posed a false alternative and, Sir Robin, I shall keep my decisions open to see precisely how we would react to that circumstance. You know I might, indeed I would, consult my Cabinet colleagues – the very thing you have accused me of not doing.

RD I didn't accuse you of anything, Prime Minister. You keep on accusing me of accusing you of things. I want to ask you one more question – which the undecided voter might be influenced by your answer. If you score a hat trick and if you get – if you go on for another term of office, is it your intention to make way in a couple of years for a younger person?

THATCHER I am often asked that and if I were to say yes, and I have not made up my mind, I would like to go through to a fourth term, I don't know what will happen. I don't know what will happen to me for a start. What I do know is that eventually someone will want to come up just in exactly the same way that I did and of course one has to judge that time. I would like to go on for the end of a fourth term, to do the things I believe in. That would be my intention at the moment but nothing is absolute. My party has to re-elect me every year –

RD The end of a *fourth* term? So what you are asking for is another *eight* years?

THATCHER No, I am so sorry, to the end of a *third* term.

RD Ah, a Freudian slip?

THATCHER Up to, no, up to submitting oneself to the judgment of a people. I cannot be absolute. Events: we do not know what they hold.

RD Thank you, Prime Minister.

THATCHER Thank you, Sir Robin.

'I don't think politics by invective and insult are the way to get a message across to people about their future.'

JOHN
MAJOR

This was the first interview I had ever done with John Major. By the time he became a minister in 1985 my work as an interviewer had dwindled away. This was because I was chairman of *Question Time* from 1979 to 1989.

So this election interview in 1992 with Prime Minister Major was not between old sparring partners as had been my election interviews with Wilson, Heath, Callaghan or Thatcher. Though I had seen him interviewed by others, he was an unknown quantity to me. I did not know him personally. I had spoken to him only a few times. I had never argued or joked with him. I was not sure what kind of a Conservative he was. I had read about him. I had watched him in the Commons. I heard, of course, he was Thatcher's chosen heir, but I could not see any great similarity in him to her. When she confronted, he seemed to conciliate. Where she insulted, he was polite. Where she would hotly dramatize an issue, he tended to cool it down calmly. But these were superficial impressions which I was ready to revise. Friends and colleagues, whose judgment I respect, had spoken admiringly of him. I knew he was not an orator nor someone given to colourful language. On the other hand I could see (in the House and on television) that he had a quiet firmness and a refreshing clarity of expression. But what, I wondered, made him angry?

As my election interview with him drew near my task as interviewer became clearer. Mr Major had a problem. His hope of election victory seemed to depend on showing how different he was from his belligerent predecessor, yet at the same time he had to hold the enthusiasm of those who thought him the right man to stand in her shoes. Furthermore John Major's campaign did not appear to be well run. Perched on a bar stool, he would chat to staged gatherings of the party faithful. The Prime Minister's campaign was seen as lacklustre and uninspiring. Heseltine and Clarke were drafted in to beef up the Tory campaign.

When this interview was done, we were midway through the campaign. Polling day was two weeks ahead. The opinion polls gave little or no hope to the Tories. Most commentators assumed that Neil Kinnock would be the Prime Minister on 9 April, either of a majority Labour government or as the leader of the largest party in a hung Parliament. But one person, at least, appeared totally convinced that John Major would be elected Prime Minister with a clear majority. That person was John Major himself.

This interview took place at what seems to have been a turning point. The dull election campaign had suddenly erupted into life. The so-called 'war of Jennifer's ear' had broken out between the big parties and among the press. For those with short memories, this was the row over a Labour Party election broadcast about a little girl and her NHS treatment. It was to illustrate Labour's campaign argument about the NHS.

This 'Jennifer's ear' episode was the first stumble in Labour's smooth and professional red-rose campaign. The little girl's identity leaked out. Tory Central Office accused the Labour Party of propaganda exploiting an innocent child. The Tory Chairman, Chris Patten, even declared that Neil Kinnock was unfit to hold public office. But the Prime Minister noticeably refrained from going that far when I raised the episode of Jennifer's ear with him.

There are several questions reflecting criticism of his campaign style. One of my suggestions appears to have borne unexpected fruit. A week later, Peterborough in the *Daily Telegraph* carried this paragraph:

> Who persuaded John Major to adopt the soapbox? Not, it seems, one of the supposedly bright young things at Conservative Central Office, but Sir Robin Day. In his television interview with Major last week, Day asked: 'What has happened to the soapbox that you used to speak from in your younger days in Brixton? Couldn't you bring that into play somehow as a means of addressing the people?' Major parried the question but was clearly impressed, and within days produced his best election trick.

Needless to say, my soapbox point had been put metaphorically. I did not know that the Tory Central Office had a soapbox ready. But it was better than the bar-stool.

If some viewers found the Prime Minister's interview unexciting, others (including non-Tories) thought him refreshingly unpompous and direct. His admission of three mistakes (poll tax, our belated entry to the ERM, the reduction of interest rates after the 1987–8 slump) was welcomed. As also was his view that people don't want 'politics by invective and insult'.

As for what the papers said, the *Daily Telegraph* reported that it was a 'confident performance by Mr Major, who emerged unscathed from his encounter with Sir Robin'. *The Times* headline was 'Major survives a difficult Day'. The Prime Minister's answers, judged *The Times* correspondent, were anodyne and awestruck. Sir Alastair Burnet, who had been wheeled out of retirement to pass judgment on his lesser contemporaries, noted that my questions were 'short and pertinent', which 'encouraged short answers, and a news pace which got in Europe, the poll tax, Nigel Lawson's judgment and Scottish devolution'.

John Major's language is not striking, but on certain matters he strikingly commits himself without equivocation or reservation. He is against a United States of Europe. He is adamantly opposed to Scottish devolution. He is opposed to proportional representation 'under any circumstances'. His words are not magic but they are not minced.

The Rt Hon. John Major, Prime Minister

Interviewed on Thames Television for This Week
26 March 1992

SIR ROBIN DAY Prime Minister, although there are more important things to deal with, I must start with this wretched row about the Health Service broadcast. Now, the Chairman of the Conservative Party said that as a result of Mr Kinnock's part in this broadcast he, Mr Kinnock, was unfit to hold public office. Do you share that view?

RT HON. JOHN MAJOR, PRIME MINISTER Well, frankly, I think the whole episode's been distasteful. The idea of a broadcast of this sort, carefully scripted, carefully prepared, and building on the difficulties of an individual family in order to make a party point, I think, is very distasteful. It shouldn't have happened. And I am very surprised Mr Kinnock did it.

RD But do you think it was fair of Mr Patten to say that Mr Kinnock was unfit to hold public office?

MAJOR I think that Chris Patten is referring to the fact that no previous leader of the Labour Party would have sanctioned a broadcast like that. It's unthinkable to think that Lord Attlee would, that Mr Gaitskell would, that Lord Callaghan would. And I think to that extent that sort of exploitation of an individual isn't attractive, shouldn't have happened. And I hope, frankly, it will never happen again.

RD But do you think the broadcast was, in some way, dishonest or reflected on Mr Kinnock's integrity?

MAJOR Well, it seems to have been a fake broadcast, that's the point. It seems to have been a fake broadcast, and it does seem to exploit the difficulties of one particular individual in the Health Service. Now the Health Service has a million people working for it. It treats millions of people during the course of a year. For every single thing that may go wrong or be delayed there are a thousand operations and treatments that go right. And I think to single one out in this way and seek to make a political point is – is, well, frankly, it's not the way a political leader should behave.

RD Yes. But that is not going as far as to say he's unfit to hold public office, which was a very serious charge, going beyond the normal cut and thrust of an election campaign, is it not?

MAJOR I don't think it is going beyond the normal cut and thrust of an election campaign, and neither do I think it is unreasonable. I think it is reasonable to accept certain standards. I don't want to be pious about it or pompous about it. But I think it is reasonable to accept certain standards from political parties and leaders of political parties. I myself do think this was a distasteful episode. It should not have happened. And it wasn't something that happened in the heat of the moment, this was carefully prepared, carefully scripted and carefully intended, in order to make a party political point for the Labour Party.

RD Mr Kinnock –

MAJOR In the heat of a debate, anyone can say something that, subsequently, they regret. It often happens. The best of politicians do it. But this was carefully prepared.

RD But Mr Kinnock would say that the broadcast illustrated an important truth, that under the Tories there is a two-tier Health Service – one free with delays, and one without delays for those who can pay.

MAJOR What you're actually seeing in the Health Service in recent years is several things. Firstly, a dramatic increase in resources. I won't tediously quote the figures, though they are dramatic and they are proposed to continue in the years ahead; and, secondly, far more people being treated better and more speedily than ever they have been treated before, and having a much wider range of treatment. Now there are very few people in this country who aren't proud of the Health Service. There are very few people who haven't used it at some time in their life, or have used it all their life. And I don't think we should concentrate on things which seem to denigrate the Health Service, rather than praising the remarkable improvements we've seen in it.

RD Well, of course, the Labour Party would say that if it is denigrating anything it is denigrating the record of the Tories in looking after the Health Service.

MAJOR Well, I'm happy to debate the record of the Tory Party looking after the Health –

RD On television with Mr Kinnock?

MAJOR I'm happy to debate it at any time, and we debate – I debate it with Mr Kinnock – in the House of Commons twice a week. But if you wish, I'll deal with some of the record of the Health Service.

Consider the number of operations that simply weren't available a few years ago. Now, I spent this morning at York Hospital, a remarkable hospital, and I saw one of the surgeons who, that morning, had performed four heart by-pass operations. Now, that's remarkable. They weren't readily available some years ago. Hip replacement operations, they weren't available some years ago. And year upon year science improves, the National Health Service absorbs those improvements and treats more and more people in a quite astonishing way. It is, frankly, one of the great success stories of the Western world, and I am determined that it will continue.

RD Now you referred to today's events as – about this broadcast – as distasteful. You denied that the Tories had anything to do with giving out information about the girl or her family, but subsequently in the afternoon Mr Waldegrave admitted that the Tory Party advised the consultant if he thought it was a good thing to do, or that it would be a good thing to do to contact the press about it.

MAJOR The fact of the matter is we had no information about the child or the incident. The first time we knew the name of the child and any details about the child were when we actually saw it in the press the following day. I gather the consultant approached us, not the other way round.

RD Was it right for the Tory Party to tell the *Daily Express* who the consultant was?

MAJOR I think the question that really should be asked is was it right in the first instance to drag an incident like this into the middle of the political arena. It isn't the first time it's happened. I hope it will be the last. Because we've many important matters to debate in this election: Europe, the hugely important constitutional issue in Scotland, which, thus far, hasn't had the prominence it deserves, and many other matters.

RD I'd like to get on and discuss those, if I may. But the question I put to you, Mr Major, which I hope you'll think is fair and relevant: was it right of the Tory Party to tell the *Daily Express* the name of the consultant so that they could contact him?

MAJOR The consultant, as I understand it – I have asked questions – as I understand it, the consultant first approached us. There was no initiating action to the consultant by the Conservative Party, neither did the Conservative Party have any information whatsoever about the child or details about the child. I repeat the central point – we did not raise this issue. We did not prepare this broadcast. We did not carefully script it, we did not broadcast it. That was the Labour Party bringing that particular incident smack in the middle of the political arena.

RD So you –

MAJOR I hope it will never occur again.

RD So you feel that you've got completely clean – you and the Tory Party have clean hands in this matter, just as Mr Kinnock feels that the Labour Party has clean hands.

MAJOR Well, it's self-evidently the case that it was their broadcast and not ours. I haven't come forward with shroud-waving on matters in the National Health Service of any sort.

RD I'm interested in that phrase, which I've not heard before. I heard you make it earlier today. What does 'shroud-waving mean?

MAJOR Well, I think it's where – you know very well what it means, Robin.

RD I don't, no. I'm not sure. But people watching may not.

MAJOR It's picking out an incident in order to illustrate something that seems to be wrong, when mostly the work of the National Health Service is right, and splendidly right.

RD Let me get on to another aspect of this campaign, Prime Minister. Are you aware that a good many of your supporters would like to see you leading the Tory campaign in a more forceful and dynamic way?

MAJOR Well, I find it interesting that you should say that. I spend half my time being told by some people that I've suddenly become too aggressive and half my time being told by other people that I ought to be more aggressive. I rather suspect in the midst of that I've got it right. But the –

RD Who told you you've got too aggressive?

MAJOR Well, I rather fancy that a number of people have. But the important issue really, is not just the question of style, it's substance. It's whether we're raising the issues that really matter to people in this election and that really matter for their futures. That's what the election's about. It's not about trivial incidents. It's about who governs Britain in the future, what their programme is and what that programme will mean for the people of Britain.

RD Yes, but the remarkable impact of Mrs Thatcher's very brief appearance on the streets of this country a few days ago drew a lot of people's attention to what they see as the weakness of your campaign.

MAJOR Well, I don't believe we have got a weak campaign. I think our campaign is extremely strong. I think if you had travelled with our campaign round the country you would have formed that judgment yourself. Anyone who's been with us, who has seen the reception on the streets, would, I think, understand that. Anyone who's attended any of our rallies, I think, would certainly understand that.

RD What has happened to the soapbox you used to speak from in your younger days in Brixton, couldn't you bring that in to play somehow, in the manner of addressing the people?

MAJOR Well, in a sense I am. The rallies we've had, of course, are set-piece speeches, but I've also been more open to answering questions, I think, than any other party leader in this campaign, and I'll say so.

RD What I'm getting at is, is it good enough to put across what you believe are sensible and wise policies for the country, is it good enough to put them across in a nice, reasonable, mild-mannered and quietly-spoken way?

MAJOR I think people in this country want to be convinced. They want to know what someone stands for, what their policies are, what they would mean and how they would carry them out. I don't think politics by invective and insult are the way to get a message across to people about their future. This election campaign, one way and another, has gone on a long time. The Labour Party started it the moment the Gulf War ended. Oppositions do, I make no criticism of that. But we have to discuss the substance of what it means for people. Our education policies, how we'll carry health forward, what we'll do on defence, Europe. These are matters that need to be discussed in detail. It's people's future at stake.

RD But is it not the problem that some people, some Tory supporters, don't yet understand what John Major does stand for. What sort of Tory is he, they ask? Is he Thatcherite fish or Heseltine fowl?

MAJOR Then ask me the detailed questions and all will become clear.

RD All right, I'll ask you a question about Europe.

MAJOR But I think people do know that. Do.

RD Are you in favour of the Thatcherite vision of Europe – namely a Europe of independent nation states, or another Europe, a federal Europe, with a single currency, a single central bank and, therefore, a single government?

MAJOR Well, I've dealt with this matter in my speeches. I've been dealing with it and I'm happy to deal with it again. I don't believe a United States of Europe is the right way ahead. I do believe a Europe bound together closely, a Europe of nation states bound together, is the right way. And not a narrow Europe with a girdle thrown round the rich countries of Europe. I do think we have to open Europe up, open it to the North and bring in the countries from EFTA and then, in due course, even more important, perhaps, open Europe to the countries of the East. Those newly democratic countries that were once part of the Soviet empire. They've now got their own elected governments, they're searching towards a free market system, they want firstly some form of relationship with the community and then, in due course, bring them in the community. Because there is a great prize to be had there. The greatest prize of the European Community is not its economic advancement. The greatest prize is this. Twice in this century Western Europe has been at war and the whole world has been at war. It is unthinkable that that could happen again. If we can open Europe to all those nations right the way across Europe – Hungary, Poland, Czechoslovakia, even Russia, we can do that, perhaps not in my political lifetime, but when we manage to achieve that we will have made the whole of our continent a much safer and more secure place than ever it has been before. And that's the sort of Europe I want to see.

RD Why do you deserve, why does the Conservative Party deserve, under your leadership, what the British people have never given any political party in modern times – a fourth successive term of office.

MAJOR I think because we have a vision for Britain that goes with the natural grain of the instincts of the British. What do people want these days? I believe increasingly they want more control over their own lives, more opportunity, more choice, more reward when they have performed well. That is the direction which our policies lead. Perhaps I can put it this way. In the 1980s Mrs Thatcher made very remarkable changes in this country. She practically took a hatchet, carved her way through the undergrowth and produced a path towards opportunity and choice, but we need to widen that path. I want more people to pass down it, become home-owners, have their own pension, have their own choices, have their own freedoms. And then when they build something up in their lifetime, have too, yes, have too, the opportunity to pass it on to the next generation. That's what I want to see.

RD That is all very well, but will that answer cut much ice with the unemployed, the homeless, those who have suffered repossession and the many bankrupt businessmen who feel betrayed by the policies of your government?

MAJOR Who are the people who are going to gain most from a successful economy and the expansion of choice? The people who will gain most are the people who at present have least. That is what I call the classless society; to expand a society of opportunity and choice, to bring more people in it, to expand that path of opportunity Mrs Thatcher started and make it wider, and bring more people in. Hence, originally, the policy of selling local authority houses, to make more people home-owners.

RD But why is there no –

MAJOR An extension of those policies that we now have.

RD Why, in your election programme, is there no emergency crash programme of public works to build homes for the homeless and to provide jobs for some of the unemployed?

MAJOR Because it's in the public expenditure programme. What people concentrate on when they look at the Budget, just a few days ago, they say – well, why did you make tax cuts. But what they have neglected to look at is the public expenditure plans which were agreed in November but come into force in April, and they expand public expenditure very dramatically, and in key areas – on housing, on health, on education. And there is an increase of over three times as much on public expenditure in their areas as there is a reduction in taxation in Norman Lamont's Budget.

RD May I put to you a remark made by Dr David Owen in one of his few speeches in this campaign. He said you, the Prime Minister, are not the architect of the recession. He conceded that. But he said you should admit that the depth of the recession in the UK is due to serious misjudgments by Lawson and Thatcher during 1987 and 1988. When, if I may remind our viewers, you were a senior Treasury Minister.

MAJOR I was Chief Secretary.

RD Yes.

MAJOR I was responsible for public expenditure at that time. But there is nothing new about that comment, for I have said it myself. In the wake of the stock exchange crash everyone thought, including the government, the Labour Party, industry, TUC, that there was a danger of a slump, not just here, but around the world. And in this country, and in other countries people then reduced interest rates quickly to avoid a slump. In retrospect, but only in retrospect, that was a mistake. And I think it is to that point that David Owen is referring, and I agree with him about that. We've said that repeatedly.

RD Why not a further cut in interest rates so as to jerk more life into the economy and to help you in the election?

MAJOR Well, we have reduced interest rates by –

RD Again?

MAJOR – by – well, I'll come to that point. We have reduced interest rates by $4\frac{1}{2}$ per cent in the last sixteen months or so. When it's appropriate on the foreign exchange markets further reductions may be made. But there are several ingredients that are necessary to build a prosperous future. And I think there are three I would mention. One is the lowest possible inflation, nil inflation when we can get it, and that's my target. Secondly, a stable exchange rate. I don't want the exchange rate falling because it sucks in inflation and puts prices up. And the third is the right sort of economic climate for investment. That's what's necessary to deal with the problems of the people who are unemployed. We need the sort of society that will create jobs and give them not temporary jobs, but permanent, sustainable jobs with a proper career pattern that they can be proud of and can depend on. It can't be done overnight.

RD But Prime Minister –

MAJOR It can only be done this way.

RD But Prime Minister, why should you expect the people to trust your economic judgment, and your economic management, when they remember the colossal fiasco of the poll tax.

MAJOR When I first became Chancellor I said that my priority was to get inflation down; inflation was on a rising trend, it went up to 11 per cent. I persisted, despite unpopularity. Inflation is now 4.1 per cent; underlying inflation in terms of producer prices is well below that, and there is not a single commentator who doesn't believe that inflation is coming down still further.

RD No, but –

MAJOR I kept my word on that.

RD – but some commentators –

MAJOR And I will keep my word on other matters.

RD Some commentators do say, and you will, doubtless, have read this comment that any fool can get inflation down if he is prepared to lay the economy on its back.

MAJOR The one thing that lays the economy on its back is rising inflation. The Labour Party, if I may remind you, in the 1970s, had 27 per cent inflation and still had a recession.

RD But that's a long time ago, Prime Minister. Could we come back to the poll tax, which was the point of my last question: how can people trust your judgment when they remember this appalling – I won't use the word that came to my tongue, but you know what I mean.

MAJOR I think I know what you mean. When a government makes a mistake, there's one thing it can do – change it. The first thing I set in train when I became Prime Minister was the replacement of the community charge with the council tax. Not only did I say I would do it, I have not held a General Election until that is on the statute books and we have a new system for local government taxation. I promised I would do that, and I have done it.

RD Do you agree with what Nigel Lawson said, that had we joined the ERM – the Exchange Rate Mechanism – in 1985, that's several years earlier than we did, the boom in the late eighties would not have been so great, nor the recession so prolonged as it has been. Wasn't that another mistake?

MAJOR I think it would have been desirable, in retrospect, if we joined the Exchange Rate Mechanism earlier.

RD You shared in that mistake.

MAJOR But I – no, I was not in the Treasury in 1985.

RD No, no, but you –

MAJOR I was in the government in 1985 but –

RD The following years, when we were still waiting for the time to be right.

MAJOR – but not in the Treasury in 1985. But may I remind you that I am the Chancellor who did take us into the Exchange Rate Mechanism. I believed it was the right thing to do. I persuaded all my colleagues in government that it was the right thing to do –

RD Including Mrs Thatcher?

MAJOR – all my colleagues in government that it was the right thing –

RD That must have been difficult.

MAJOR All my colleagues in government and Mrs Thatcher and I took sterling into the Exchange Rate Mechanism. It was the right thing to do, and it has helped us bring inflation down to the benefit of industry and every individual in this country.

RD You mentioned Scotland, Prime Minister. Why are you so adamant against any measure of Scottish devolution? Because in 1976 – fifteen years ago – Mrs Thatcher, Mr Heath, Viscount Whitelaw as he now is, that wise old Knight of the Thistle, said I don't think anyone could deny that a directly elected Scottish assembly, which is what they proposed, is consistent, he said, with the political and economic integrity of the UK. Why have you gone back on that policy?

MAJOR What is proposed in Scotland at the moment by the Labour Party and the Liberal Party is a tax-raising assembly in Parliament. Follow the thought through.

RD But you're proposing nothing.

MAJOR No. Let me follow the thought through and you'll understand why I feel so seriously about this, so deeply and passionately about it. If there's a tax-raising assembly in Edinburgh in which they have sole responsibility for certain areas of policy: health, education, industry perhaps, that will have several effects on the Westminster Parliament. If Scotland are to determine those matters solely for themselves, Scottish MPs could not come to Westminster and then decide upon the same issues for England, Wales and Northern Ireland. And what would that mean? That would mean two sorts of MPs at Westminster. MPs from Wales, Northern Ireland and England who could vote on everything, and MPs from Scotland who were second-tier MPs, who could only vote on some subjects.

RD Are you saying that that means we can't have any reform at all?

MAJOR I'm not saying that. Just one moment. And that, undoubtedly, would mean at Westminster you are changing the constitution – a government couldn't be sure of its majority. And where would that end? What bitterness and chaos and frustration would that cause in Scotland? And if it did cause the bitterness and frustration I suspect, would that not lead them to take the extra step towards separation? This is a dangerous and a slippery slope for the proposals for devolution that the Labour Party have.

RD But why don't you put forward better proposals for a devolution?

MAJOR Well, I'm arguing very strongly for the union. We've had a union –

RD A union isn't inconsistent with devolution, as Viscount Whitelaw said.

MAJOR The sort of tax-raising assembly that is proposed now is inconsistent, over time, with maintaining the union for the reasons I have just set out.

RD Why have you changed your mind on the desirability of Proportional Representation?

MAJOR I never have.

RD Oh. But I –

MAJOR I know exactly what you have there.

RD What do I have?

266

MAJOR You have a cutting, very probably, from a Sunday newspaper saying I was in favour of Proportional Representation. If you have, you would find they corrected it and apologized a week later, because what they had quoted was something I had said previously – that had been said previously not by me, but by my Liberal opponent at a General Election –

RD So you've never wanted Proportional Representation, never thought it was a good idea at all?

MAJOR I don't believe it's a good idea.

RD And you don't think you're going to have to talk about that after the election with Paddy Ashdown?

MAJOR No. It isn't a good idea. It leads to weak government. There are a number of governments in Europe who have Proportional Representation who wish they hadn't got it. They can't form their – How long did it take the Belgians to form a government? A hundred days. You can't run a country that way. A country like Britain. There are many countries with Proportional Representation who wish they had a first-past-the-post system in order that they have a strong government. I'm not in favour of Proportional Representation.

RD Under any circumstances?

MAJOR Under any circumstances.

RD And you would under no circumstances co-operate with the minority party in order to maintain government?

MAJOR I would not weaken our constitution for short-term party advantage of staying in government, no.

RD Will you resign as Prime Minister if you don't win an overall majority?

MAJOR It's purely hypothetical. I am going to win an overall majority and I'm –

RD Yes, but all questions in an election are hypothetical, Prime Minister. What will you do if this, what will you do if that?

MAJOR Prime Ministers answer questions when they're reality, not when they're hypothetical.

RD Not in an election?

MAJOR And in this circumstance, I can absolutely assure you that I am confident that we are going to win a clear overall majority sufficient for five years.

RD Of course, it's possible that God may smile upon the Labour Party.

MAJOR I think the electorate will smile upon the Conservative Party.

RD What do you say to those people who think that after thirteen years of Tory rule it's only fair for the other team to have an innings in the interest of a healthy democracy?

MAJOR This isn't a game of Tag. It isn't a question of fairness. It's a question of who is going to run this country in the best way for the future of this country. I have no doubt that our policies are the right policies for this country and, equally, I have no doubt that the policies the Labour Party have in mind would be a very dramatic step back into the past.

RD Why? Why a dramatic step back into the past?

MAJOR Well, let me set out some of them for you.

RD Yes.

MAJOR They would repeal the trade union legislation.

RD Not all of it.

MAJOR They would repeal the trade union legislation, almost all of it, if not all of it, and they would offer fresh freedoms to the trade unions. Nobody wants to go back to that. They will have policies of much higher taxation rather than leaving more money in people's pockets to decide for themselves. They would stop the education reforms. The concentration that I believe is vital on the very basics of education: reading, writing, adding up. They'd go back to the old theories that have failed. They would stop the reforms that are making this a better and more efficient Health Service. They certainly wouldn't proceed with the strong defence policy that we have. They have a policy of cutting defence by 27 per cent. And the Liberals now, I think, by 50 per cent. So there are sharp differences. No one can be sure from one day to the next whether the Labour Party are in favour of being in Europe or out of Europe. They've changed their mind upon that matter six times.

RD Do you think that it would be a good idea, in view of the fact that the campaign is now getting rough and the polls don't look very good for you, though you think they're all over the place, do you not think it would be a good idea to reconsider your refusal to have a face-to-face debate with Mr Kinnock and, perhaps, Mr Ashdown?

MAJOR I'm having my debate with the electorate, day after day and night after night. That's the debate I want to have. I want to put to them our ideas for the future of this country, listen to what they have to say and persuade them that we have the right policies. That's the way forward.

RD So judging by your description of the alternative which Labour offers, you don't just regard this as another General Election, but as a very

serious election affecting the whole future of the country and whether
we make progress or go back. Most people don't quite see it in that
way, do they, they think of it in terms of tax.

MAJOR No. Well, tax is a very important matter, but the election's far
more important than just about tax. Tax is vital, it is central. But
there is a gulf between the two major parties, one of whom will form
the government after this election, a gulf down a whole range of
issues. I believe we have to build on what's been achieved in the
1980s, we have set out the policies to do that. I'm sure that's the
way forward.

RD Prime Minister, thank you very much.

'I think that the way in which there was a complete adherence to the idea of unilateralism may have been an error of judgment.'

NEIL KINNOCK

One week before polling day in the 1992 General Election, Neil Kinnock looked supremely relaxed, his confidence of victory boosted by the opinion polls and by the pundits.

As it happened, that day turned out to have been a day of significant misjudgment by the Labour leadership. In the morning Kinnock had appeared to open the door to discussion about electoral reform with Paddy Ashdown. Kinnock denied that he had done anything of the kind. But his mention of the subject, one week before polling day, at once suggested to me and others that behind his swaggering confidence a doubt was forming as to whether Labour would get a majority after all. Hence this last-minute hint about Proportional Representation to win Liberal voters over to Labour.

Correct or not, that was a reasonable interpretation, and one which should be put straight away to Neil Kinnock. In characteristic style and at characteristic length, he gave his explanation. This might have been more convincing if he had not, with uncharacteristic brevity, refused point-blank to reveal his own views on Proportional Representation.

When the result of an election is widely seen as a foregone conclusion, a heavy responsibility falls on the television interviewer. His duty is to ignore the predictions and the prevailing opinion. He has to do what he can to pursue the election argument. He should not let the issues be obscured by the pollsters' predictions. I felt this responsibility strongly in my approach to this Kinnock interview. My questions had to be such as not to give credence to the prevailing opinion that Labour was home and dry. I had to remember that the election was not in the bag but was still to be decided, and would be decided not by pollsters or newspapers but by the voters on the issues. I was determined not to appear influenced by the premature triumphalism of Labour's campaign.

I could remember from 1970 that it was dangerously easy to be brain-washed by the prevailing wisdom. Ted Heath was written off then as a loser and, to the surprise of the pundits, won the election.

My interrogation of Kinnock was to be vigorous and persistent. As in the interview with John Major, I put direct questions concerning past errors of judgment which he might wish to admit. As did Major, Kinnock makes some admissions. His confessions of error were seized on by the Tory press. KINNOCK ADMITS GRAVE ERRORS was the *Daily Express* banner full-page headline, with the somewhat exaggerated sub-heading, 'Robin Day skewers Labour leader'. Sir Alastair Burnet handed down his judgment in the *Sunday Times*: 'Neil Kinnock was enjoying himself, what with the polls and his Wednesday rally in Sheffield. Then he ran into Sir Robin Day on Thursday's *This Week*.'

Would Kinnock have been a great Prime Minister? He certainly showed courage and skill in his long struggle to make the Labour Party electable. If he had greatness in him, it had yet to be proved. The same could be said of John Major.

I admired Kinnock's guts and his sense of humour. I had enjoyed his company. Before he was leader, I had more than one lively evening of singing with him in conference hotels. After one of his appearances on *Question Time*, I took him home for a drink and played him my treasured recording of Aneurin Bevan (one of his heroes). This was the historic speech against unilateral nuclear disarmament at Brighton ('Don't send the British Foreign Secretary naked into the Conference Chamber') in 1957. Neil had never met Nye nor, he said, had he heard the recording before. We got on well.

The Rt Hon. Neil Kinnock, Leader of the Labour Party

Interviewed for Thames Television in This Week
2 April 1992

SIR ROBIN DAY Mr Kinnock, by your clear hint about electoral reform to Paddy Ashdown today, have you not, at last, had to concede the possibility that you may not get an overall majority and that the Parliament will be well and truly hung?

RT HON. NEIL KINNOCK No. And it wasn't a hint to Paddy Ashdown either. It was a quite natural part of a process that I started in the Labour Party over two years ago in establishing the Plant Committee, in undertaking a very thorough appraisal, for the purposes of promoting the public debate, on the whole question of electoral reform.

RD But if people read tomorrow in their newspapers, as they will, and hear on the television bulletins tonight that you, Mr Kinnock, have been seeking to open today the door to some PR deal with Ashdown, when you made it clear that the Liberal Party and other parties could join your commission of inquiry.

KINNOCK Well, I think that's a fairly natural development of what we have been doing. And you – you may –

RD So you are – you are opening the door.

KINNOCK No, I'm not.

RD Or seeking to.

KINNOCK I'm not opening the door at all. I will most certainly –

RD Well, you're not shutting it, like John Major is.

KINNOCK – I will most certainly welcome participation of other parties, and of church leaders and trade unionists and business people in the deliberations and in the recommendations of the Plant Committee. That becomes possible because the Plant Committee, instead of only reporting to an Opposition party, will be reporting to a government. You may recall that a few weeks ago we made it clear that that was going to be the intention. All I did today was to confirm that. But as I say, I think it's important for everybody to acknowledge before they start –

RD You've chosen a very significant moment in the campaign to confirm it. Captain Ashdown, as you call him, says your offer is fudging and fence-sitting.

KINNOCK Well, I'm not obliged to respond to him. I will certainly do that. But I think it's important, since I know you are absolutely obsessed by accuracy, to recall that it is over two years since I started the process, and it would be peculiar, wouldn't it, if I'd started that process with the purpose of ensuring that there was some great addition to it just a week before a General Election, when it is, as I said, a natural part of what we've been doing in the Labour Party, what I instigated over two years ago –

RD But you instigated it –

KINNOCK – and I think will be of interest to the general public and certainly not any part of any proposed horse-trading with any other party. When we form the majority government I am certain that the process that I inaugurated will continue and will meet with public satisfaction.

RD But when you started the process two years ago, you had the coming General Election in mind, and the possibility of the need of Liberal co-operation about PR, didn't you?

KINNOCK Well, as it happened, at the time that I started it we were running 10 and 12 per cent ahead in the polls. So –

RD But you knew that wouldn't last.

KINNOCK Well, whether it would last or not, it has to be said that I didn't begin the process in any supplicant way. It was an independent proposition. It's been endorsed by the Labour Party. It's been carried out under the chairmanship of Professor Plant, and the idea that it was inaugurated by, or is now sponsored in any way by the feeling that we won't get a majority is wrong, we will get a majority. And the idea that it's all part of some great plot to build a bridge to Paddy Ashdown, is also wrong, is nonsense.

RD You have your own views about PR at Westminster, don't you?

KINNOCK I do.

RD Would you tell us what those views are?

KINNOCK No, I won't. Because I –

RD Oh?

KINNOCK – said at the outset that what would occur, of course, if I said very clearly what my conclusions were likely to be about the whole process of electoral reform, or the system of electing that we should have in this country, we would translate what I hope would be a very constructive activity, as it has been, into one of a test of loyalty to the leadership, divisions in the Labour Party, splits and all the other distractions, so I wasn't having that, and I'm still not going to.

RD But Mr Kinnock, you want to win our votes, we want to hear your views.

KINNOCK I want to hear other people's views. I want to provide them with an opportunity for the –

RD But why are you so shy, why are you hiding your views under –

KINNOCK It isn't shyness at all. It's the action of a confident person who has got such confidence in his party and in the public's ability to conduct this debate on a well-informed basis, that I've been determined to ensure that the additional information is available in the most non-partisan fashion.

RD But if you're a good leader, as you believe you are, why don't you lead your party towards what you think is the right view on Proportional Representation, instead of hiding and finding refuge behind a commission.

KINNOCK Because this is one of the few areas that I believe should not be partisan property. I've believed all along that because there was a discussion taking place, because it was subject to various kinds of influences, dyed-in-the-wool opponents of any change, dyed-in-the-wool proponents of just about any change, that there was a danger of what is a profoundly important debate becoming completely polarized. It was up to us to take the ground that said let us undertake the fullest analysis, make the international comparisons, see what the possibilities are, in British terms, and what would be the outcomes, and to – if I can just make this last point – and to do it on the basis not of achieving a partisan outcome, convenient or inconvenient, but of ensuring the two questions were answered: Would change produce a better system of representation in Britain? Would change produce a better system of government in Britain? And those have still got to be the two basic criteria on which any proposition for change or any proposition for staying with the current system have got to be decided.

RD Would it be cynical for me to suggest, Mr Kinnock, that if you do win an overall majority under our first-past-the-post system, any idea of Proportional Representation for Westminster will be dumped by you promptly to the bottom of the Thames?

KINNOCK The problem wouldn't be of cynicism, because I know that cynicism is entirely absent from your personality, but the problem would be the question of accuracy. We have set up the process.

RD OK, we've had that.

KINNOCK The process will continue, and it will continue in all circumstances. I'm happy to report that it will continue with the majority government in power.

RD Now Mr Kinnock, as you have absolutely no experience in government yourself, would it be unreasonable for undecided voters to ask whether you are up to the job of Prime Minister?

KINNOCK Not unreasonable, but I hope they'd come to the right conclusion, and consider my record of bringing a party back from the point of abject defeat in 1983 to where we now are – going to form the next government – and to understand that that hasn't been done without application, without the ability to lead, without an ability to look into the future, an ability to put together a highly effective and talented team, and to adopt policies that are relevant to the condition of our country now, and capable of equipping our country better for the future. Now I think they're qualifications for the leadership of a country, and I hope people will judge me on the basis of those accomplishments, and the potential that it shows for leadership of the country in the future.

RD Well, let us, then, consider your record, as you suggested. Why should voters trust your judgment when you were a member of the Campaign for Nuclear Disarmament for many years, and advocated that Britain should give up her nuclear weapons, even though a potential enemy still possessed theirs?

KINNOCK I just asked that two matters were referred to. The first is that the argument that I put forward, and you will have heard it, was that there was a total log-jam, indeed a continuing build-up of nuclear weapons on both sides and no prospect appearing over the horizon of any kind of change. The moment that that change – secondly – became apparent, that there were ways of ensuring that the arms race stopped and a process of disarmament was undertaken, on the basis of negotiation, verifiable disarmament, I thought that the Labour Party should be part of that. And since I've never been a pacifist, it was perfectly natural, indeed, quite easy for me to say here are a new set of opportunities, and it is up to us to take full advantage, sustaining security for our country, an alliance, in the process, with seeing that we are part of that process of ending what George Bush called the 'peace of tension', and replacing it with what he called the 'peace of trust'.

RD But if the country had followed your judgment in the past, Britain wouldn't have nuclear weapons now.

KINNOCK Well, I think that we'd have been talking in terms of a different world in many respects in any case. But what we –

RD Is that correct?

KINNOCK – but what we have to deal with –

RD Is that correct?

KINNOCK Well, what we have to deal with is the situation that's confronted us since 1985 and the situation confronting us now. And it would be, would it not, a failure to do one's duty if you didn't relate to the circumstances as they exist and are likely to exist, rather than ones that might have existed in a previous period in history.

RD Yes, but many –

KINNOCK Even though relatively recent.

RD Yes, but many – many voters may ask this, you see, why is it you wanted to scrap our nuclear weapons when the Soviet Union was our potential enemy and had them of their own, yet you now want to keep them when the Soviet Union doesn't exist and isn't a danger to us?

KINNOCK Well, through those years, as I candidly acknowledged, and I have since –

RD You made a mistake?

KINNOCK – I did believe that it was the only way to promote a change in the relationships and to secure an ending to a continuing arms race and a shift in the direction of disarmament.

RD Was it an error of judgment?

KINNOCK I think that the way in which there was a complete adherence to the idea of unilateralism, that the only way to promote the change may have been an error of judgment –

RD By you?

KINNOCK Well, yes, by me as an individual.

RD May have been or was?

KINNOCK Well, as an individual, I had the view that the only cir-cumstances in which there would ever be profit from trying to change the direction of affairs was by taking unilateral action. I believe that the opportunities that have been provided by the action of President Reagan, now President Bush, Mr Gorbachev, changed situations, changed conditions very radically and made it necessary, not just providing the opportunity, but made it necessary for a change of policy to take place.

RD If you are Prime Minister in a week's time, Mr Kinnock, you will have Britain's nuclear weapons under your control. Are you prepared to use them?

KINNOCK No one ever gives, and you know it very well, a yes or no answer to that.

RD Why not?

KINNOCK The presumption of retention of weapons is a readiness to use. But nobody ever has given a yes or no answer to that question, because it would be utterly unconvincing. For the potential aggressor the view would be if you said, yes, I am prepared to use them, they'd have to work on the basis that possibly, given the conditions in which nuclear weapons would be used then, perhaps, that resolution wouldn't be carried through. If you said no, that you wouldn't use them, well, of course, the point of retention would go. So we are retaining nuclear weapons, nobody will tell you yes or no. But everybody will make the presumption that as long as they exist and as long as they are possessed the likelihood of their use is there.

RD But why should voters trust your judgment on foreign affairs, Mr Kinnock? Because if we'd followed your declared opinion in 1983 Britain would not now be in the European Community, for which you are now so very enthusiastic.

KINNOCK Well, on the European Community I've explained on other occasions, and I happily do so now, that my view of our participation in the European Community changed some time before 1983, but such was the turmoil and weakness in my party, to which I owe a duty, that I wasn't going to inflict an additional division. The moment that that 1983 election was over I made my opinions clear in a very long article and counselled the radical change in direction of the policies of the Labour Party. I was accepting collective responsibility. That is something I expect anybody in a senior position in an Opposition party or in a government to do, and it's the discipline I accept for myself.

RD When did you become a marketeer, having been an anti-marketeer?

KINNOCK Oh, I'd say certainly in the late seventies, early eighties.

RD Was it an error of judgment?

KINNOCK And the only regret that I have, I believe I did make an error of judgment in the wake of the 1975 Referendum.

RD Did you vote for or against?

KINNOCK I campaigned against continuing –

RD Yes. Was that an error of judgment?

KINNOCK No. Not at the time. But I should have decided in 1975, when the Referendum result was so complete, that it was a cause that could not be pursued, and what we had to do was to exercise maximum influence from the inside and not to continue to court the idea of trying to get on the outside. Now I should have made that change of view then, that was an error of judgment. But I must say that the first chance that I really got to manifest the change, without inflicting harm on my party, was to do so in the wake of the 1983 election.

RD Will your Foreign Secretary definitely be Gerald Kaufman?

KINNOCK Gerald will be the Foreign Secretary.

RD But is it wise to appoint as Foreign Secretary, who will be President of the British – of the European Community, someone who was against, like you, the Common Market?

KINNOCK Very wise. Because he's a very effective advocate, as you know yourself. He's a very patriotic Britisher and representative of this country. But he is someone who also profoundly comprehends both the need for us to make our way clearly, and make our presence felt in the European Community, but also to treat it as a community which has to solve many problems that commonly face us with common answers. And on all three grounds I'd say that Gerald is not only capable of doing the job but will prove to be brilliant in the job.

RD You may have seen an article in the *Guardian* which is neither anti-Labour nor anti-Semitic, which said that some Jewish voters may not want to vote Labour for fear that Gerald Kaufman may become the Foreign Secretary.

KINNOCK I think they would be mistaken if they were to have reservations on that account, because Gerald, whose knowledge of the Middle East, and of the position and necessary continual status of the State of Israel, dates back a very long way, and the consequence of that is that he is prepared and able to bring to bear on the vexed question of the Middle East a dispassionate attitude that is capable of promoting peace. And I am glad to say that because of other changes he will get even more of an opportunity to do that because of the way in which a peace process is now under way, something for which he has argued much longer than he has been Shadow Foreign Secretary, and

I think that he will be provided with opportunities to make his presence felt and his wisdom known, because that process is under way.

RD Let us take the important question of devolution in Scotland. Now in an interview last summer with the *Scotsman* newspaper, you said this, Mr Kinnock: 'I think that people can trust my word and my attitude because I have always been in favour of devolution.'

KINNOCK Yes.

RD That produced a reaction of stunned incredulity from your interlocutors because they said some people – 'most people would think of Neil Kinnock as a man who has not always believed in devolution'.

KINNOCK Well, I said to my interlocutors that they should find anything that I've ever offered in argument against devolution, against the decentralization of power, against the realistic establishment of more effective systems of executive action and democratic decision-making. And, of course, they didn't begin to try because they knew I'd never done that. What I did argue against was a particular form of devolution that was proposed by the then Labour government in the late 1970s. I am very happy that I've been partly responsible for securing changes which mean that the changes that we will make, so far as the establishment of a Parliament in Scotland, an assembly in Wales is concerned, they will be in the context of continuing devolution, continuing decentralization of power in England as well. So that the danger that I think you may recall me drawing attention to fifteen years or so ago of what I called 'sore thumb' devolution, of isolation of Wales and Scotland, will not arise, because we will be going through a process that is familiar in the European Community of decentralization of power to the different component parts – the nations and regions of Britain. I think this will be a better place in which to live as a result.

RD Could we come to the important question of economic management. Won't your sharp increase of income tax on middle and high earners be bad for wealth creation and for the generation of growth, the very growth you need if you're going to be able to afford to carry out your manifesto commitments?

KINNOCK No, it won't be. And I put it to you on two grounds that it won't be. First of all, the only years of vitality, in the last thirteen, were in the middle to late 1980s and that was under Mrs Thatcher. It proved to be giddy, it proved to be unsustainable, but they were years of growth. They were also the years that were said to be the years of enterprise. But, of course, the top marginal rate of income tax at that time was 60 per cent. If you combine together our top rate of 50 per cent, starting at £40,000, and 9 per cent National Insurance, it still doesn't come to 60 per cent. Secondly, there is absolutely no study that can demonstrate a connection between the vitality in the economy and the strivings of enterprising individuals and the marginal rate of tax. I suppose it is possible.

RD Well, is it not – it may not be research or studies, but a certain amount of commonsense will tell you that it won't be very encouraging to, say, a manager on £40,000 a year whose tax burden and National Insurance under the Labour government – if you form one – will increase by 19 per cent.

KINNOCK Well, there are several people in that position and, of course, they include you and myself, whose strivings will not be diminished at all by that. And there are, secondly, other people in that position who, realizing that whatever take-home pay they got, this could become an incompetent country and an ill-served country if the Health Service and the education system were both under-invested, and would be ready to make an additional contribution to ensure that they live in a country which is well served in terms of health care and is well served in terms of the education of its children.

RD But do you think you could convince the undecided voters that by stinging the better-off you will be able to benefit the poor?

KINNOCK We're not stinging them, we're asking them to make a fair contribution –

RD What, not taking 60 per cent of an extra pound that –

KINNOCK – that is in line – that is in line with their capacity – in line with their capacity to pay, which, as I say, several will do because they recognize their obligations to themselves, as well as the rest of society, and because the payment of that taxation to get better public services in essential areas is not an entirely selfless act, it's an act of common sense. But, of course, all it does is to ensure that at the top levels of income there is a fairer system of taxation just as people on under £22,000 a year have to pay a fair system of taxation.

RD Yes, but may I remind you of what your old comrade Denis Healey said in his memoirs. He said: 'Any substantial attempt to improve the lot of the poorest must now be at the expense of

the average man and woman, since the very rich do not collec-
tively earn enough to make much difference, and the average man
does not, nowadays, want to punish those who earn a little
more than he, since the average man hopes, ultimately, to join
them.'

KINNOCK Well, the average man and woman, and Denis is correct about
the way in which it has to be distributed. But I think that if he were
to define the average man and woman, he would talk of people on
the average wage of £13,000 to £14,000 a year. Or if he was talking
about households in Britain, the figure would be £19,000 a year.
Now, in both cases, those people are actual beneficiaries of our tax
changes and not in any sense obliged to pay additional taxation. To
get £22,000 a year is to be well above average. And we are recognizing
that it is not possible just to squeeze the most rich in order to help
the average and the below average, but to require that there is a fair
taxation system followed through that course, which is why we are
asking people on over £22,000 a year to pay 9 per cent National
Insurance on all their income, as does everyone else; and to have a
top rate of tax which we will not increase, that begins at £40,000 a
year. Even when we've done that, the people in those brackets will
not have a tax obligation which is as high as their counterparts in
France or in Germany. That's how fair it's going to be.

RD Under a Labour government, would the trade unions recover much
of their pre-Thatcher power?

KINNOCK We've made the propositions and we will put into effect those
propositions, that there is universal balloting, that there is a system
of industrial tribunals, that the membership shall be in control of the
trade union, and there will be no flying pickets. What we will have,
of course –

RD Secondary picketing?

KINNOCK I'll explain. What we will have, of course, is a legal procedure
that ensures that British trade unions and British employees have the
same civil rights as exist on the other side of the Channel in the rest
of the European Community, and that means that there can be no
secondary action, unless it is directly related to a primary action and,
secondly, that if any action is proposed it still has to enjoy the majority
in a ballot taken of all of the concerned workers.

RD Can you assure the voters that there will be no return to abuse of
union power under the Labour government, if you form it?

KINNOCK Because of the legal procedure we'll introduce, certainly, there will be no return. There are no favours involved. It's only fairness that brings us into line with procedures in other democratic industrialized countries.

RD Do you think – do you really think, Mr Kinnock, that Mr John Major does not believe in the National Health Service just as sincerely as you do?

KINNOCK Well, if he does, he's got a very funny way of showing it. If he does, he wouldn't have sat on the secret committee that set up this so-called market system. If he does believe as sincerely as I do, he will realize that the market principle is in collision with the idea of a universally free National Health Service – free at time of need. And if he did believe in the way that I do, in the National Health Service, he wouldn't be embarking upon a system of general practitioner arrangements which would turn the attempts by a doctor to get his patients into hospital in due course, if there were many more of the general practitioner arrangements, the fund-holding arrangements that they've offered, would turn that whole business into a sickness bazaar. Like a kind of stock market.

RD But will it help the patients or the doctors or the nurses or the hospital workers for the National Health Service to go through another upheaval, while you undo and reverse the reforms which the Tories have put in only just now?

KINNOCK But there's no great upheaval. First of all, only fifty-two hospitals have thus far opted out. There's another tranche that are in the first week of the process, but there's no great turn-around on that. And it's very easy, of course, for them to re-enter the mainstream of the National Health Service, much less of an upheaval than leaving it. And certainly, it's not going to cost the tax payer £500 million pounds, which this –

RD We're at the end of our interview, Mr Kinnock.

KINNOCK – which this bureaucratized market system has so far cost the tax payers for the hospitals to return to a National – underlined four times – Health Service.

RD Despite your bitter criticism of the Tory record, may not some undecided voters prefer to remember the old advice: 'Always keep a hold of nurse, for fear of finding something worse.'

KINNOCK For fear – for fear –

RD Yes.

KINNOCK – is the active part. And I want the nation without fear.

RD Thank you, Mr Kinnock.

KINNOCK I hope the people will make their decision on 9 April with confidence and courage.

RD Thank you very much, Mr Kinnock.

'We both hold strong views. I am hired to express mine. You, Robin, are hired not to express yours. Isn't that really rather odd?'

ROBIN DAY

interviewed by

BERNARD LEVIN

My friendship with Bernard Levin* goes back a very long time. In 1955, when I started on television in ITN, he was a TV critic for the *Guardian*. We were both beginning to make names for ourselves, he as a brilliantly original writer on anything (drama, politics, parliament, music, food, books), I as one of a new breed of mediamen – a television journalist (newscaster, interviewer, political correspondent, roving reporter).

Mr Levin was a master of critical ridicule. One of the first notices I ever had of an appearance on television was by him. It was so brutal that it does not appear to have been kept in my book of early cuttings. But I remember it well. He said that I was absolutely awful. It was extremely painful to read. It was, moreover, perfectly true. I do, however, still have the *Guardian* piece which Levin later wrote in looking back on the TV programmes of 1956. He wrote that ITN had led not only its BBC rivals but most of the programmes around it. Then, declared Levin:

> May I at this point withdraw a number of horrid things I said when ITN was in its infancy about Mr Robin Day? He has improved, it seems to me, out of all recognition, pomposity having been replaced by incisiveness, off-handedness by application, and buttonholing by a genuine intimacy. And as an interviewer, Mr Day has always been in the very highest flight.

Years later, in 1980, I celebrated my twenty-fifth anniversary in television. Bernard, by now Britain's columnist laureate, devoted one of his columns in *The Times* to a generous eulogy which was (almost) too embarrassing to read:

* CBE in 1990.

You have to be as old as I am to remember what the interviewing of politicians was like on television before Robin established himself in the field. If a politician in a fix took refuge from a question in a labyrinth of verbiage, the interviewer simply went on to the next question. If the politician, in answer to the next question, told an obvious lie, the interviewer behaved as though it was the truth. If the politician behaved as though the interviewer should have used the tradesmen's entrance, the interviewer made it clear that he thought so too.

Nous avons changé tout cela. But we have done so almost entirely by virtue of Robin's talent, determination and integrity. And he has achieved his success, on our behalf, not by bullying but by courteous insistence, and not by taking sides but by the most scrupulous fairness.

So in 1980 when Bernard invited me to be one of his guests on his BBC 2 series, *The Levin Interviews,* I accepted – but not immediately. His other guests were great creative people of our time, geniuses of literature and music. Was he not scraping the barrel by inviting me, a mere television man? He needed variety in the series, and so would I please accept?

I journeyed to Bristol where the programme was to be recorded. I submitted to Bernard's civilized cross-examination. On the train back to London he seemed quite pleased by our joint performance, but not unduly excited.

I was stunned a few days later to get a delighted telephone call from Bernard who had seen a playback of the interview. It was, he said, just what he wanted and went on to speak of it in words too flattering to repeat here. What gratified me even more was the mail I received from viewers. I had argued that television had contributed to the spate of unreasoned violence and conflict in our society. The response was overwhelming (the biggest I have ever had), from all kinds of people of all political opinions. Virtually every single one supported me. That, of course, proved nothing except that I was not alone.

If our conversation was entertaining or stimulating as a programme, this is due to Bernard who probed with skill and charm. He brilliantly hit on a simple difference between us. He said we both held strong views. 'Now I am hired to express mine, you are hired not to express yours. Isn't that really rather odd?'

That simple distinction had not occurred to me. My off-the-cuff response was the best I could think of. But as I had already explained, I was frankly grateful that it was not my job to express my opinions on every issue. I simply did not have a clear opinion on how to conquer inflation, or how to end bloodshed in Ulster, or how to stop the increase in crime. But Bernard Levin coaxed more expressions of opinion out of me than I had ever uttered before or since on television. I am grateful to him, and count it an honour to include the transcript in this book.

Robin Day
interviewed by Bernard Levin

Recorded for BBC 2 series The Levin Interviews
*3 May 1980**

BERNARD LEVIN This is a man who in 1980 is celebrating, if that's the word he would use, his twenty-fifth year in television. He began as, and remains, a very distinguished television reporter, but perhaps he is mainly known for having devised, almost single-handed, the modern form of the television political interview. His appearance is intimately familiar in almost every household in the land, with his trademarks, his polka-dot bow tie, and what Frankie Howerd once memorably called 'those cruel glasses': Robin Day.

Robin, you once wrote that if the interviewer loses his nerve, and fails to ask the crucial questions, he betrays the public who are relying on him. Nobody who knows your work would deny that you have always lived up to that self-imposed obligation. But I think you would not wish to relieve me of that responsibility on this occasion. So let's begin with a question that you have been asked many times. It's a charge that has been levelled against you very frequently, and that is that in your manner, and whatever is behind that manner, in interviewing politicians, don't you really delight in bullying them, hectoring them, and telling them off in a way which perhaps is none of your business?

ROBIN DAY Can you give me an example of when I have ever hectored or bullied a politician, and can you think of a politician whom one *could* hector or bully?

LEVIN Well, let's say tried to. You've interrupted politicians many times.
RD Oh, certainly you have to interrupt, because otherwise you wouldn't cover the ground. I hate interrupting, I honestly tell you that. I hate interrupting because it looks rude, and it's not meant to be rude. But if one didn't interrupt, some politicians would never end their answers, and one has to come in with supplementaries, and to cover other aspects of the matter. I would say that in recent years I have had far fewer letters complaining of what you've complained of, or what you

---

*First published in the *Listener*, 18 and 25 December 1980.

have quoted, than I used to, because people have now got used to the vigorous, relevant interview. It may also be because people have had a chance to hear Parliament broadcast on the radio. They now realize how polite and deferential I am, by comparison to our elected MPs.

LEVIN Of course, there is this, isn't there, that the politician, the government politician certainly, and the alternative government politician, has a responsibility which you don't have, which I don't have in my writing. Obviously he's trying to get the economy right if he's the Chancellor, or grappling with questions of crime if he's Home Secretary. You have no such responsibility. What is your role *vis-à-vis* that politician when you think, 'Here is this man who is really doing the job; who am I to tell him off for not doing it properly?'

RD I quite agree; I do feel that responsibility very acutely, and whenever I go before a politician or a politician comes into the studio, I have that feeling in my stomach, in my guts. But I have to not let it unnerve me, because I have to remember not only that he or she has enormous responsibilities and burdens, but I have also to remember that history shows that politicians make mistakes. Also that there are people out there who are angry, or bewildered, or disturbed about some matter. And I like to remember some words of Montaigne, which translated say, 'Sit he on never so high a throne, a man still sits on his own bottom.'

LEVIN Do you think politicians forget that, and that your job is to remind them?

RD No, I don't. They don't. They're invariably ready to answer the questions which I want to ask, for the simple reason that they live in an atmosphere of debate and controversy. If I have to interview, say, Mr Jim Prior about his industrial relations proposals, he has been living with those for months, debating them in Committee, in Parliament, in Cabinet. There's virtually nothing I can ask him which he hasn't been asked before. Therefore he is prepared. Though he doesn't know the details of my questions, he's ready for them.

LEVIN But doesn't it then become a game, really? Almost like, in some respects, but only in *some* respects, advocacy in a courtroom: that everybody knows the rules? The politician you say has been up and down this a thousand times, he's probably been interviewed by you twenty times. Is it worth it? What's gained from it nowadays?

RD They may have been interviewed by me twenty times or more, but there are always new situations and new problems. If you say answers are predictable and politicians don't say what you don't expect them to say, I can only refer you to an interview I had the privilege of doing with the Prime Minister in Downing Street, when I asked her whether it might not be better, perhaps, to have industrial relations law which enabled people to get at union funds by means of legal action. Much to my surprise, and that of every other journalist, she gave a clear indication that she personally was inclined to favour that point of view, even though it wasn't in Mr Prior's proposals. So what might have been a routine interview elicited some very interesting information, and it has happened on other occasions.

LEVIN Do you feel ever, after such an interview, 'Ha! I got him there'?

RD No, I don't. Occasionally, after an interview, Harold Wilson used to take me aside and say, 'I thought you were going to ask me that, you missed that one. I didn't know what to say if you'd asked me that. Why didn't you ask me that?' You see? And he'd tick me off for not, as you would put it, playing the game in the proper way. But I never regard it as a game. If you have twenty minutes with a Minister of the Crown, or a senior politician, and you have to cover Northern Ireland and Rhodesia and inflation and the latest industrial crisis, you don't think of it as a game. You say, how on earth do I get all this in in the time, what are the questions I need to ask, what are the people in this industrial crisis going to want to ask, what are the people who've been wounded or mutilated in Northern Ireland going to want asked?

LEVIN Then you think of it, by the sound of you, you think of yourself as a representative of the viewers, is that so?

RD I try to ask questions which will reflect what the viewers may wish to know. But also I try to ask questions which the viewers ought to want asked if they knew a little more about the subject. I try to say, 'What does the ordinary person want to know about this?'

LEVIN Well, then, what duties do you, so to speak, lay upon yourself in your role? Not merely as an interviewer, because you're not only an interviewer after all, you've done a great deal of reporting, from abroad, for instance. Now, what code of conduct, if you like, what duties, what responsibilities do you lay upon yourself, apart from the one which I mentioned right at the beginning of the programme?

RD I don't lay any duties at all upon myself. I accept a contract from the BBC, or any other organization, as the case may be, and I'm hired and employed to perform the function of a television journalist. I know that, having regard to the responsibilities of that organization,

I must ask questions in a particular way and have regard to the editorial policy of the programme or the editorial responsibility of the programme. I don't put any duties upon myself, I accept duties imposed upon me by other people.

LEVIN But that really sounds like far too neutral a role for the Robin Day we know. You're a man with decided opinions of your own.

RD Oh, yes, but my training is not to express them.

LEVIN Does that irk you, not being able to?

RD Not at all, because in fact, if I have a strong opinion on a particular issue, which comes up in the middle of an interview with a senior politician, my instinct and training is to be very careful to suppress my own point of view, because I don't want my employers saying, 'While you were hammering away, you were grinding your own axe.' And indeed it doesn't happen, because on most of the major issues – this may sound like cowardice – I don't have the solution or even a strong prejudice: I don't know the solution of the Northern Ireland problem; I didn't know the solution to the Rhodesia problem or the Vietnam problem; I don't know how to conquer inflation. I may have particular views on particular aspects of government or opposition policy at a particular time, but, no, I'm sometimes relieved that I don't have responsibility for expressing opinions. I don't think I could do your job because I don't have your tremendous self-confidence, in that you are able to pronounce words of wisdom three times a week.

LEVIN Well, that's another matter, but, you see, in one respect we're certainly similar, in that we both do have strong views. Now, I am hired to express mine, you are hired not to express yours. Isn't that really rather odd?

RD No. Because if I were given a choice between having one of two rights, the right to ask questions and the right to express my opinions, and I could only have one of them, I would choose the right to ask questions, because I believe that disclosure is a greater journalistic weapon than the expression of opinion. I don't say that the opinionated, polemical journalist hasn't an enormous function to play in the editorial, but more things have been changed, more influences have taken place through journalists disclosing facts and inquiring into things – say, the appalling scandal of the Crimean War by Delane in *The Times*. That did more than editorials.

LEVIN You've been abroad a great deal, in your *Panorama* days, for instance, when you were reporting. You were showing the viewers something. That's a different kind of responsibility, isn't it? You can see it, you're the eyes. What are you trying to convey? You're trying to convey the way you see it, obviously, but you see it through your mind, your personality. You can't be totally objective as you might say. Which of us can be?

RD You can't be totally objective but you can try to be. And there's all the difference between a reporter who sets out to be objective and a reporter who sets out to be prejudiced, and you can see that in somebody's work. I've done programmes on South Africa where I might have had strong views on something, but I think I produced a reasonably objective report. And indeed, by so doing, I think it was more effective than producing a prejudiced report. But I think that one of the things I came not to like about film reporting was that it is a committee job. I would go sometimes with a producer. We would argue and discuss, sometimes in a friendly way, sometimes not, but generally in a friendly way, how to cover it. There would be a cameraman to consider. Then there would be the editing of it when one got home. And therefore it was inevitably a committee job, and I don't think a committee could write one of your articles. But a committee on the whole does a reporter's film. I quite enjoyed that, but sometimes I had a lot of freedom and went without a producer and there was very little trouble when I got back. But I prefer 'live' television, because although I don't have total responsibility – I'm responsible to people and my duty is imposed on me – none the less, it is a more personal form of journalism than the committee journalism of making a film.

LEVIN Well now, with those views, those attitudes, and that kind of work, you've been in business for a very long time, haven't you – twenty-five years, as I said before.

RD Not a long time for many professions: showbusiness, the law or industry or politics. But it is a very long time for television, which spews out its products with remarkable speed.

LEVIN Yes, and incidentally, you're quite right in saying it isn't a very long time by the standards of most professions. Now why is that? Why is television omnivorous? In the sense that there's a lot of television pouring out every day, obviously ...

RD Yes.

LEVIN But then you do your job within that flood. You keep your head above the water in it. Why does television use some people up?

RD Well, I think I've been lucky, because first of all I don't make my own material like a comedian does, I don't depend on other people writing me good plays. I have a vested interest, I'm sorry to say, in disaster and conflict, in political crisis and new political battles.

LEVIN There's never any lack of those ...

RD No, and therefore when people watch me do a programme or an interview, some people may turn on to watch *me*, but the vast majority of people are turning on to watch the report on this crisis, the presidential election, or the new Prime Minister or whatever. Naturally, if I do it well, that may impress them or not, as the case may be, but basically it is the event and the issue which keeps me alive. Of course, if I hadn't done it reasonably well, to my employers' satisfaction, I would have been chucked out. And also I haven't appeared all that often. Now you and some of the people watching may think I have. But in fact I appear relatively rarely compared to some people.

LEVIN Do those twenty-five years virtually cover the most important period in the life of television?

RD They're the years when television began to grow up.

LEVIN Really began to be important. So you've seen it all, virtually from the start to the present day. It's changed a great deal in that time. How do you feel about those changes? What kind of changes do you see, for the good or ill, both no doubt?

RD No, I think for good, and I'll say that to be fair. Briefly, I think it's been an enormous social advance to have television in every home, with all the pleasure and information that it can give to people who would not otherwise get it. They have the trash and the triviality, but they also have the treasure which television can give them, people of all classes and all educations. And I think it's a great social boon in that respect. But as regards television journalism and current affairs and news, I began by being very excited about this. ITN in the early days had a motto 'See it happen on ITN'. That was in the fifties and sixties, and suddenly one felt what a tremendous impact this information medium was having. But then I began increasingly to become aware of the limitations and dangers of television; that it was a medium of shock rather than explanation; that it was a crude medium which strikes at the emotions rather than the intellect. And because of its insatiable appetite for visual action, and for violence very often, it tended to distort and trivialize. In my opinion, and I'll stop here, otherwise I'll go on too long, it has contributed to the spate of unreason and violence and conflict in our society.

LEVIN Don't *stop* there. *Start* there, because that is the difference. The next question I was going to ask you was, if that is so, what is the effect that this has had, and does it matter? You obviously, by the sound of you, think it matters a great deal.

RD I do think it matters a great deal; I think our presentation of news and events has been affected by television's appetite for violence and action. Our news bulletins, I think, have become too much a kaleidoscope of happenings, visual happenings, rather than explanations of issues. Not always, but I think that has been the tendency. Take the Nigerian civil war. Television showed pictures of the starving Biafran babies – I'm not taking sides in that war now, that's irrelevant – but it was very, very difficult indeed to give any television balance to the pictures of the starving babies, yet there *was* an argument on the other side: that you didn't want to break up a great nation and Balkanize Africa. But try doing a dramatic or exciting item on the Balkanization of Africa, because it has to be a discussion of some kind. Yet I say those in charge of television must restrain themselves from using the power of television solely to project the visual aspects of world affairs, because the most important things are not always visual.

LEVIN You said, in the course of that, that it's television's appetite for violence, etc. Isn't it *our* appetite for violence, the people's attitude to violence, the *viewers'*, because television, like newspapers, will not long survive if it gives its customers something they don't want? Or do you not agree, do you think that television in that sense has a duty, not just to inform, which it obviously has, to educate, but to, as it were, direct public taste, public attitudes, all that? At any rate, even if it doesn't have a duty to do it, that's what it does, and it can lead them downwards as well as upwards.

RD I don't think it should direct public taste, but I do think those in charge of television should try to put its power on the side of reason. I think they should try to restrain the capacity of television to encourage unreason and what Bertrand Russell called 'the anti-rational philosophy of the naked will'. I think that television could do a great deal of good by redressing the balance, because we don't want our society to slide into violence and unreason. In your question you raised the question of 'Don't the public want this?' That doesn't interest me in the slightest. I mean that the public would flock in their thousands to see a public execution, but as a society we don't allow it. As a civilized society we take decisions which will not pander to the lowest instincts of human nature.

LEVIN Robin, you're a man who clearly lives by reason, by mind and reason and argument. Don't you really think that there's something missing in your make-up here, in that the world is on the whole not governed by reason? And if we go on thinking – I have suffered, heaven knows, from the same failing, if it is a failing – that the world is a rational place and that everybody is as reasonable as we are – of course we all like to think we're reasonable – then terrible things will happen. We will first of all be disillusioned. That perhaps doesn't matter, but that we will fail to take account of the deep unreason in human beings which is, goodness knows, exemplified in what you've just been saying about certain kinds of potential public appetite ... Can man live by reason alone? I think not.

RD Well, he can't live without it.

LEVIN No ...

RD And living by reason, and being reasonable, doesn't exclude the use of force and violence if and when it is necessary; for instance, when we fought the war against Hitler. I don't believe that violence is necessarily always an unreasonable course to take. What I do believe – I'm talking about our society – is that we're not responsible for the world any more; we were for a long time but we're not any more. That is what I'm primarily concerned about. But, none the less, I think that in *this* country we have got to concentrate on preventing this country sliding into a society which is unreasonable, which is full of hate and conflict in practically every aspect of our society. You see it in industrial relations, you see it in sport, you see it in education, you see it in journalism. I'm concerned now that our society should be a reasonable society, and that absolutes should be thrown away and that dogmas should be thrown away, and we should seek to reason together to work out solutions. Now this may seem an awful, a frightful platitude, and I can see people yawning at home as I say it. But every branch of our society, professional people, working-class people, politicians, they speak too often with the language of violence and hate and conflict.

LEVIN I entirely agree with you, but there's a point here that you must face, which is that there are people in our society who want to encourage that. You said our society would slide down into, I think you said, barbarism. So it might, and we've got to be on our guard against that constantly. But there are forces who don't mind about that. And there are others who would actually welcome it for political and other similar reasons of their own. But this you must also face: that there are real grievances in our society, there are people frustrated, their lives worthless to them, their conditions intolerable. Are we to say, 'Sit down, we'll discuss this calmly and reasonably'? 'I don't feel reasonable,' the reply might be, 'I feel very *un*reasonable. Filthy, terrible things are happening to me, why should I be reasonable?'

RD I wasn't talking about extremist minorities when I was complaining about unreason. I was complaining about something which seems to have infected the professional classes and all sorts of other people. But taking your point that there are people who are deprived and bitter and have a grievance, I do not see *any* grievance in this country (in many other countries, perhaps, but not in this country) which cannot be solved by peaceful debate and protest and by legislative or other reform. There is no justification whatever for anyone in this country murdering people or throwing petrol bombs or doing what has happened in certain recent events. I don't say that people haven't got grievances, but there is no justification for that. There is every argument for ensuring that people don't want to behave like that, but that's a different thing from saying people are justified in doing it if they feel aggrieved.

LEVIN Do you feel pessimistic about the course of this phenomenon you're talking about?

RD Deeply pessimistic.

LEVIN Do you think we are, in fact, going to slide down that hill?

RD Yes. I think we are sliding down unless we pull ourselves together, and that's a loose phrase to use, but I think television has a part to play in this. I think it should do its utmost to redress the balance of the portrayal of violence with the projection of reason. I think that news could be presented in a more civilized and balanced way, so as to get the reasons behind an industrial dispute and not just the scuffle outside the gate. I think that public men must give a lead. I think the trade union leaders must give a lead. I think the teachers who go to trade union conferences shouldn't scream at ministers. I think that ministers themselves should watch their words. Britain, England – that's what I believe in. I'm concerned about the rest of the world, but what matters to me is the country in which my two little sons will grow up. And I see it sliding down towards an ugly and bitter and divided society unless somehow we pull ourselves together.

LEVIN That's your view nationally. Personally – don't be angry at this question – do you yourself feel a sense of failure, in your life, in your career?

RD Yes, I do; although I've had a great deal of luck in television. I was very lucky to get in when television started. And I was lucky too, to work under very fine editors such as Aidan Crawley and Geoffrey Cox, and later others in the BBC like Paul Fox and so on, who gave me lots of opportunities. I'm proud to have made some contribution to the advancement of democratic communication by the development of television journalism. But I'm fifty-seven this year; I would like to have more responsibility than I have had. You've suggested that I have a lot, but in fact it's within very narrow limits, and most of my contemporaries have more responsible, more important jobs, with real decision-making. I would rather have gone into Parliament. I don't share your disregard for that institution; I believe in it profoundly. And, being very frank, I would like to have made more money. Because although I've had a perfectly adequate professional income, increasing over the years, and I don't plead poverty, I don't have that wealth which gives independence. I would like to have had financial independence, not for luxury or for lavish living, but for independence and the ability to say 'No' and 'I'm not going to do that series or work on that programme' and 'I'm not going to work for another year, I'm going to think.'

LEVIN You don't strike me, Robin Day, as a man who lacks a sense of independence in his own life. Thank you very much.

AFTERTHOUGHT

When the 1992 General Election result was known, I realized with a shock that I would be seventy-three at the next General Election in 1996 when the new Parliament will have gone its four and a half years. So, I thought, the interviews published in this book with Mr Major and Mr Kinnock were the last campaign interviews I would ever do. Sadly I went to see my cardiologist. I put a crucial and cunningly worded question to him: 'Do you think there will be another General Election in my lifetime?' He laughed and seemed to indicate that I should not worry unduly. But of course it was an unfair question for him to answer.

Why should a cardiologist, or any ologist, know whether the Tory majority of twenty-one can be safely held in the turbulent period of Europolitics which is ahead? May not the next General Election be sooner than we think? And what if there is a referendum? Would there be no interviewing then? Who knows?

Meanwhile I remember one of the many kind letters I received following the New Year's Honours list of 1981. Sir Robert Armstrong, then Secretary to the Cabinet, wrote to send congratulations on the knighthood conferred upon me. Sir Robert added a warning: 'But don't let it blunt the keen edge of your rapier.' This book of interviews may enable the patient reader to judge whether the rapier's edge has been any less keen in the eighties and the nineties, than it was said to be in the fifties, sixties and seventies. Vigorous, incisive interviewing is now commonplace. Thirty-five years ago it was a novelty. What then may have seemed fierce and provocative would not raise an eyebrow nowadays.